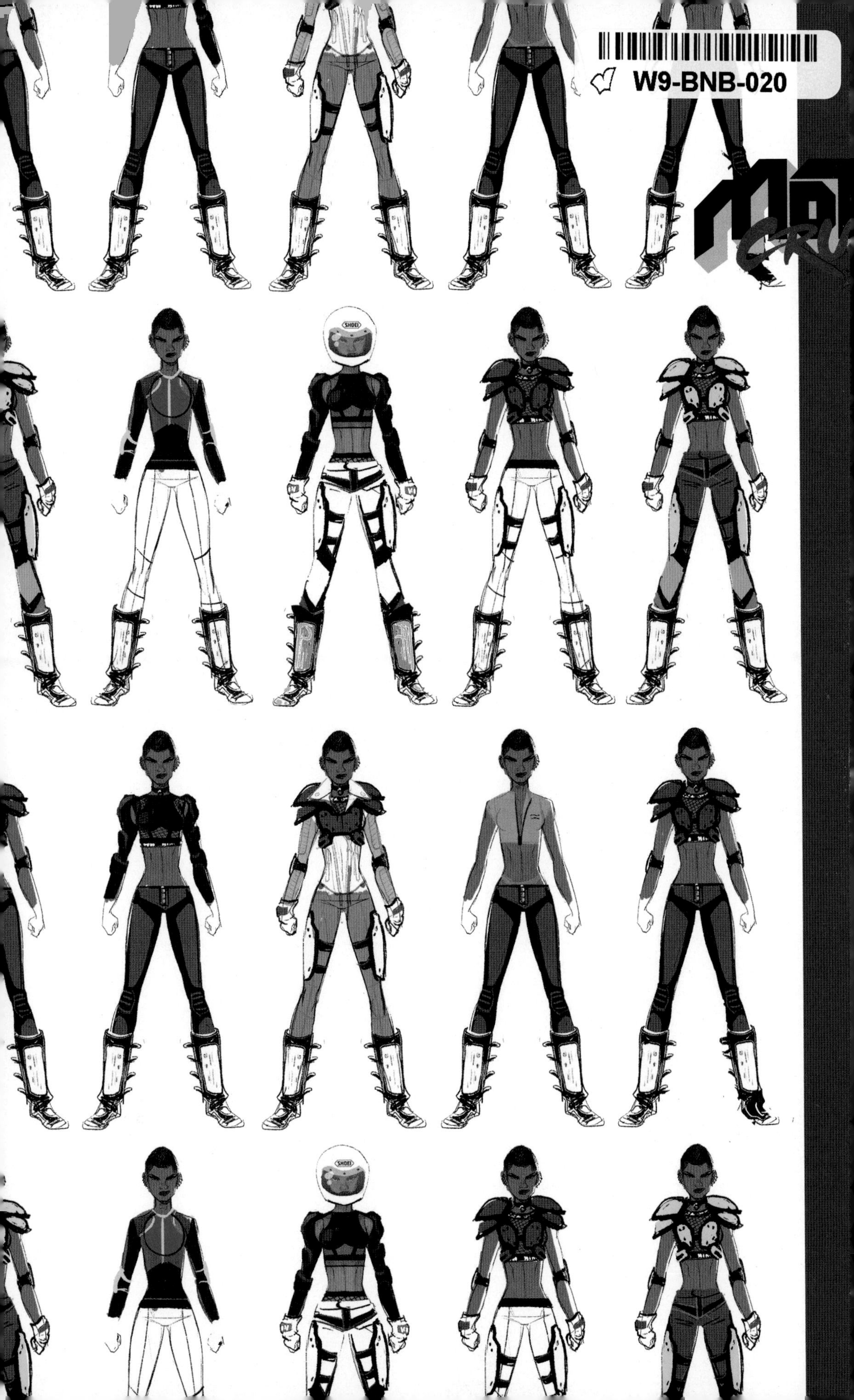
SHOEI
SHOEI

WORLD GRAND PRIX

WGP RECOMMENDS

MOTOR CRUSH MOTOR MOTOR

Vol.1

Creators
BRENDEN FLETCHER
CAMERON STEWART
BABS TARR

Original Cover Artists
BABS TARR, CAMERON STEWART, LESLIE HUNG

Color & Production Assistant
HEATHER DANFORTH

Lettering
ADITYA BIDIKAR

Logo, Publication Design, WGP In-World Captions
TOM MULLER

Editor
JEANINE SCHAEFER

Special thanks to Nate Piekos & Blambot®

MOTOR CRUSH Vol. 1 — Originally published as MOTOR CRUSH #1–5

WGP

START

INFOPOP

MOTOR CRUSH
CHAPTER 1

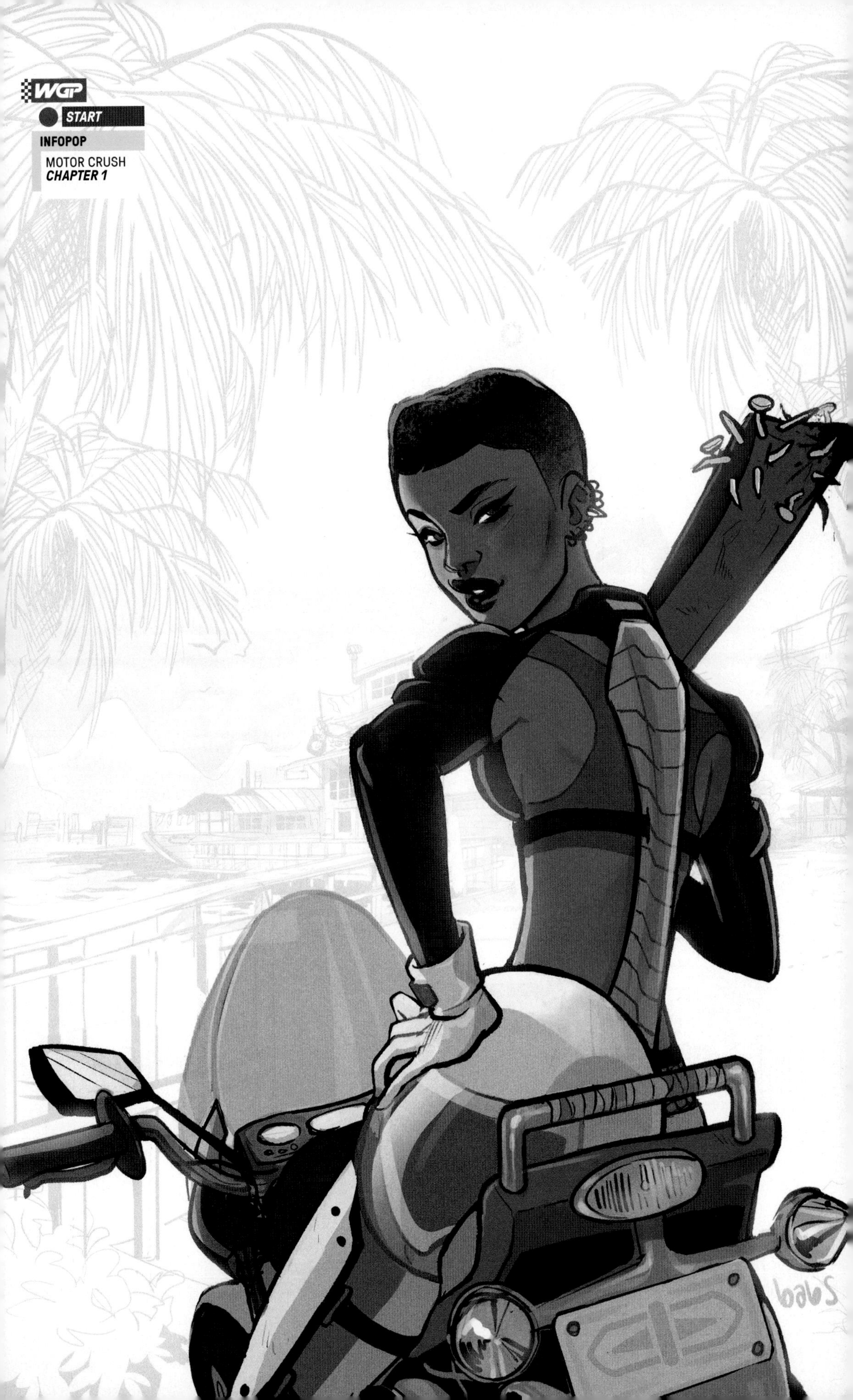
babs

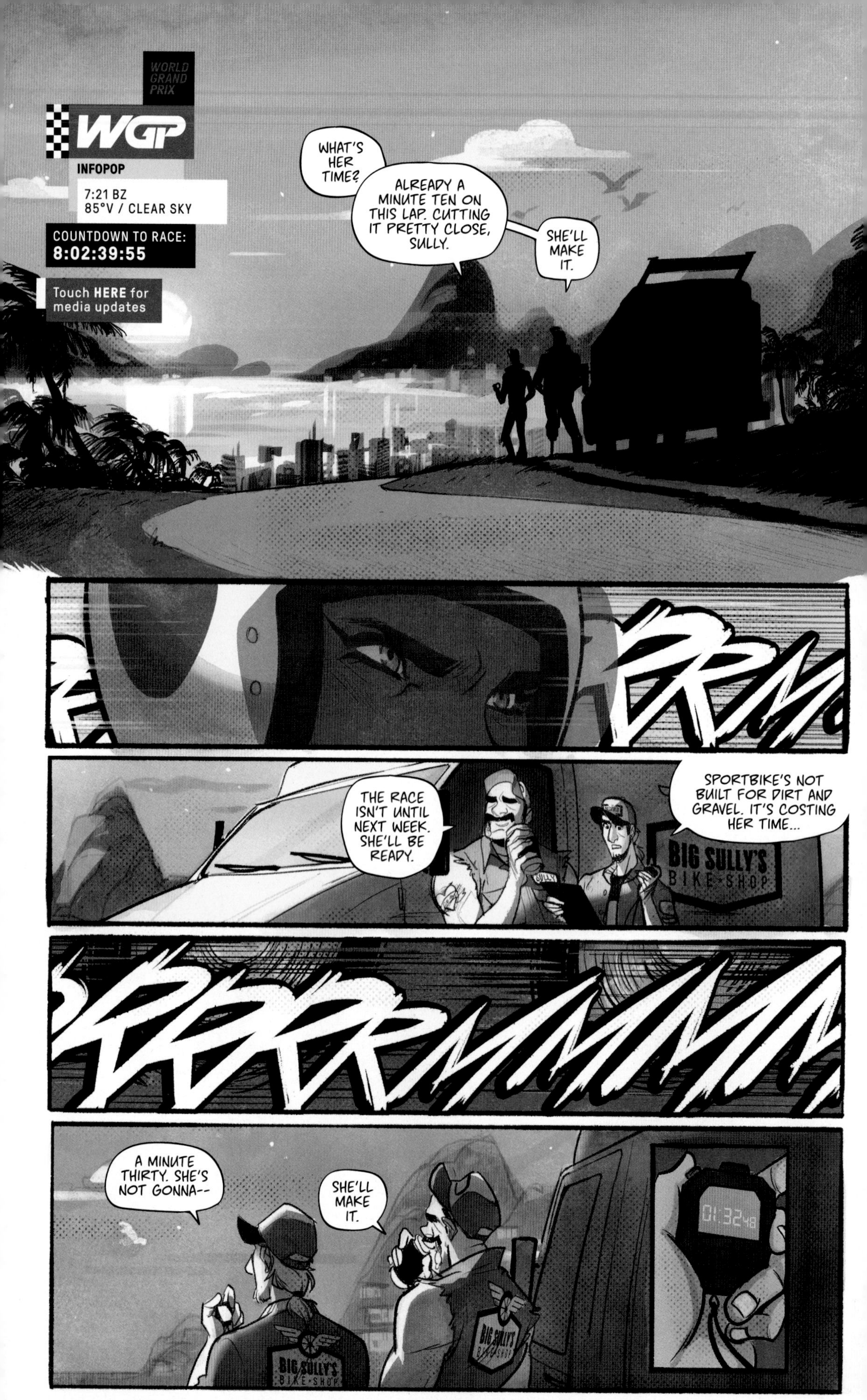
WORLD GRAND PRIX
WGP
INFOPOP
7:21 BZ
85°V / CLEAR SKY
COUNTDOWN TO RACE:
8:02:39:55
Touch HERE for media updates
WHAT'S HER TIME?
ALREADY A MINUTE TEN ON THIS LAP. CUTTING IT PRETTY CLOSE, SULLY.
SHE'LL MAKE IT.
BRM...
THE RACE ISN'T UNTIL NEXT WEEK. SHE'LL BE READY.
SPORTBIKE'S NOT BUILT FOR DIRT AND GRAVEL. IT'S COSTING HER TIME...
BIG SULLY'S BIKE SHOP
RRRRMMMMM
A MINUTE THIRTY. SHE'S NOT GONNA--
SHE'LL MAKE IT.
01:32 48
BIG SULLY'S BIKE SHOP

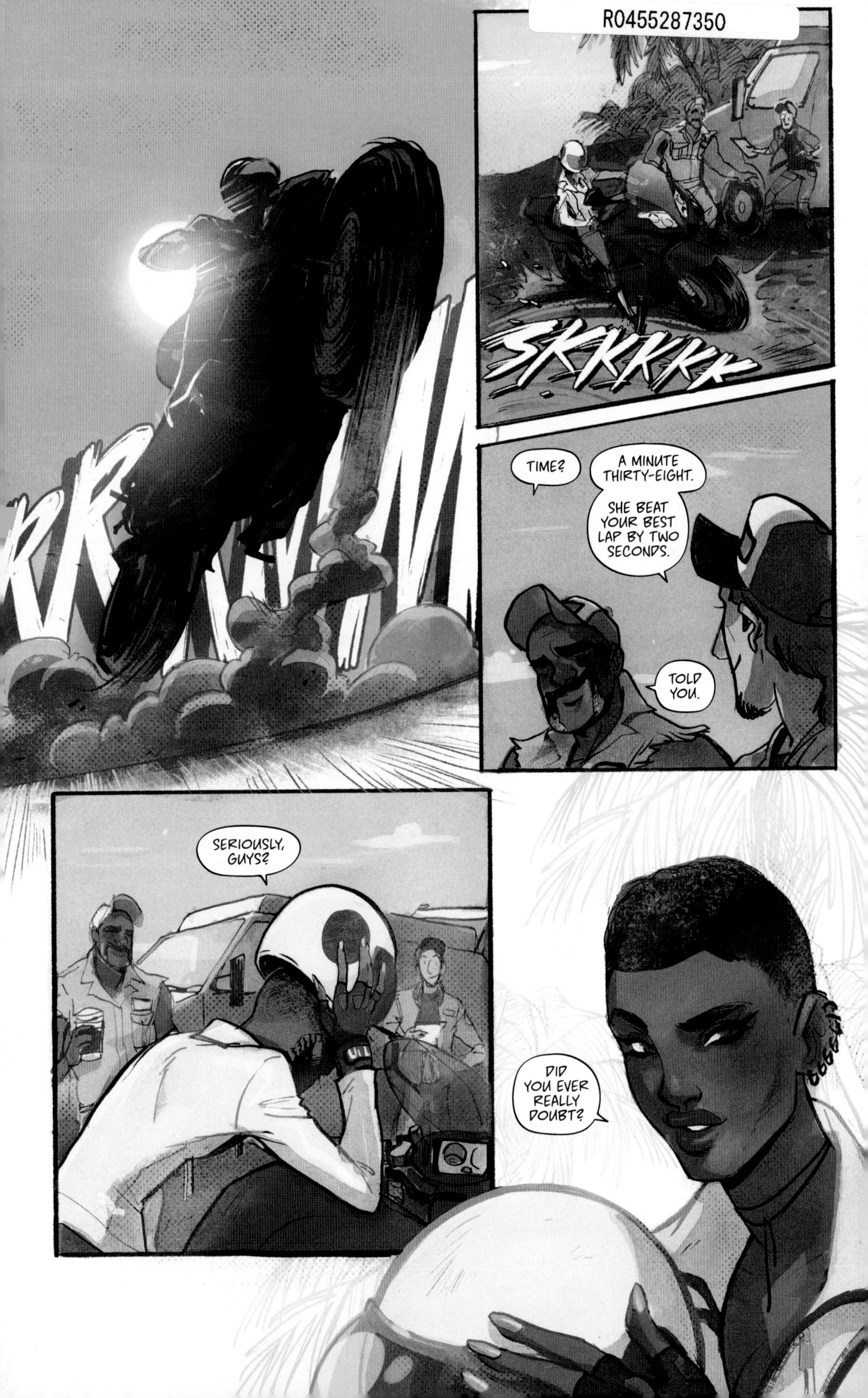
SKKKKK
TIME?
A MINUTE THIRTY-EIGHT.
SHE BEAT YOUR BEST LAP BY TWO SECONDS.
TOLD YOU.
SERIOUSLY, GUYS?
DID YOU EVER REALLY DOUBT?

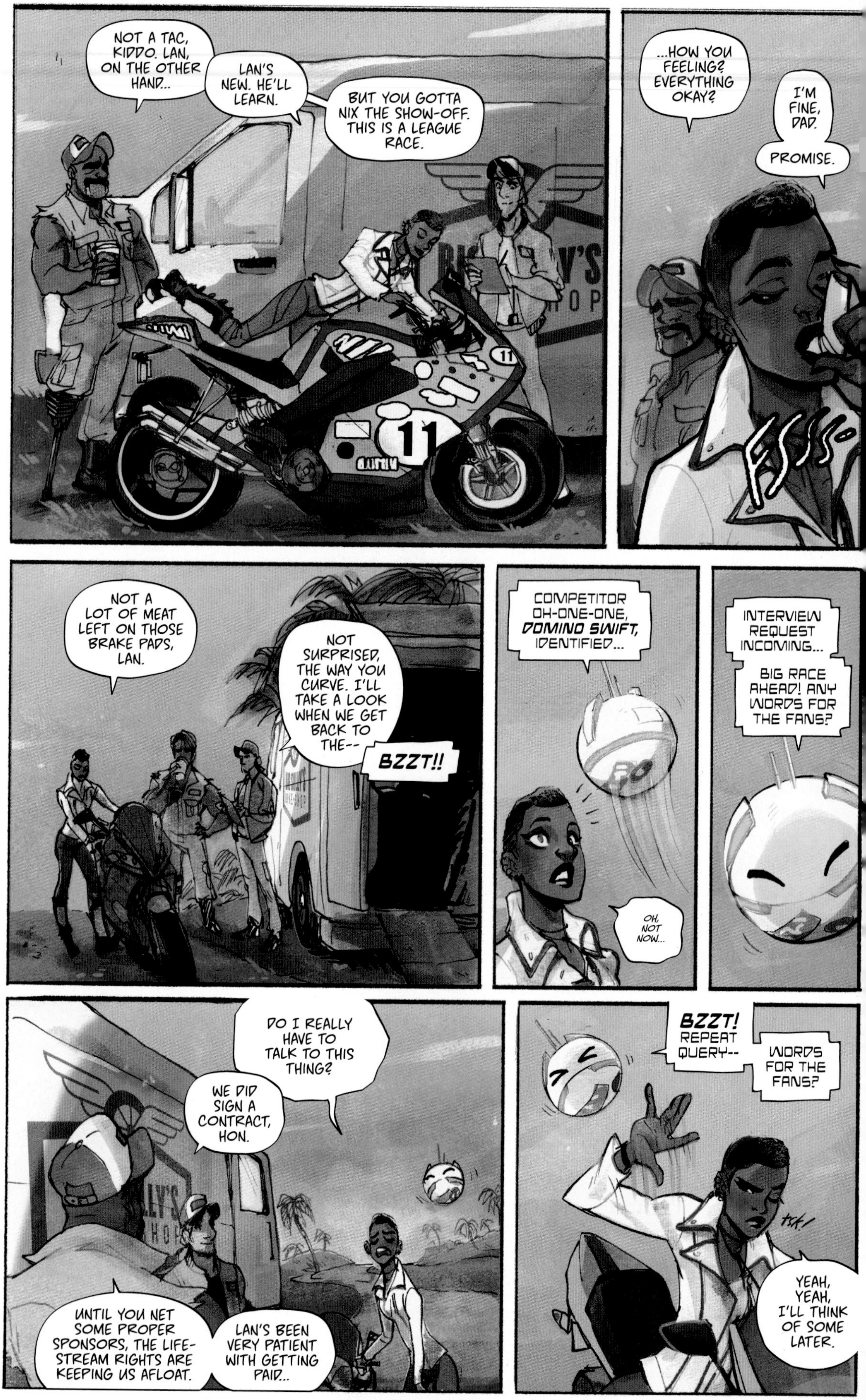

NOT A TAC, KIDDO. LAN, ON THE OTHER HAND...
LAN'S NEW. HE'LL LEARN.
BUT YOU GOTTA NIX THE SHOW-OFF. THIS IS A LEAGUE RACE.
...HOW YOU FEELING? EVERYTHING OKAY?
I'M FINE, DAD.
PROMISE.
FSSS
NOT A LOT OF MEAT LEFT ON THOSE BRAKE PADS, LAN.
NOT SURPRISED, THE WAY YOU CURVE. I'LL TAKE A LOOK WHEN WE GET BACK TO THE--
BZZT!!
COMPETITOR OH-ONE-ONE, DOMINO SWIFT, IDENTIFIED...
OH, NOT NOW...
INTERVIEW REQUEST INCOMING...
BIG RACE AHEAD! ANY WORDS FOR THE FANS?
DO I REALLY HAVE TO TALK TO THIS THING?
WE DID SIGN A CONTRACT, HON.
UNTIL YOU NET SOME PROPER SPONSORS, THE LIFE-STREAM RIGHTS ARE KEEPING US AFLOAT.
LAN'S BEEN VERY PATIENT WITH GETTING PAID...
BZZT! REPEAT QUERY--
WORDS FOR THE FANS?
TSK!
YEAH, YEAH, I'LL THINK OF SOME LATER.

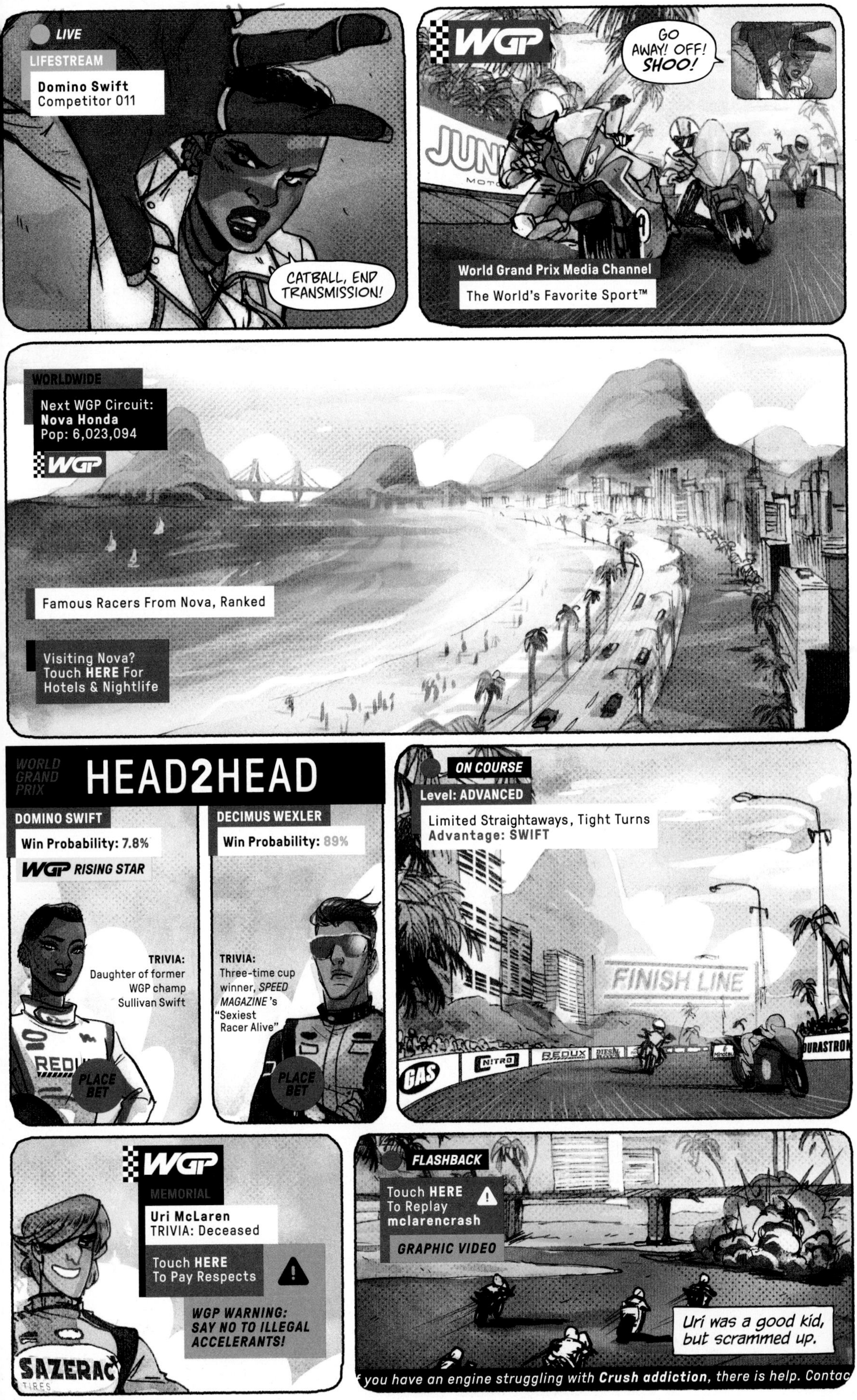

LIVE
LIFESTREAM
Domino Swift
Competitor 011
CATBALL, END TRANSMISSION!
WGP
GO AWAY! OFF! SHOO!
JUN
World Grand Prix Media Channel
The World's Favorite Sport™
WORLDWIDE
Next WGP Circuit:
Nova Honda
Pop: 6,023,094
WGP
Famous Racers From Nova, Ranked
Visiting Nova?
Touch HERE For
Hotels & Nightlife
WORLD GRAND PRIX
HEAD2HEAD
DOMINO SWIFT
Win Probability: 7.8%
WGP RISING STAR
TRIVIA:
Daughter of former
WGP champ
Sullivan Swift
PLACE BET
DECIMUS WEXLER
Win Probability: 89%
TRIVIA:
Three-time cup
winner, SPEED
MAGAZINE's
"Sexiest
Racer Alive"
PLACE BET
ON COURSE
Level: ADVANCED
Limited Straightaways, Tight Turns
Advantage: SWIFT
FINISH LINE
GAS
NITRO
REDUX
DURASTRON
WGP
MEMORIAL
Uri McLaren
TRIVIA: Deceased
Touch HERE
To Pay Respects
WGP WARNING:
SAY NO TO ILLEGAL
ACCELERANTS!
SAZERAC
TIRES
FLASHBACK
Touch HERE
To Replay
mclarencrash
GRAPHIC VIDEO
Uri was a good kid,
but scrammed up.
f you have an engine struggling with Crush addiction, there is help. Contac

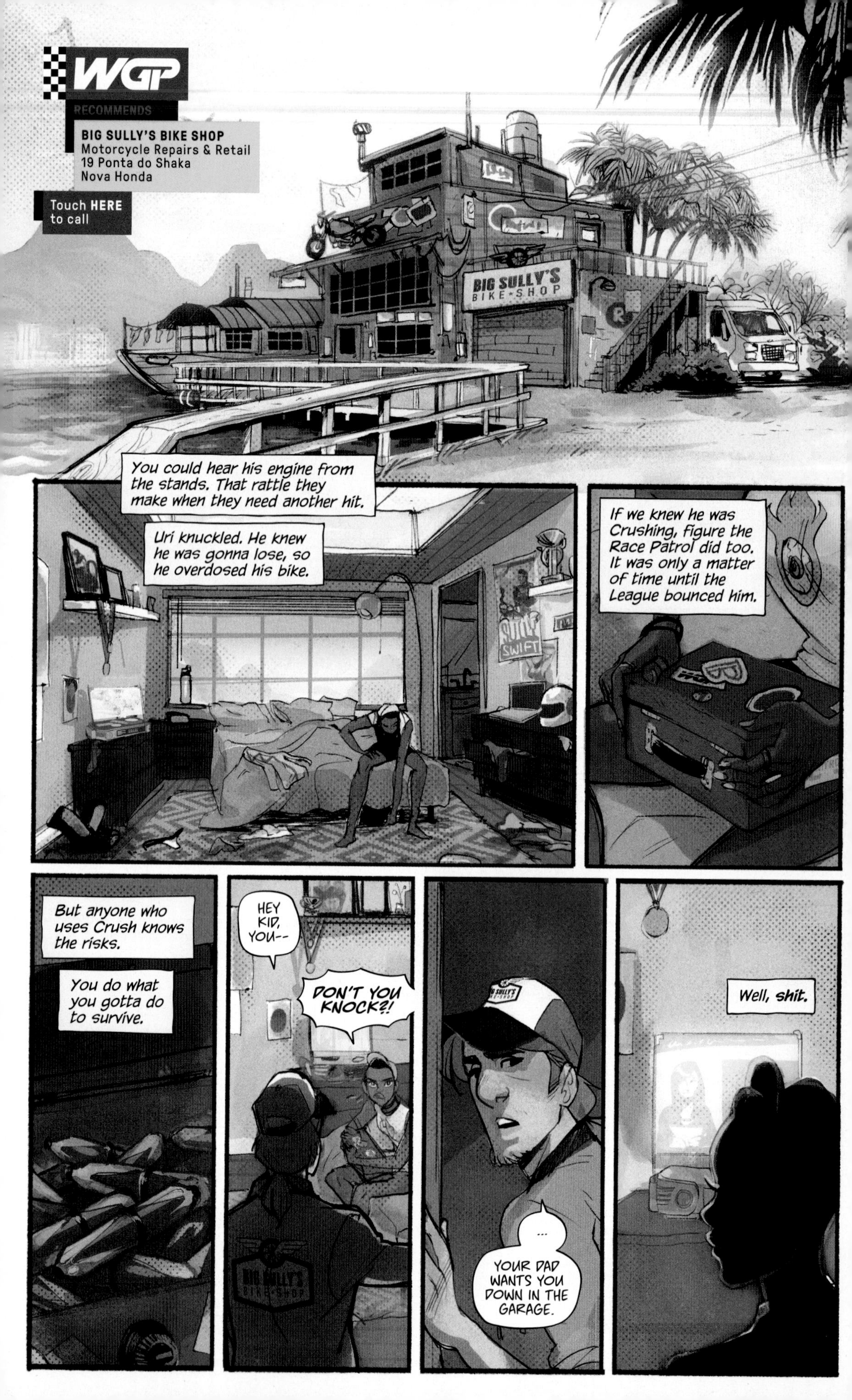
WGP
RECOMMENDS
BIG SULLY'S BIKE SHOP
Motorcycle Repairs & Retail
19 Ponta do Shaka
Nova Honda
Touch HERE to call
BIG SULLY'S BIKE SHOP
You could hear his engine from the stands. That rattle they make when they need another hit.
Uri knuckled. He knew he was gonna lose, so he overdosed his bike.
If we knew he was Crushing, figure the Race Patrol did too. It was only a matter of time until the League bounced him.
But anyone who uses Crush knows the risks.
You do what you gotta do to survive.
HEY KID, YOU--
DON'T YOU KNOCK?!
...
YOUR DAD WANTS YOU DOWN IN THE GARAGE.
Well, shit.

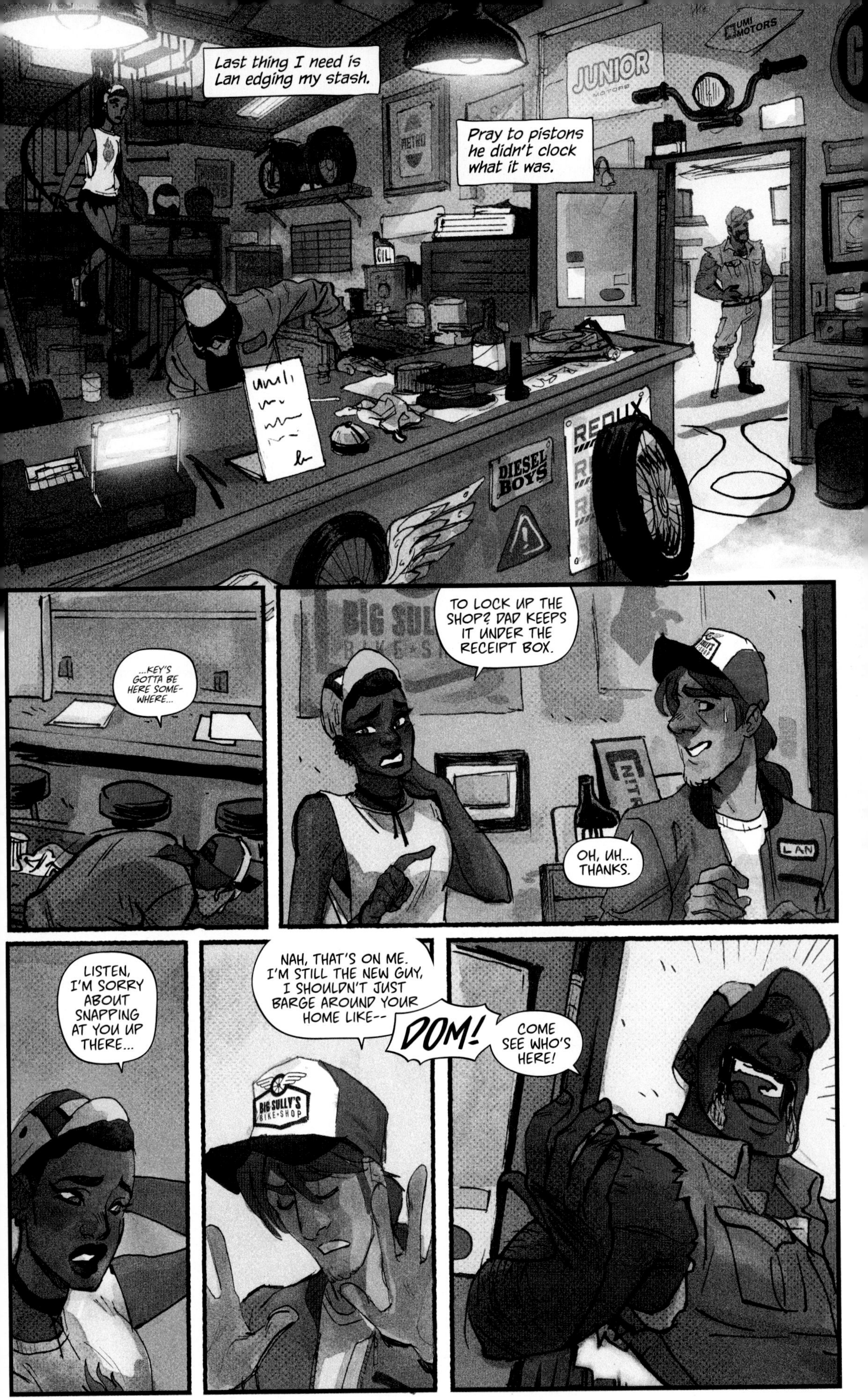
Last thing I need is Lan edging my stash.
Pray to pistons he didn't clock what it was.
JUNIOR
UMI MOTORS
METRO
OIL
DIESEL BOYS
REDUX
...KEY'S GOTTA BE HERE SOME-WHERE...
TO LOCK UP THE SHOP? DAD KEEPS IT UNDER THE RECEIPT BOX.
OH, UH... THANKS.
LAN
LISTEN, I'M SORRY ABOUT SNAPPING AT YOU UP THERE...
NAH, THAT'S ON ME. I'M STILL THE NEW GUY, I SHOULDN'T JUST BARGE AROUND YOUR HOME LIKE--
DOM!
COME SEE WHO'S HERE!
BIG SULLY'S BIKE SHOP

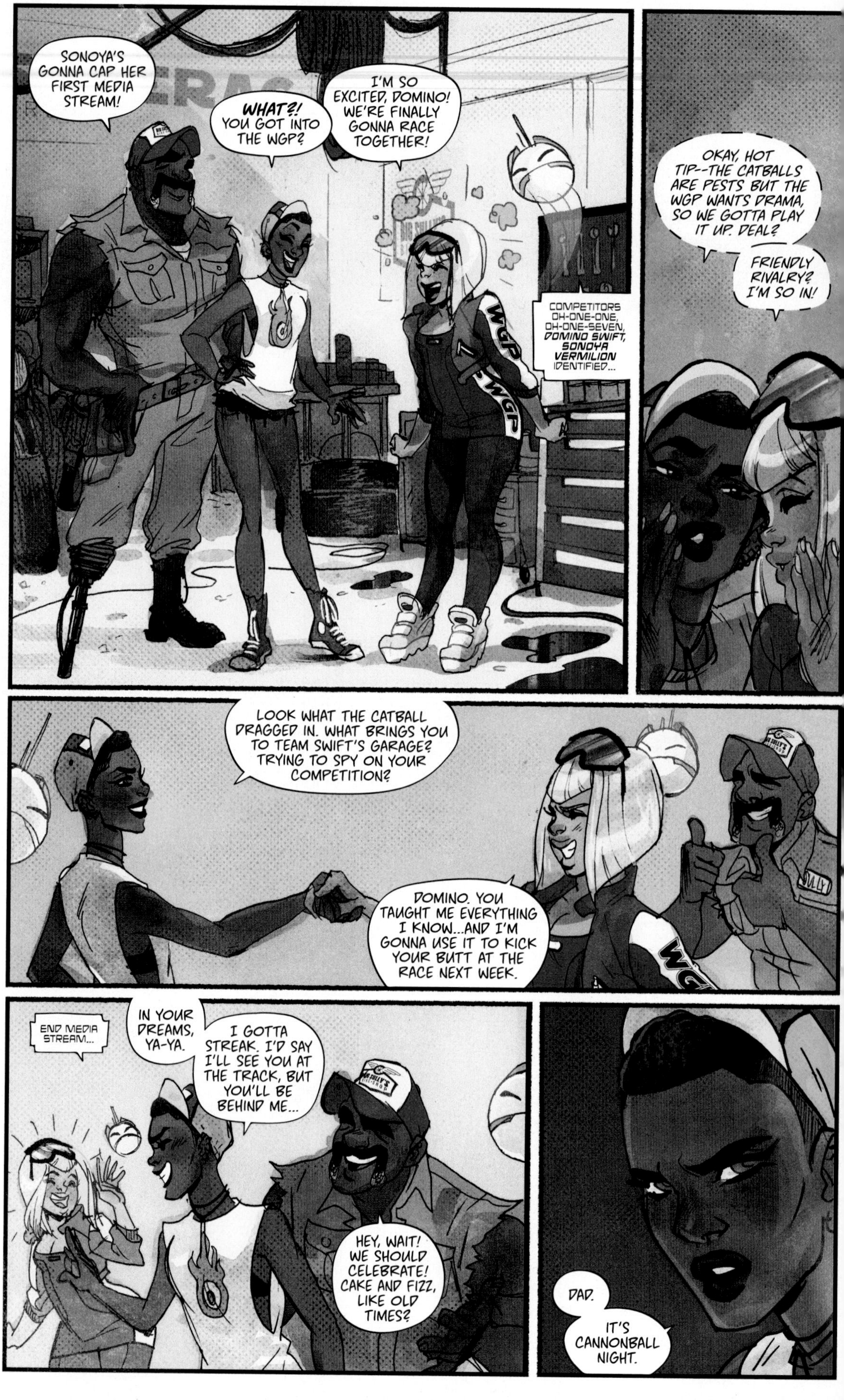
SONOYA'S GONNA CAP HER FIRST MEDIA STREAM!
WHAT?! YOU GOT INTO THE WGP?
I'M SO EXCITED, DOMINO! WE'RE FINALLY GONNA RACE TOGETHER!
COMPETITORS OH-ONE-ONE, OH-ONE-SEVEN, DOMINO SWIFT, SONOYA VERMILION IDENTIFIED...
OKAY, HOT TIP--THE CATBALLS ARE PESTS BUT THE WGP WANTS DRAMA, SO WE GOTTA PLAY IT UP. DEAL?
FRIENDLY RIVALRY? I'M SO IN!
LOOK WHAT THE CATBALL DRAGGED IN. WHAT BRINGS YOU TO TEAM SWIFT'S GARAGE? TRYING TO SPY ON YOUR COMPETITION?
DOMINO. YOU TAUGHT ME EVERYTHING I KNOW...AND I'M GONNA USE IT TO KICK YOUR BUTT AT THE RACE NEXT WEEK.
END MEDIA STREAM...
IN YOUR DREAMS, YA-YA.
I GOTTA STREAK. I'D SAY I'LL SEE YOU AT THE TRACK, BUT YOU'LL BE BEHIND ME...
HEY, WAIT! WE SHOULD CELEBRATE! CAKE AND FIZZ, LIKE OLD TIMES?
DAD.
IT'S CANNONBALL NIGHT.

WGP Street Racing in Old Nova
DANGER: Tourists should ONLY attend WGP-approved events to avoid injury
ILLEGAL RACING COSTS LIVES!

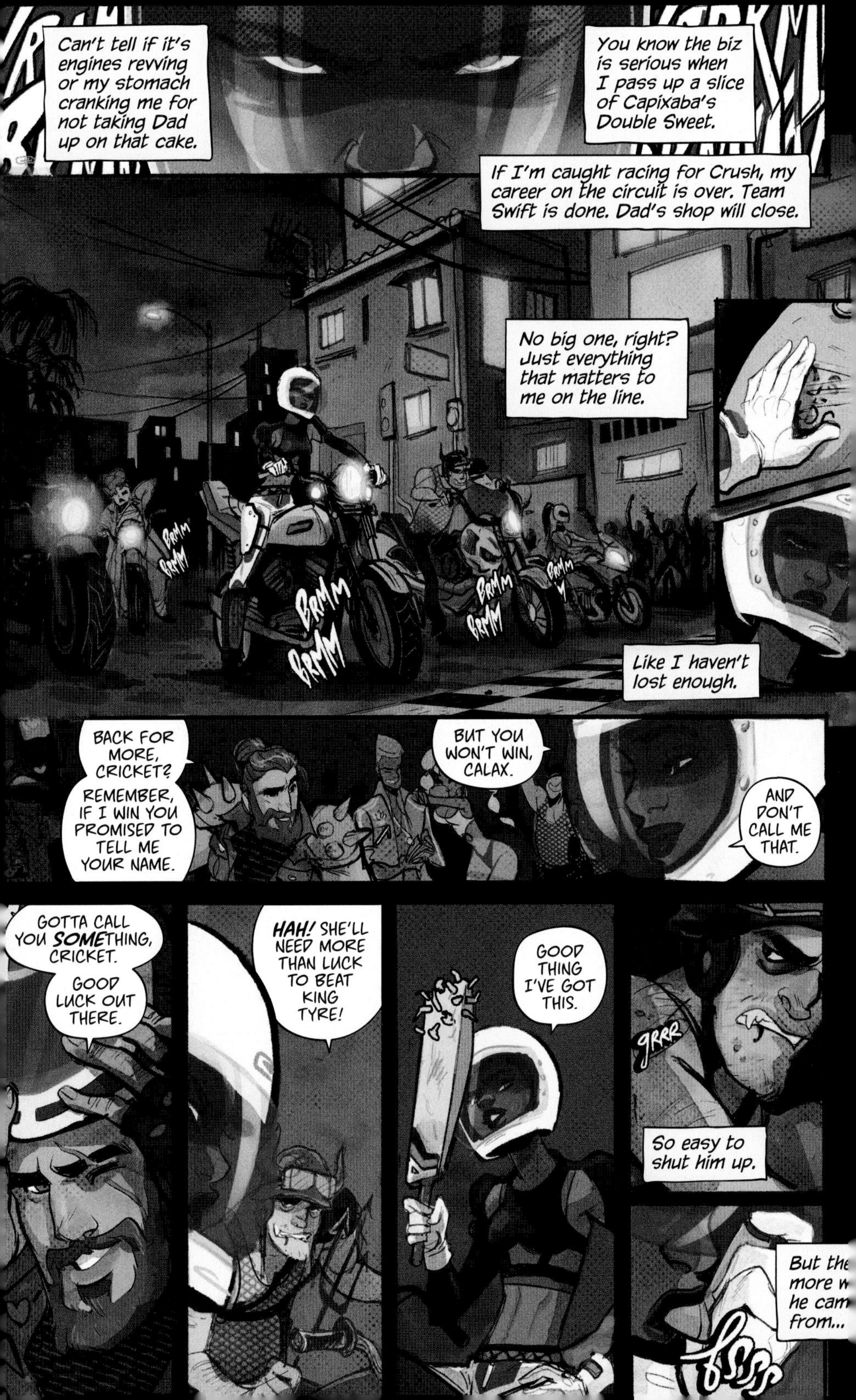

Can't tell if it's engines revving or my stomach cranking me for not taking Dad up on that cake.
You know the biz is serious when I pass up a slice of Capixaba's Double Sweet.
If I'm caught racing for Crush, my career on the circuit is over. Team Swift is done. Dad's shop will close.
No big one, right? Just everything that matters to me on the line.
BRMM BRMM
BRMM BRMM
BRMM BRMM
BRMM
Like I haven't lost enough.
BACK FOR MORE, CRICKET?
REMEMBER, IF I WIN YOU PROMISED TO TELL ME YOUR NAME.
BUT YOU WON'T WIN, CALAX.
AND DON'T CALL ME THAT.
GOTTA CALL YOU *SOME*THING, CRICKET.
GOOD LUCK OUT THERE.
HAH! SHE'LL NEED MORE THAN LUCK TO BEAT KING TYRE!
GOOD THING I'VE GOT THIS.
GRRR
So easy to shut him up.
But the more w he cam from...
fssss

MORS EX MARIBUS
AKA MARI

GANG	GLADIATORS
SPECIALITY	CHAIN AND PAIN
CRUSH COUNT	0 WINS
TRIVIA	TALKS TRASH EASY CASH

HANNIBAL HOLOCAUST

GANG	MAGIC MONSTERS
SPECIALITY	THE HAMMERDROP
CRUSH COUNT	2 WINS
TRIVIA	FUZZY FACE DAMAGED MIND

KING TYRE

GANG	ROYAL BASTARD SQUAD
SPECIALITY	STICK A FORK IN IT
CRUSH COUNT	3 WINS
TRIVIA	ROLLS WITH THE DEVIL BOWS TO QUEEN CHRISTINE

DECORA

GANG	CLUB CLUB
SPECIALITY	CHAIN AND PAIN
CRUSH COUNT	3 WINS
TRIVIA	HARD CORE HAUTE COUTURE

CALAX GOTHARD
AKA SAVAGE

GANG	DENIM FANG
SPECIALITY	BEEFQUAKE
CRUSH COUNT	3.5 WINS
TRIVIA	TOUGH GUY ACT ACTUAL PUSSYCAT

And then there's me.

AKA CRICKET

GANG	NONE
SPECIALITY	BATTER UP
CRUSH COUNT	17 WINS
TRIVIA	HATES BEING CALLED CRICKET

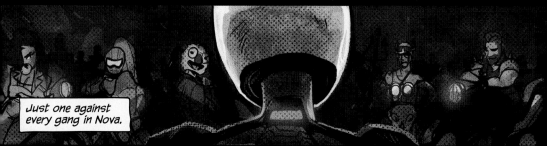

Just one against every gang in Nova.

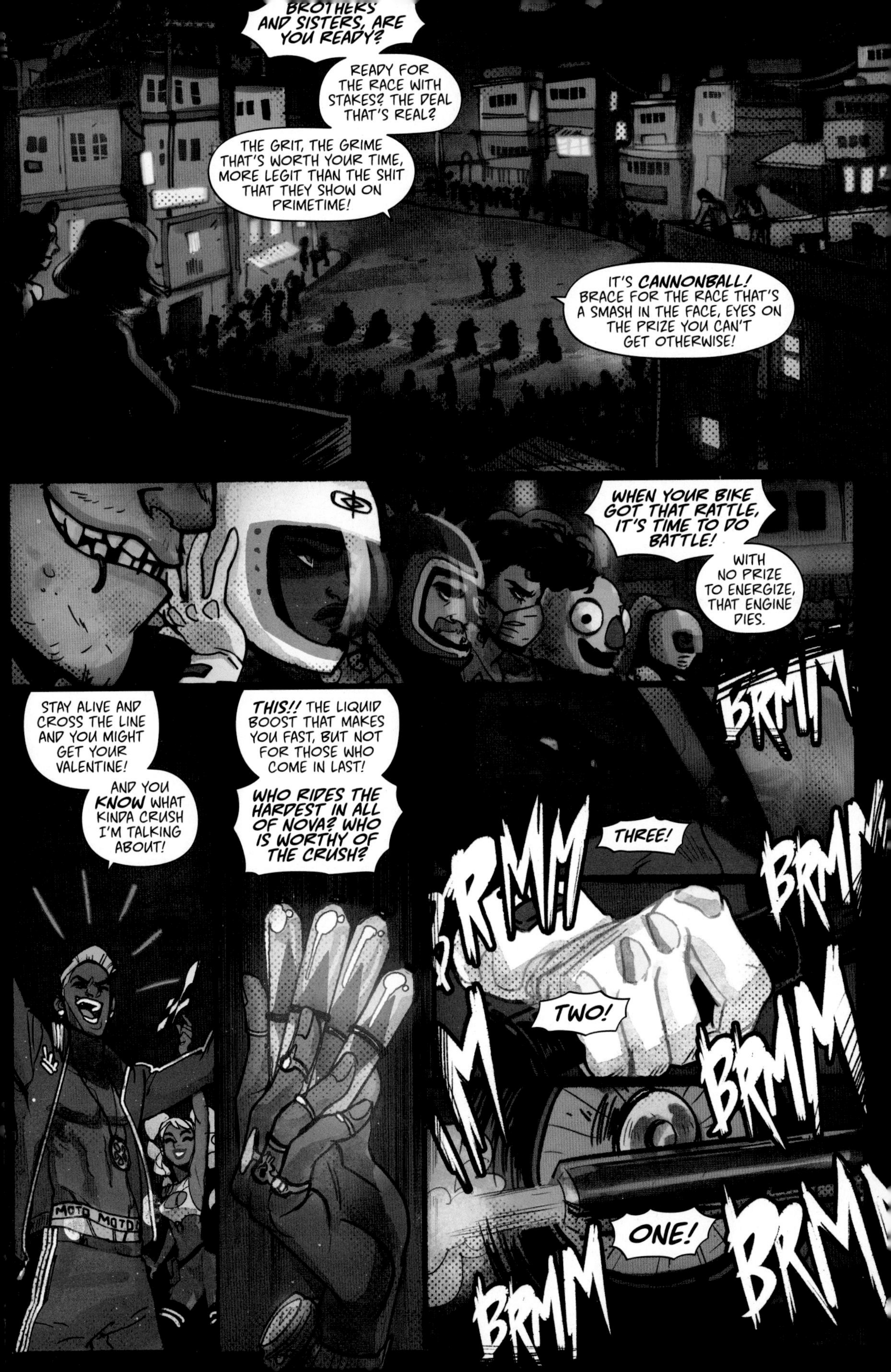
BROTHERS AND SISTERS, ARE YOU READY?
READY FOR THE RACE WITH STAKES? THE DEAL THAT'S REAL?
THE GRIT, THE GRIME THAT'S WORTH YOUR TIME, MORE LEGIT THAN THE SHIT THAT THEY SHOW ON PRIMETIME!
IT'S CANNONBALL! BRACE FOR THE RACE THAT'S A SMASH IN THE FACE, EYES ON THE PRIZE YOU CAN'T GET OTHERWISE!
WHEN YOUR BIKE GOT THAT RATTLE, IT'S TIME TO DO BATTLE!
WITH NO PRIZE TO ENERGIZE, THAT ENGINE DIES.
STAY ALIVE AND CROSS THE LINE AND YOU MIGHT GET YOUR VALENTINE!
AND YOU KNOW WHAT KINDA CRUSH I'M TALKING ABOUT!
THIS!! THE LIQUID BOOST THAT MAKES YOU FAST, BUT NOT FOR THOSE WHO COME IN LAST!
WHO RIDES THE HARDEST IN ALL OF NOVA? WHO IS WORTHY OF THE CRUSH?
BRMM
THREE!
BRMM
BRMM
TWO!
BRMM
ONE!
BRMM
BRMM

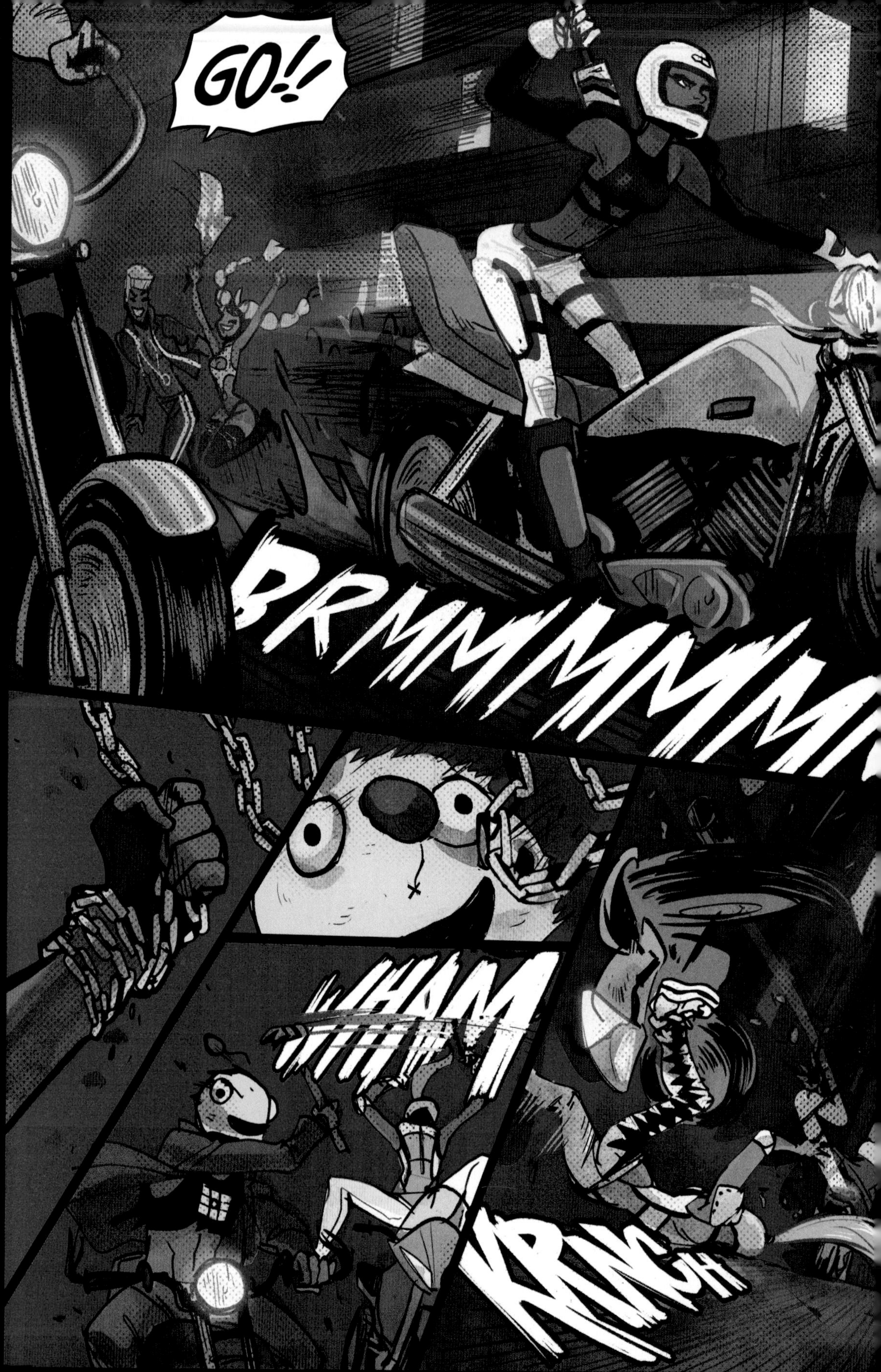
GO!!
BRMMMMMMM
WHAM
KRNCH

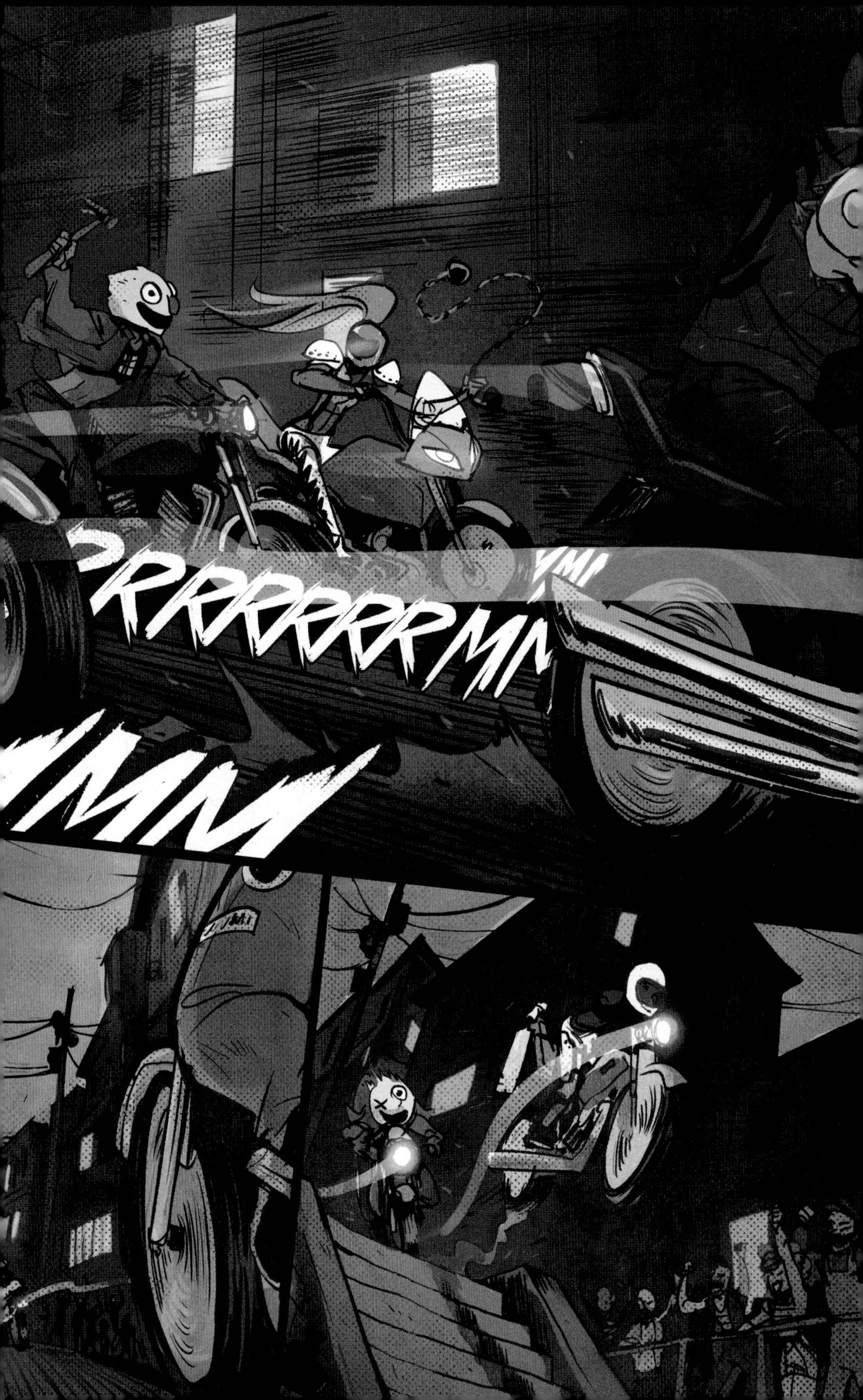
RRRRRRRMM
MMM

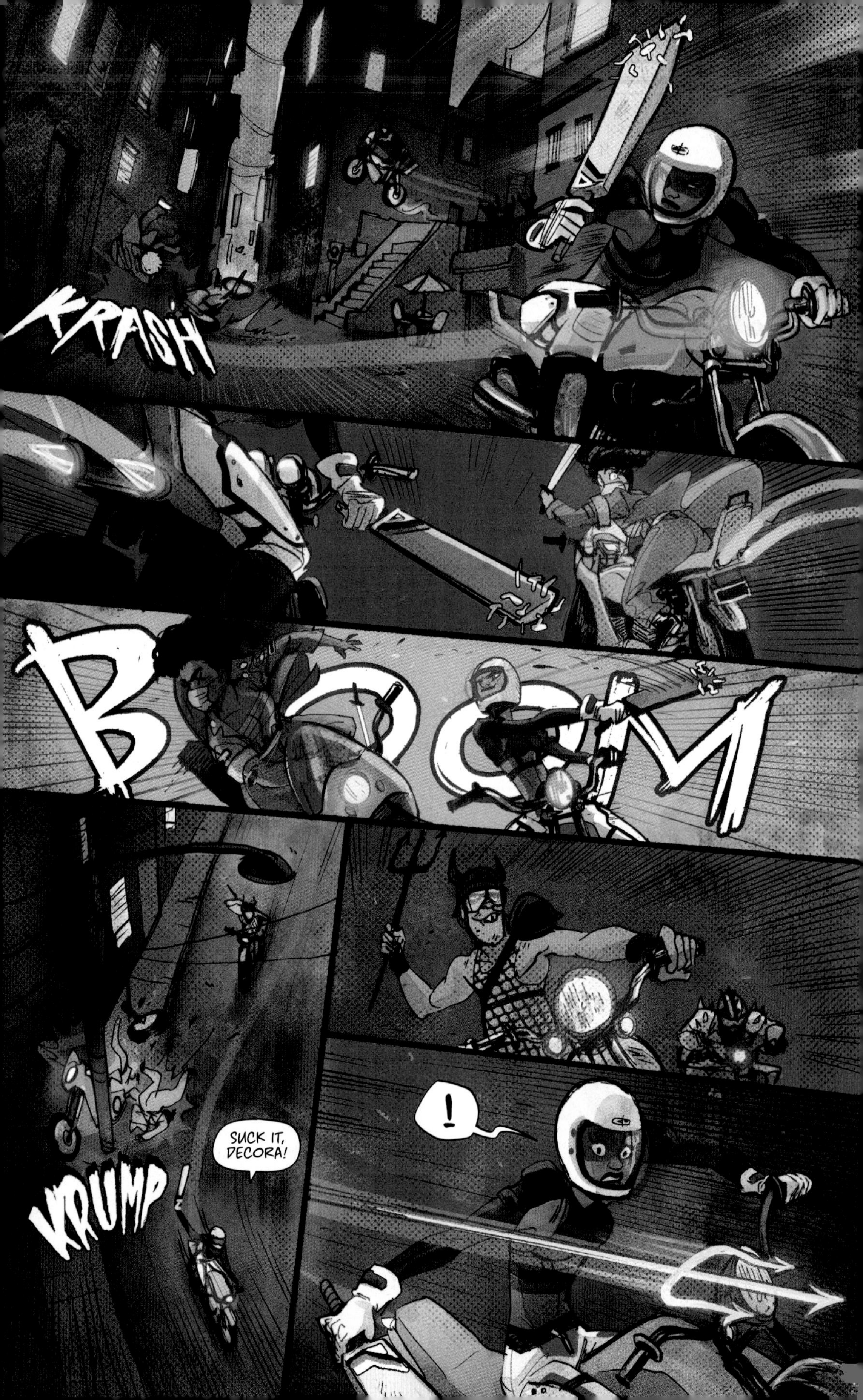
KRASH
BOOM
SUCK IT, DECORA!
VRUMP!
!

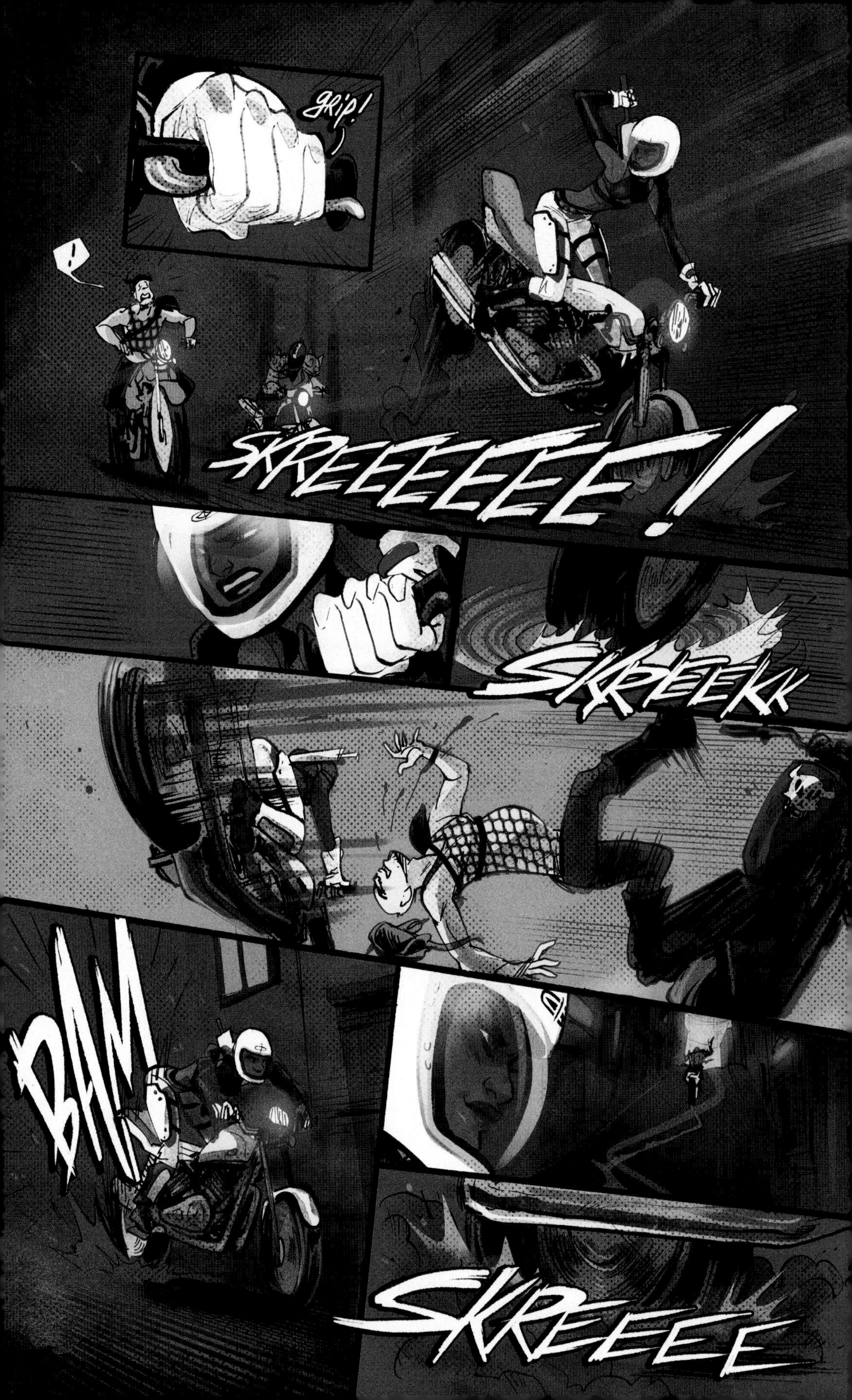
grip!
!
SKREEEEEEE!
SKREEKK
BAM
SKREEEE

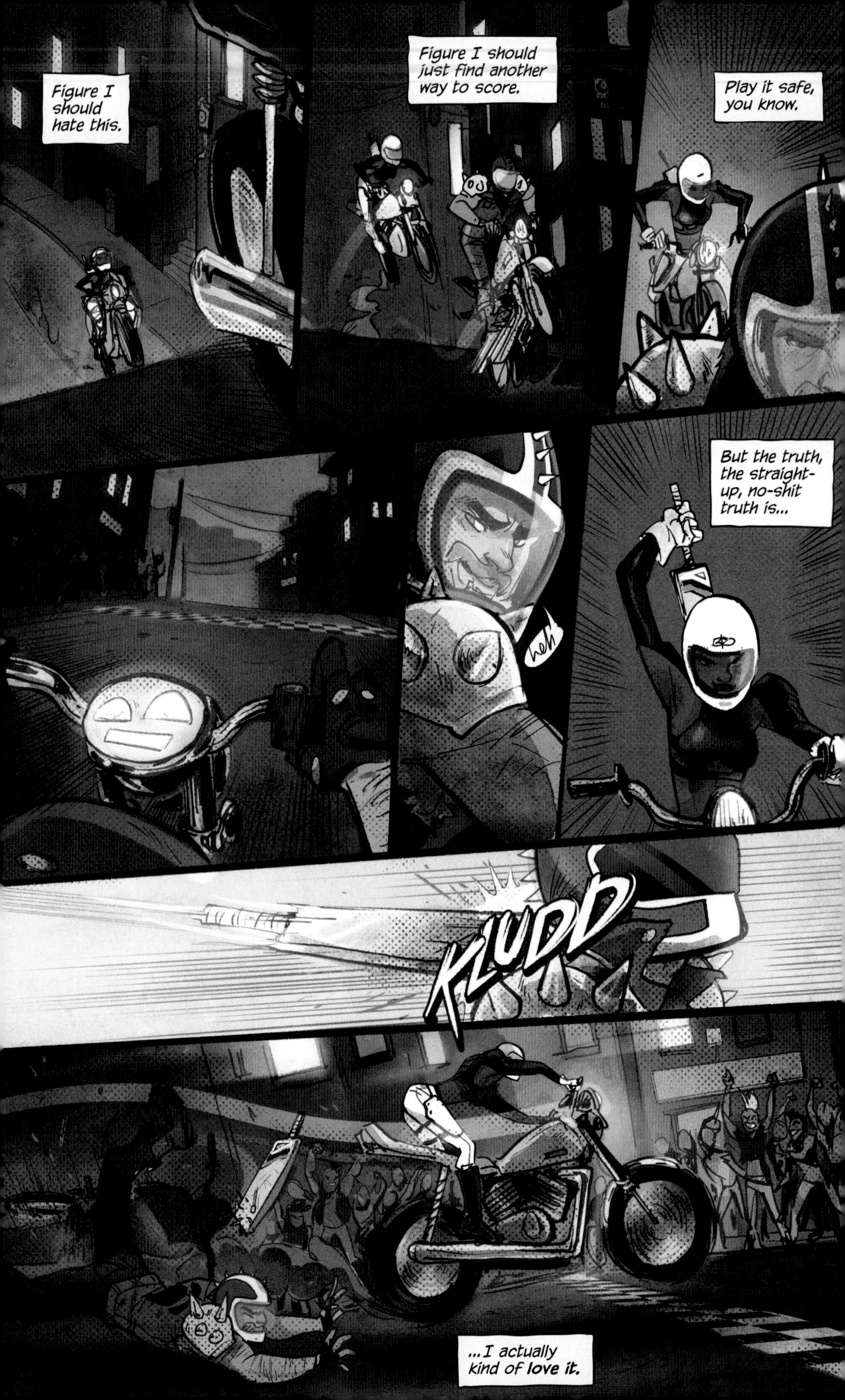
Figure I should hate this.
Figure I should just find another way to score.
Play it safe, you know.
heh
But the truth, the straight-up, no-shit truth is...
KLUDD
...I actually kind of love it.

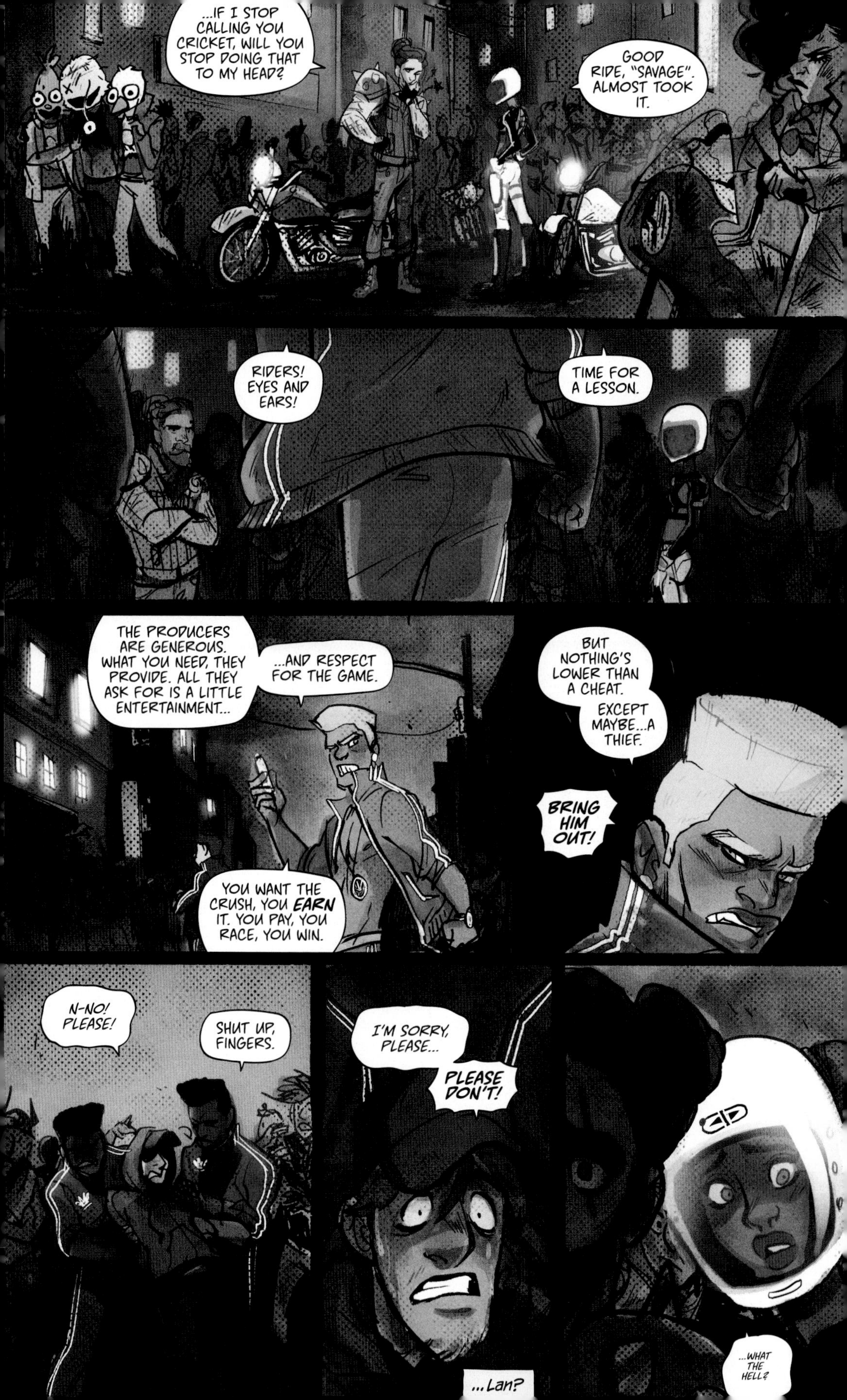
...IF I STOP CALLING YOU CRICKET, WILL YOU STOP DOING THAT TO MY HEAD?
GOOD RIDE, "SAVAGE". ALMOST TOOK IT.
RIDERS! EYES AND EARS!
TIME FOR A LESSON.
THE PRODUCERS ARE GENEROUS. WHAT YOU NEED, THEY PROVIDE. ALL THEY ASK FOR IS A LITTLE ENTERTAINMENT...
...AND RESPECT FOR THE GAME.
YOU WANT THE CRUSH, YOU EARN IT. YOU PAY, YOU RACE, YOU WIN.
BUT NOTHING'S LOWER THAN A CHEAT.
EXCEPT MAYBE...A THIEF.
BRING HIM OUT!
N-NO! PLEASE!
SHUT UP, FINGERS.
I'M SORRY, PLEASE...
PLEASE DON'T!
...Lan?
...WHAT THE HELL?

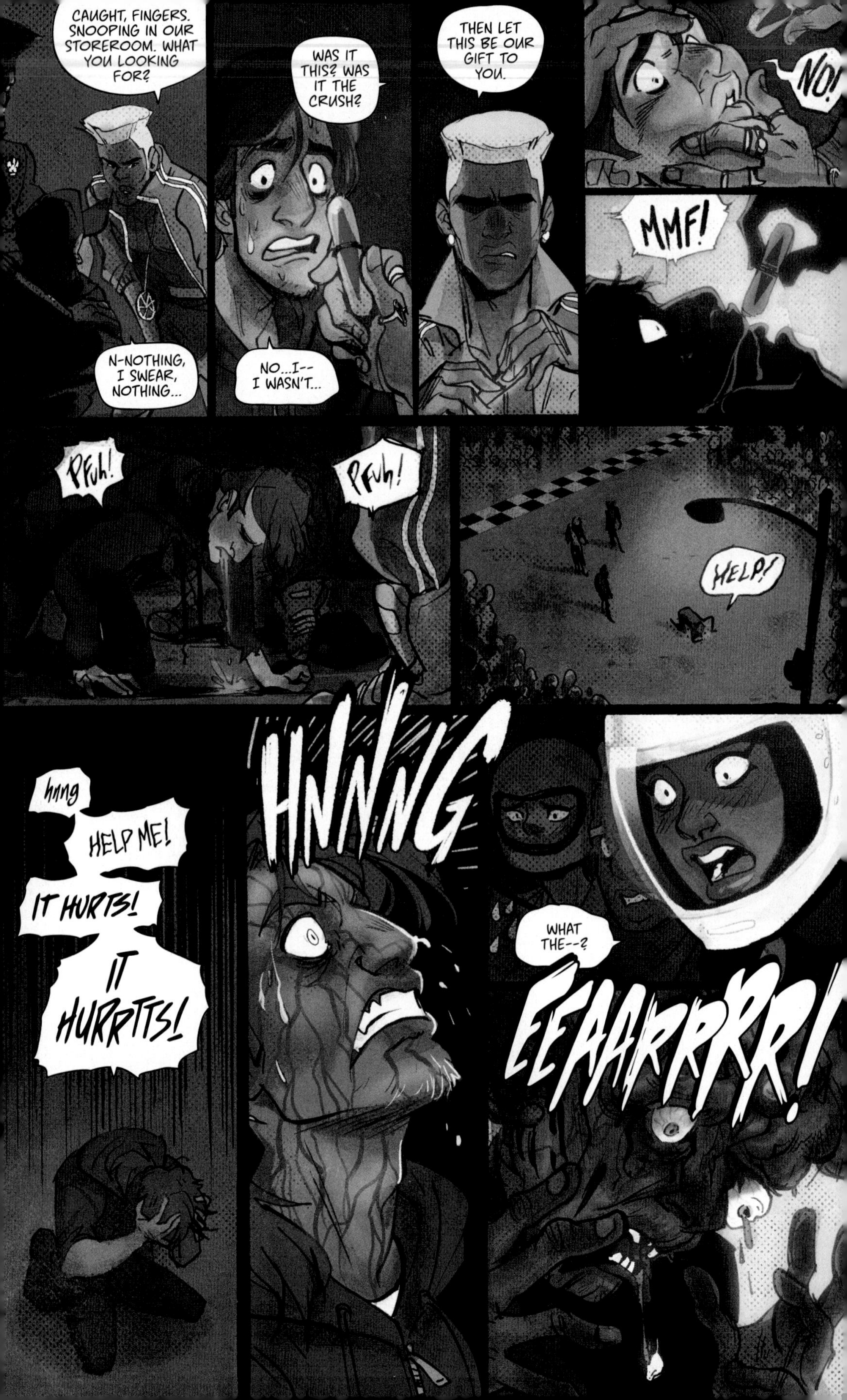
CAUGHT, FINGERS. SNOOPING IN OUR STOREROOM. WHAT YOU LOOKING FOR?
N-NOTHING, I SWEAR, NOTHING...
WAS IT THIS? WAS IT THE CRUSH?
NO...I-- I WASN'T...
THEN LET THIS BE OUR GIFT TO YOU.
NO!
MMF!
PFUH!
PFUH!
HELP!
hnng
HELP ME!
IT HURTS!
IT HURRTTS!
HNNNG
WHAT THE--?
EEAARRRR!

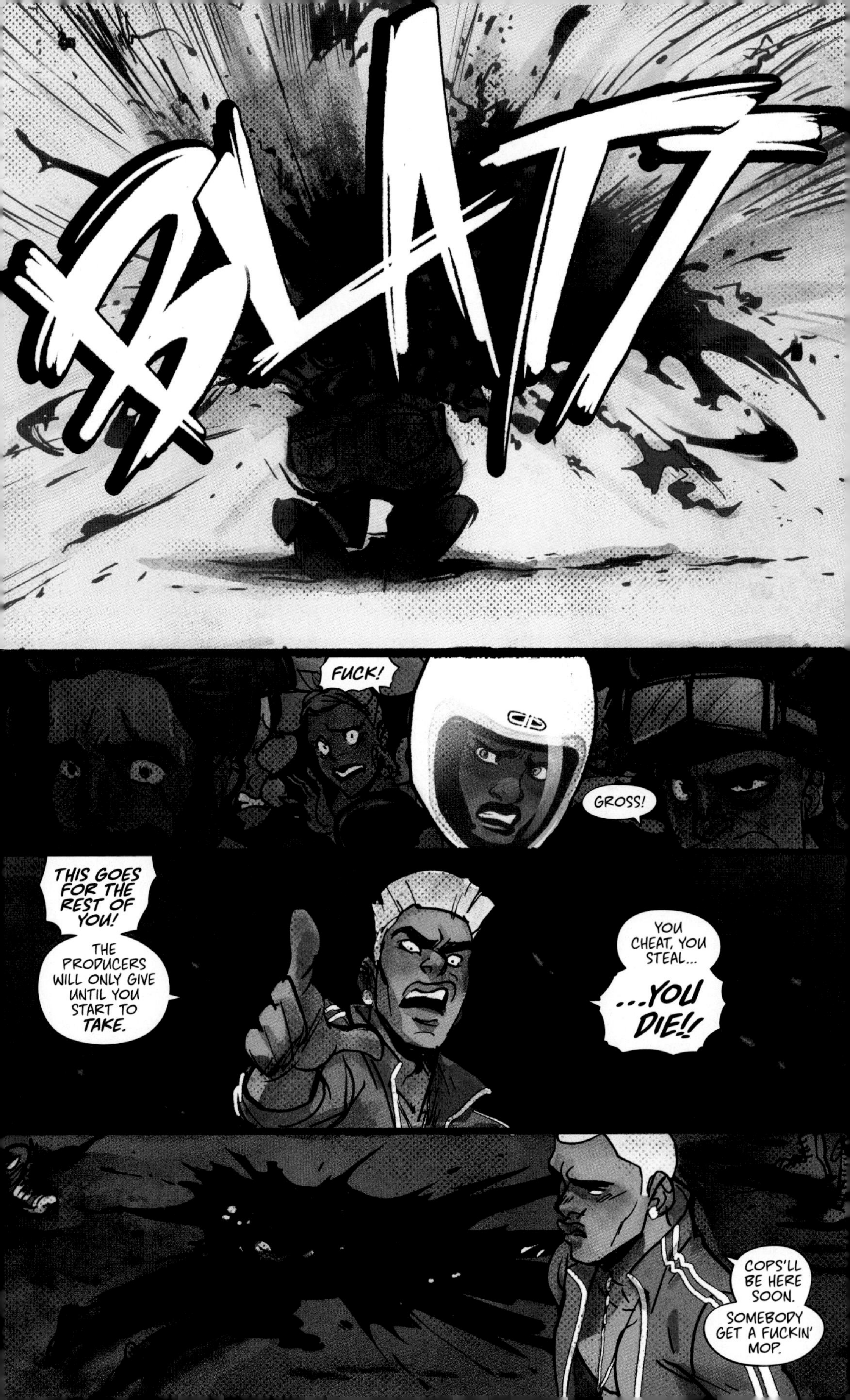
BLATT
FUCK!
GROSS!
THIS GOES FOR THE REST OF YOU!
THE PRODUCERS WILL ONLY GIVE UNTIL YOU START TO TAKE.
YOU CHEAT, YOU STEAL...
...YOU DIE!!
COPS'LL BE HERE SOON.
SOMEBODY GET A FUCKIN' MOP.

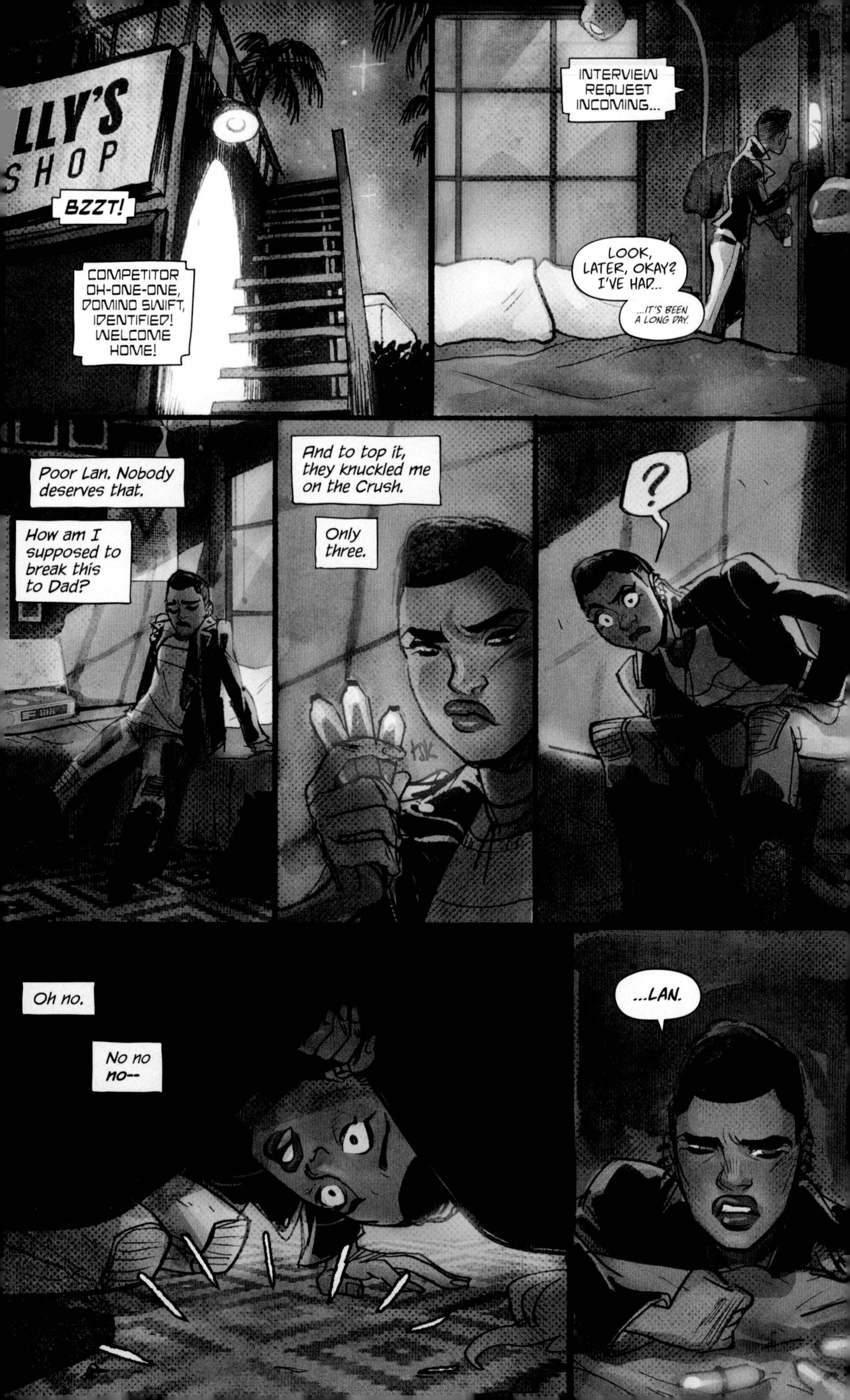
LLY'S
SHOP
BZZT!
COMPETITOR OH-ONE-ONE, DOMINO SWIFT, IDENTIFIED! WELCOME HOME!
INTERVIEW REQUEST INCOMING...
LOOK, LATER, OKAY? I'VE HAD...
...IT'S BEEN A LONG DAY.
Poor Lan. Nobody deserves that.
How am I supposed to break this to Dad?
And to top it, they knuckled me on the Crush.
Only three.
?
Oh no.
No no no--
...LAN.

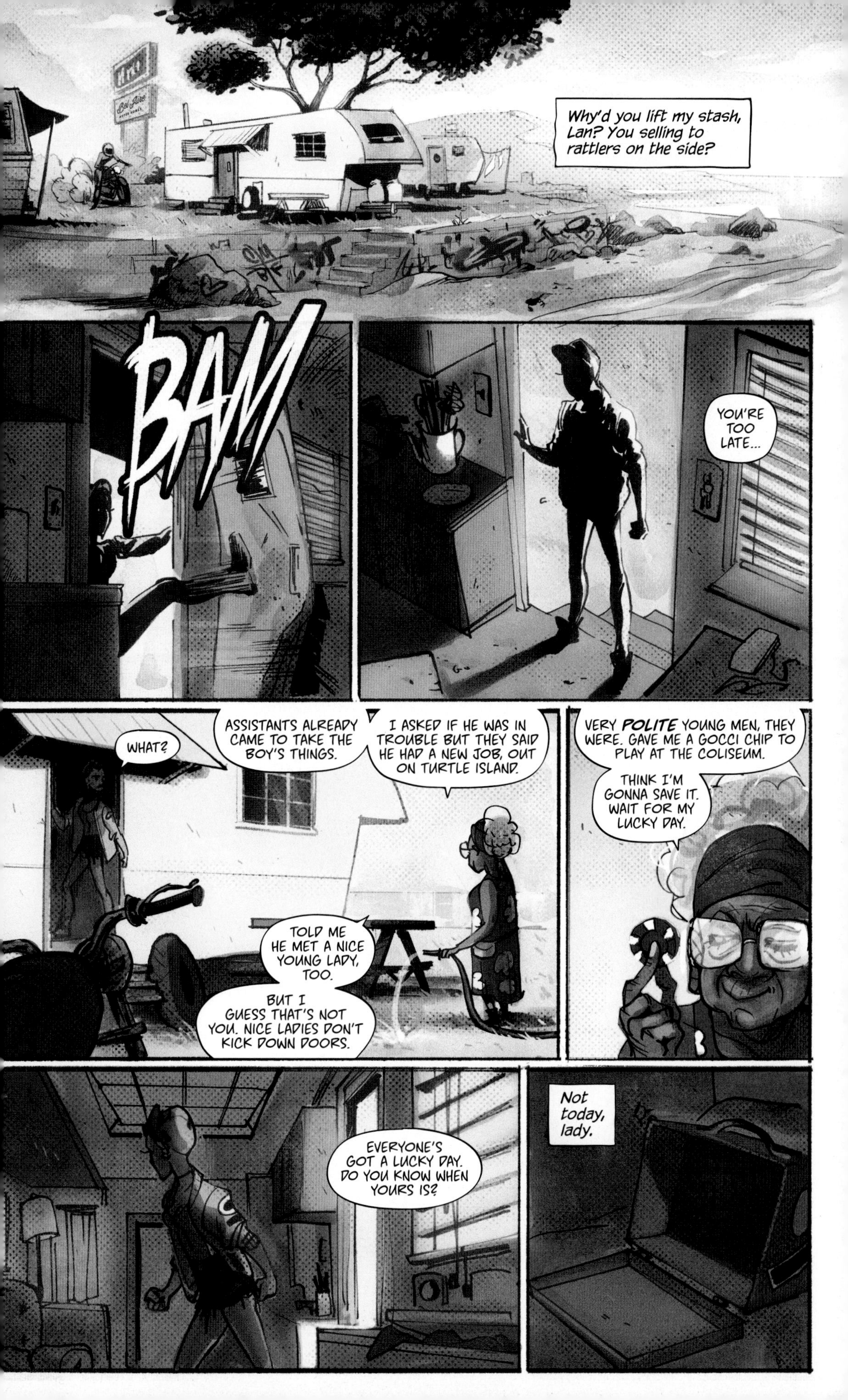
Why'd you lift my stash, Lan? You selling to rattlers on the side?
BAM
YOU'RE TOO LATE...
WHAT?
ASSISTANTS ALREADY CAME TO TAKE THE BOY'S THINGS.
I ASKED IF HE WAS IN TROUBLE BUT THEY SAID HE HAD A NEW JOB, OUT ON TURTLE ISLAND.
TOLD ME HE MET A NICE YOUNG LADY, TOO.
BUT I GUESS THAT'S NOT YOU. NICE LADIES DON'T KICK DOWN DOORS.
VERY POLITE YOUNG MEN, THEY WERE. GAVE ME A GOCCI CHIP TO PLAY AT THE COLISEUM.
THINK I'M GONNA SAVE IT. WAIT FOR MY LUCKY DAY.
EVERYONE'S GOT A LUCKY DAY. DO YOU KNOW WHEN YOURS IS?
Not today, lady.

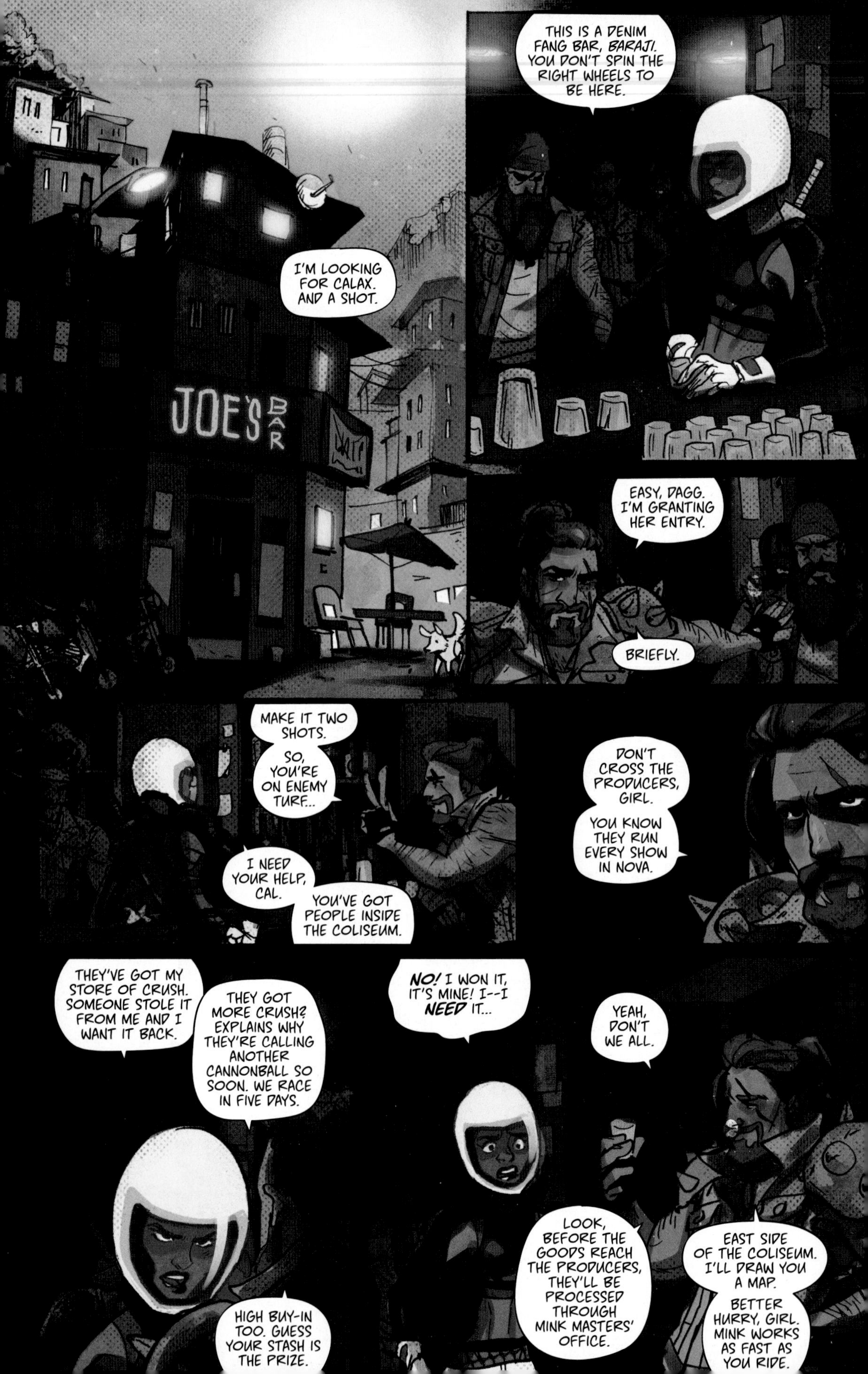
JOE'S BAR
THIS IS A DENIM FANG BAR, BARAJI. YOU DON'T SPIN THE RIGHT WHEELS TO BE HERE.
I'M LOOKING FOR CALAX. AND A SHOT.
EASY, DAGG. I'M GRANTING HER ENTRY.
BRIEFLY.
MAKE IT TWO SHOTS.
SO, YOU'RE ON ENEMY TURF...
I NEED YOUR HELP, CAL.
YOU'VE GOT PEOPLE INSIDE THE COLISEUM.
DON'T CROSS THE PRODUCERS, GIRL.
YOU KNOW THEY RUN EVERY SHOW IN NOVA.
THEY'VE GOT MY STORE OF CRUSH. SOMEONE STOLE IT FROM ME AND I WANT IT BACK.
THEY GOT MORE CRUSH? EXPLAINS WHY THEY'RE CALLING ANOTHER CANNONBALL SO SOON. WE RACE IN FIVE DAYS.
HIGH BUY-IN TOO. GUESS YOUR STASH IS THE PRIZE.
NO! I WON IT, IT'S MINE! I--I NEED IT...
YEAH, DON'T WE ALL.
LOOK, BEFORE THE GOODS REACH THE PRODUCERS, THEY'LL BE PROCESSED THROUGH MINK MASTERS' OFFICE.
EAST SIDE OF THE COLISEUM. I'LL DRAW YOU A MAP.
BETTER HURRY, GIRL. MINK WORKS AS FAST AS YOU RIDE.

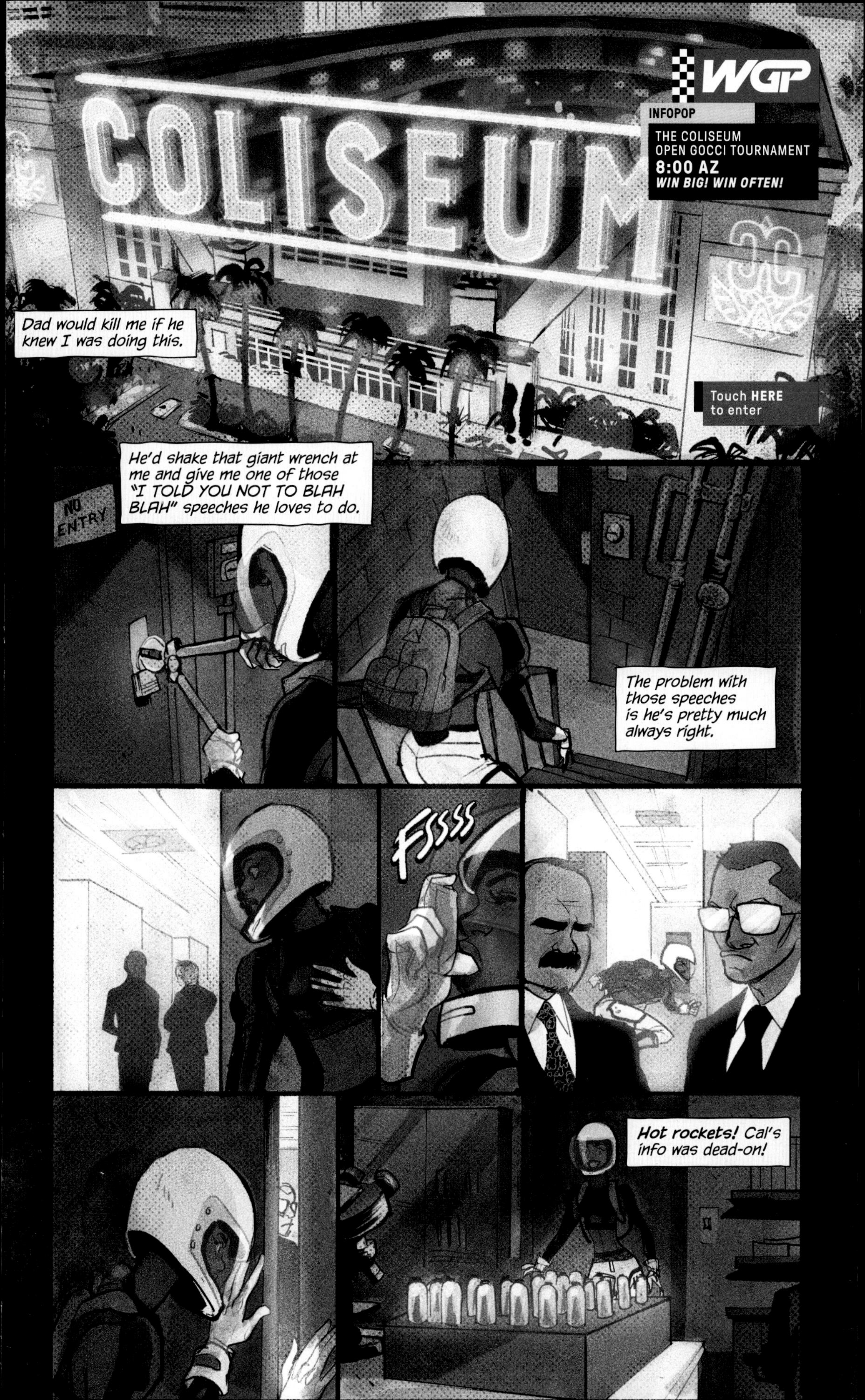
COLISEUM
WGP
INFOPOP
THE COLISEUM
OPEN GOCCI TOURNAMENT
8:00 AZ
WIN BIG! WIN OFTEN!
Dad would kill me if he knew I was doing this.
Touch HERE to enter
He'd shake that giant wrench at me and give me one of those "I TOLD YOU NOT TO BLAH BLAH" speeches he loves to do.
NO ENTRY
The problem with those speeches is he's pretty much always right.
FSSSS
Hot rockets! Cal's info was dead-on!

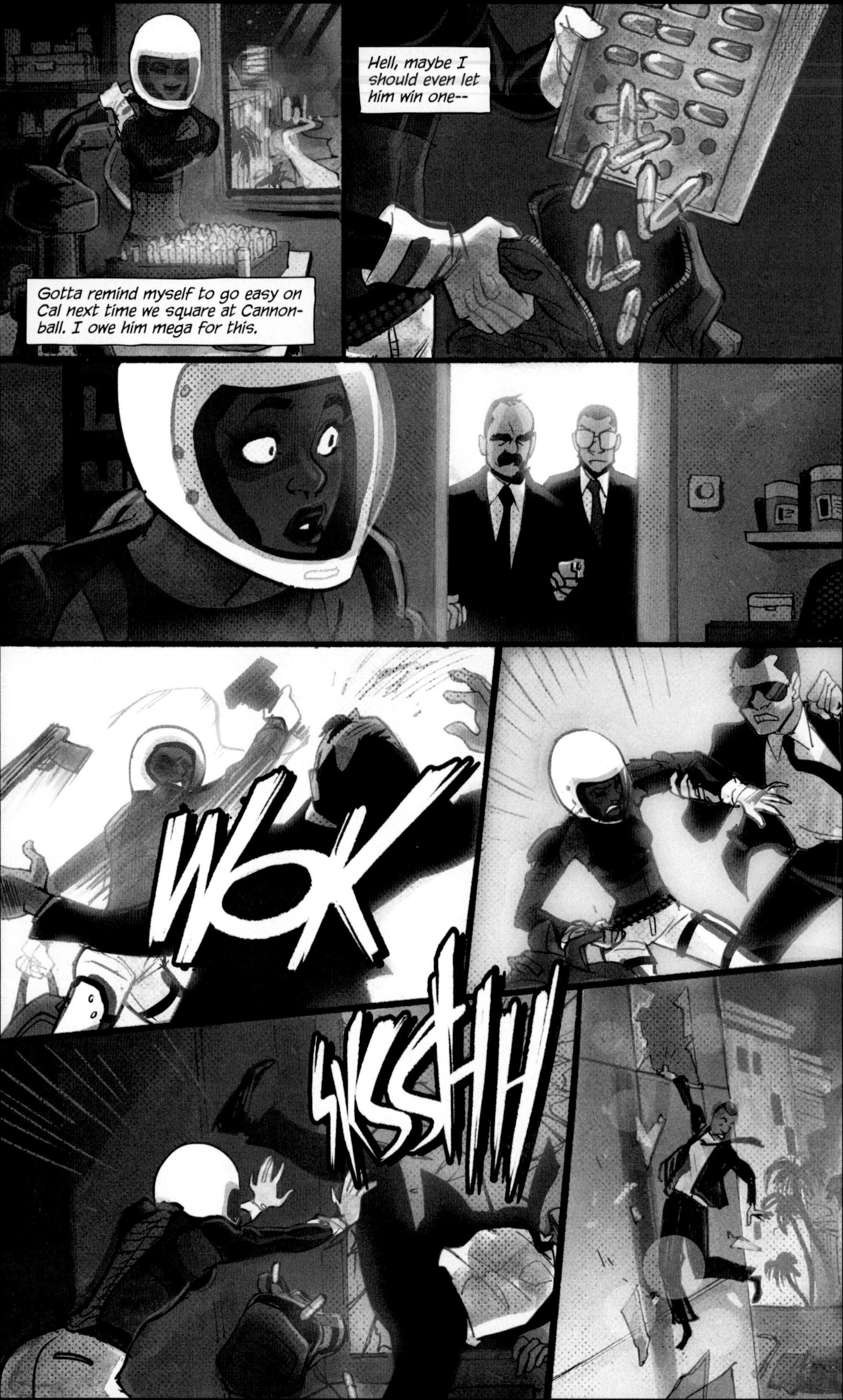
Gotta remind myself to go easy on Cal next time we square at Cannonball. I owe him mega for this.
Hell, maybe I should even let him win one--
WOK
WSSHH

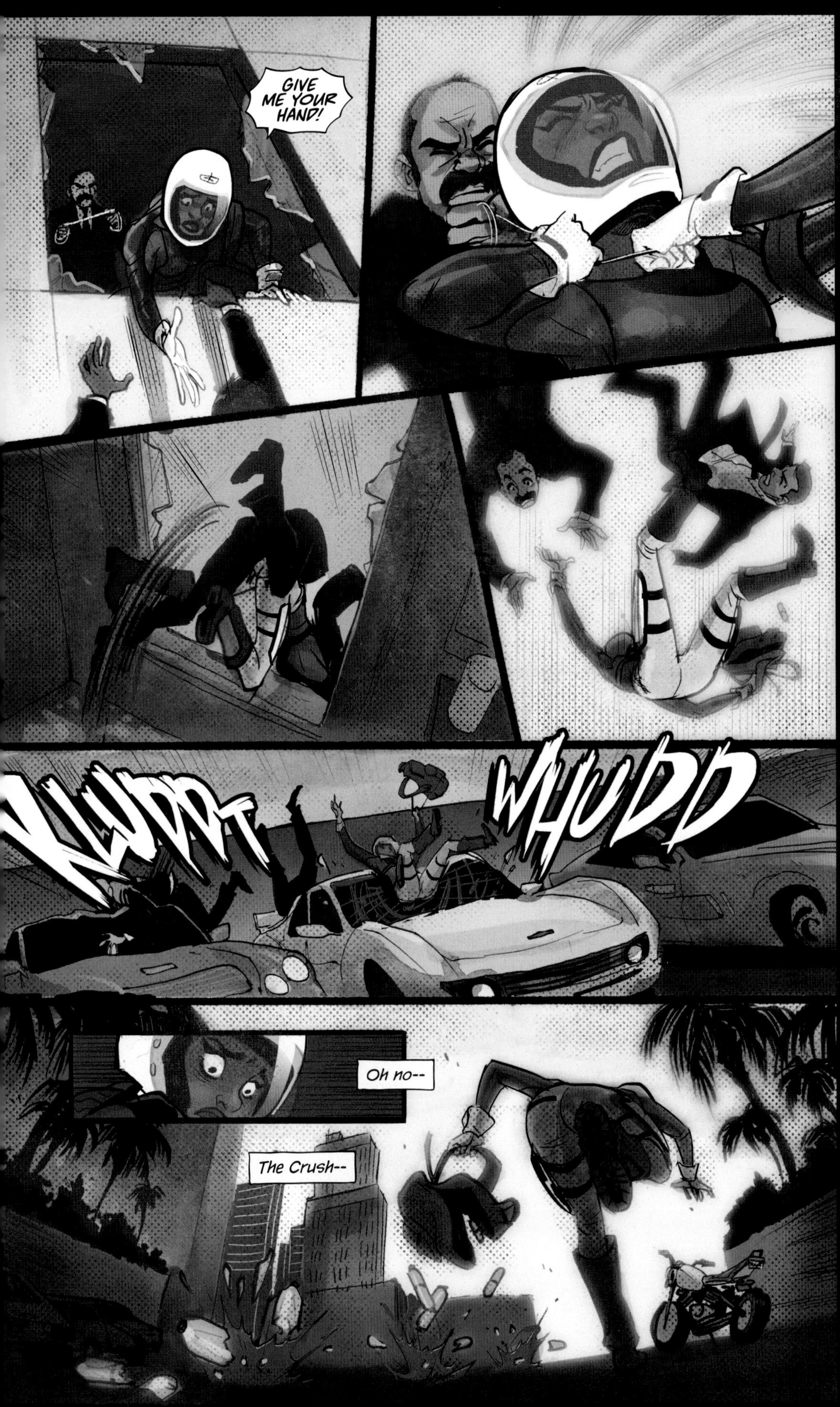
GIVE ME YOUR HAND!
KLUDDT
WHUDD
Oh no--
The Crush--

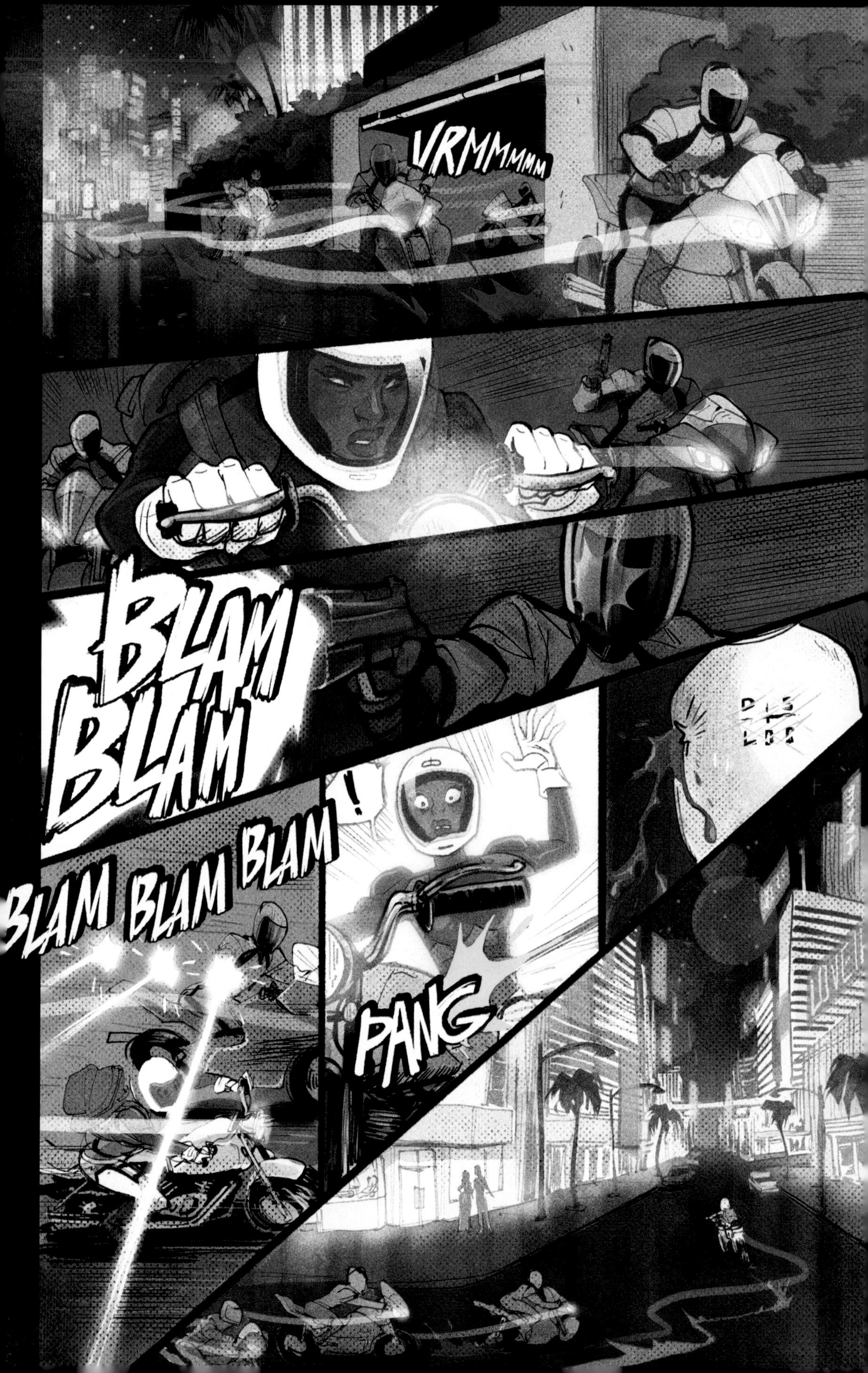
VRMMMMM
BLAM
BLAM
BLAM BLAM BLAM
!
PANG

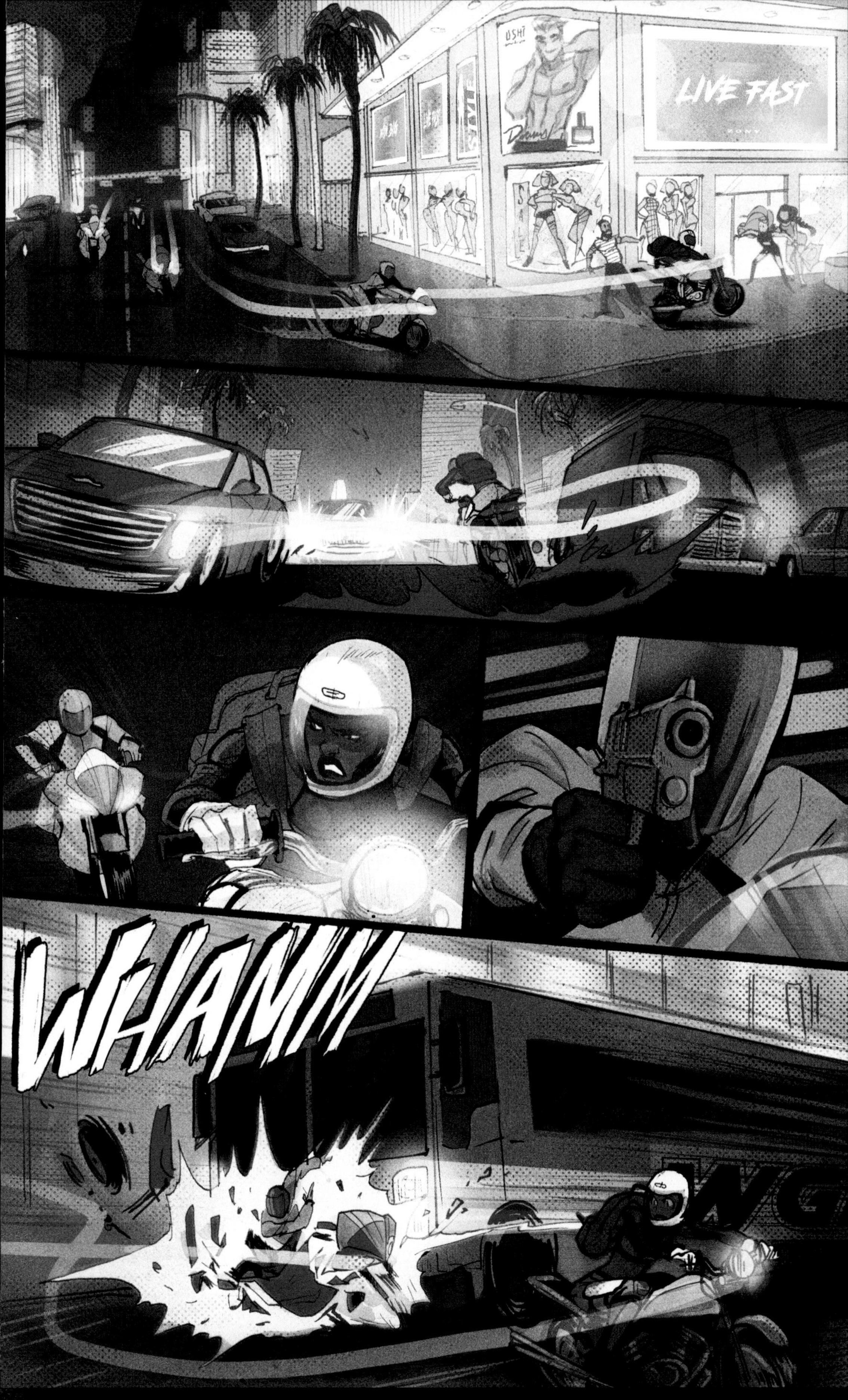
USHI
LIVE FAST
SONY
WHAMM

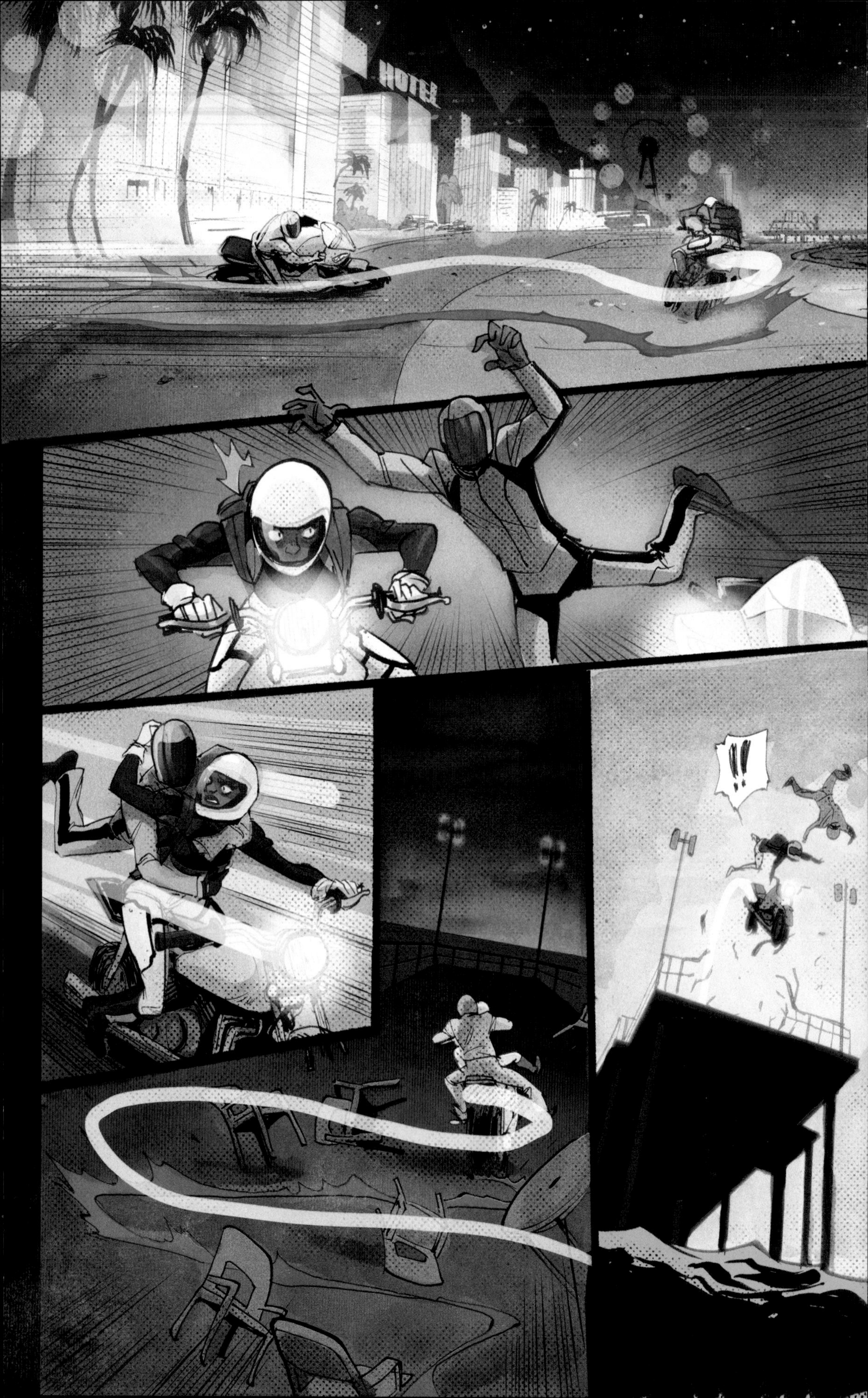
HOTEL
!!

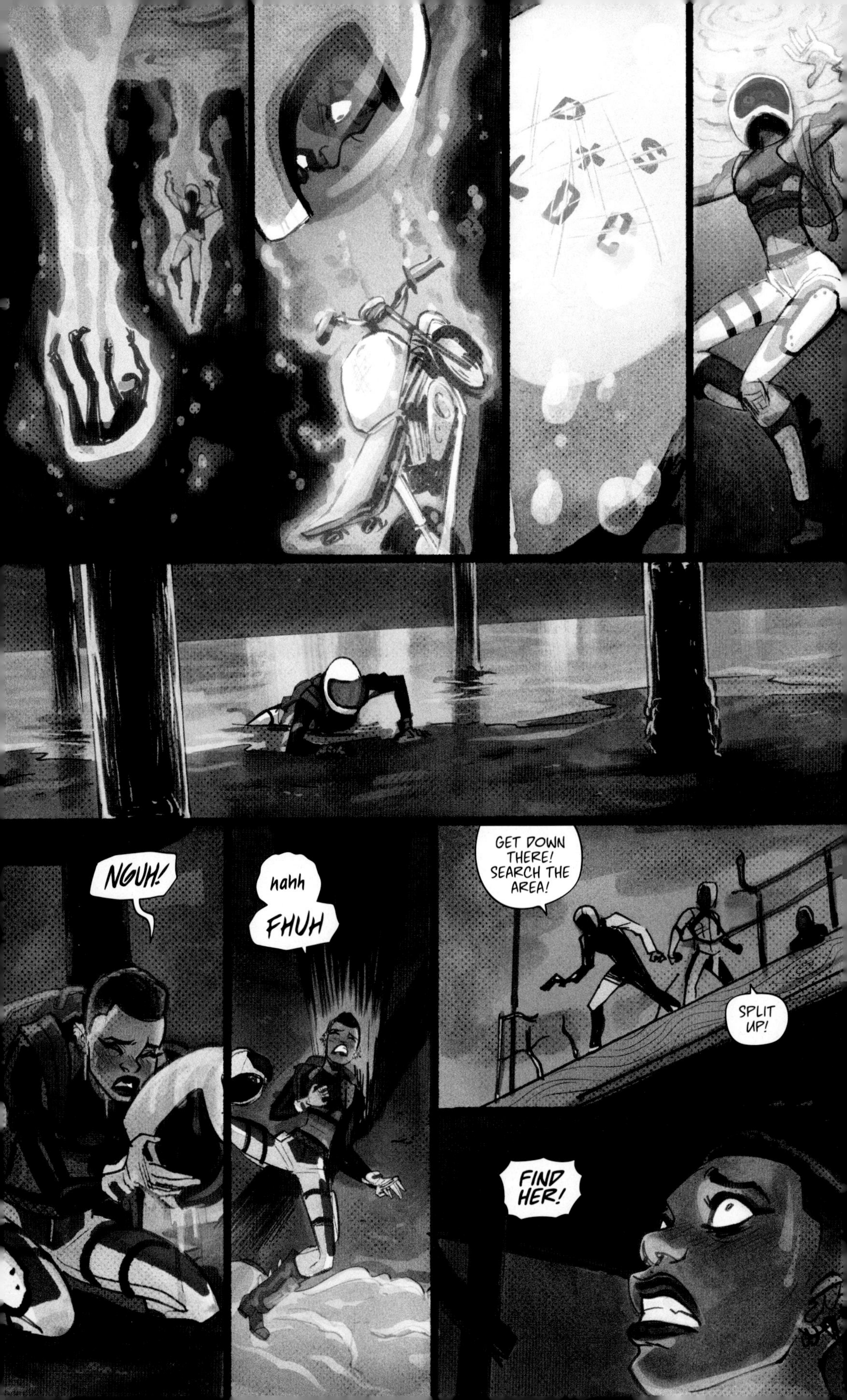
NGUH!
nahh
FHUH
GET DOWN THERE! SEARCH THE AREA!
SPLIT UP!
FIND HER!

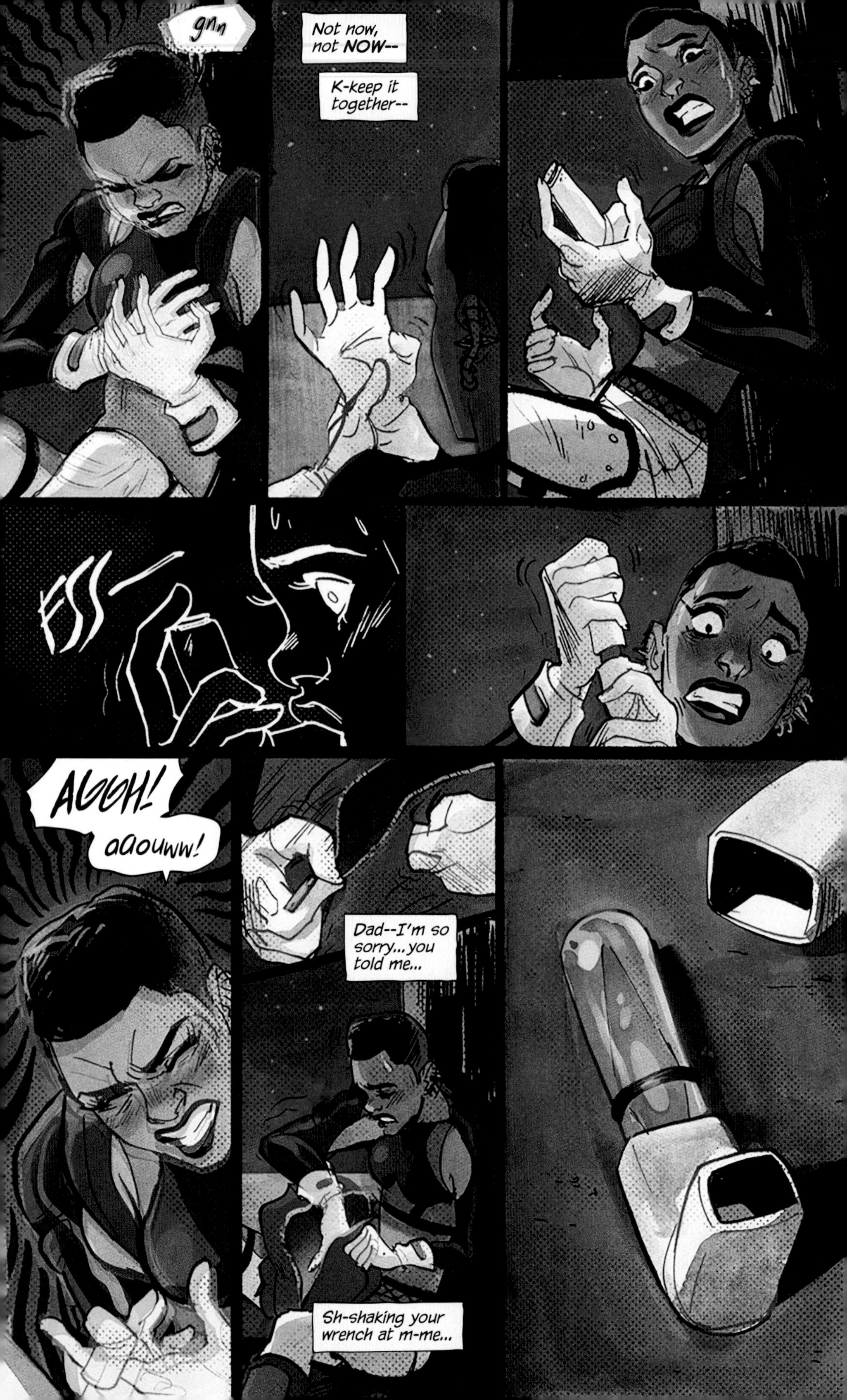
gnn
Not now, not NOW--
K-keep it together--
FSS--
AGGH!
aaouww!
Dad--I'm so sorry...you told me...
Sh-shaking your wrench at m-me...

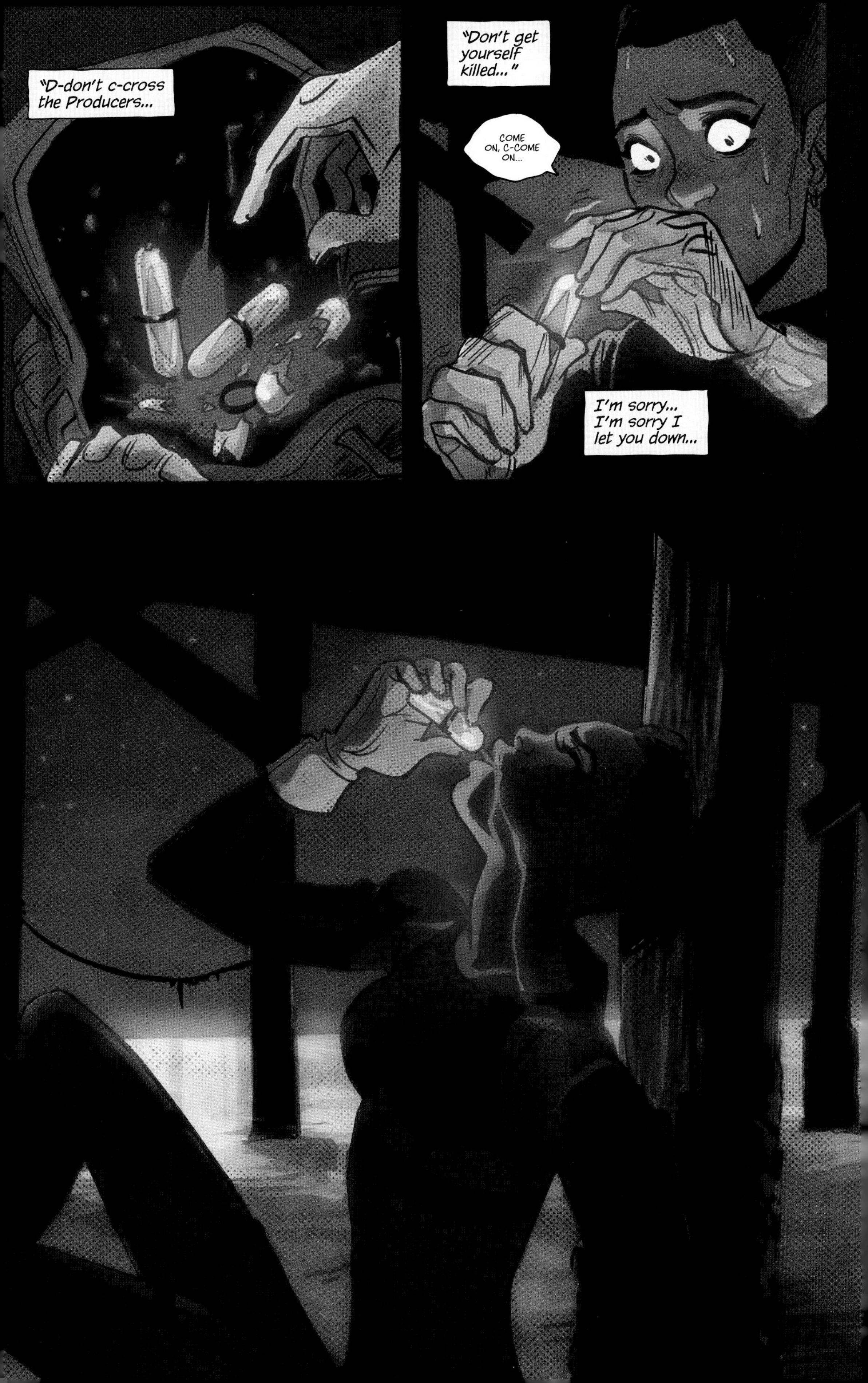
"D-don't c-cross the Producers...
"Don't get yourself killed..."
COME ON, C-COME ON...
I'm sorry... I'm sorry I let you down...

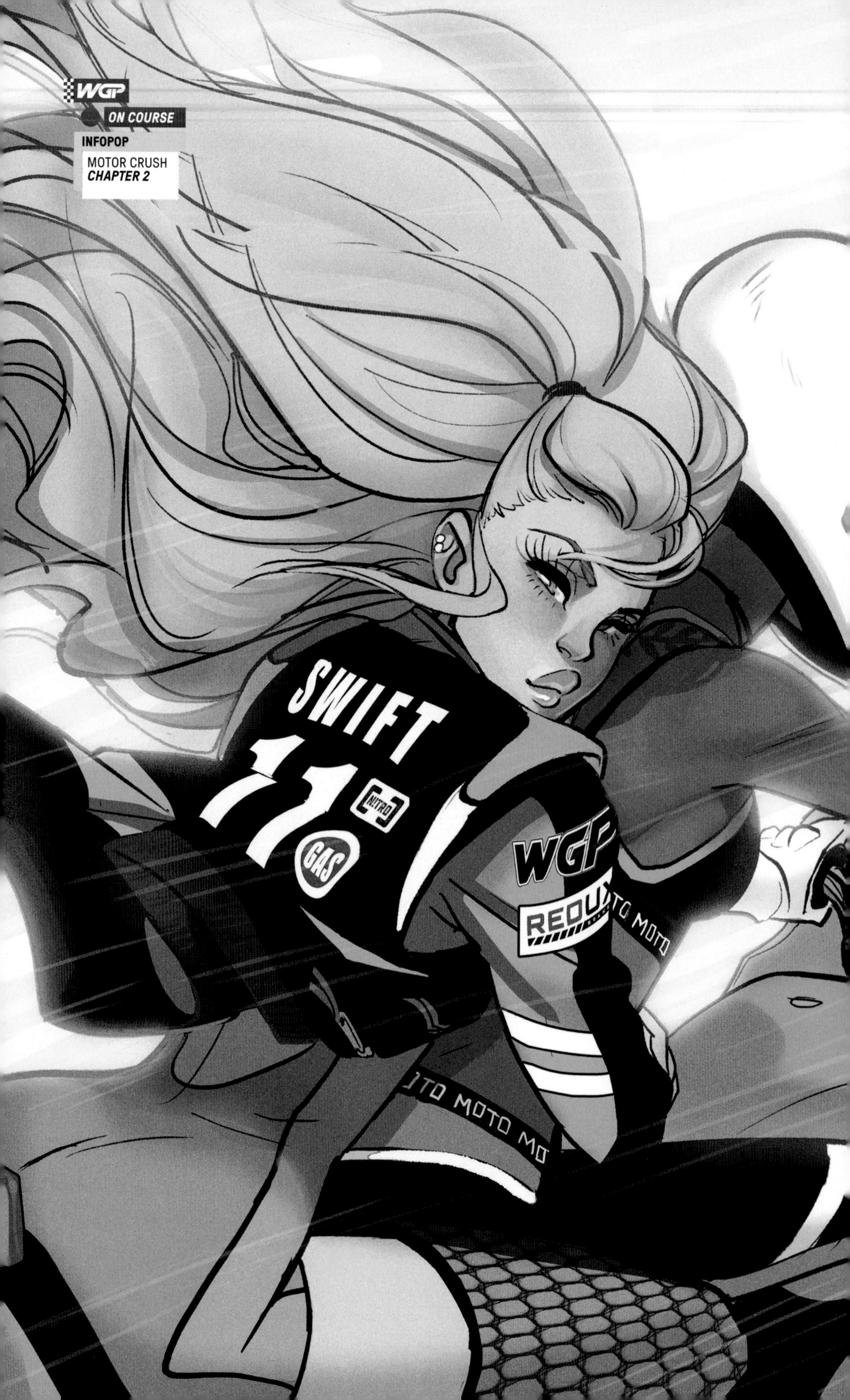
WGP
ON COURSE
INFOPOP
MOTOR CRUSH
CHAPTER 2
SWIFT
11
NITRO
GAS
WGP
REDUX
MOTO MOTO
MOTO MOTO MOTO

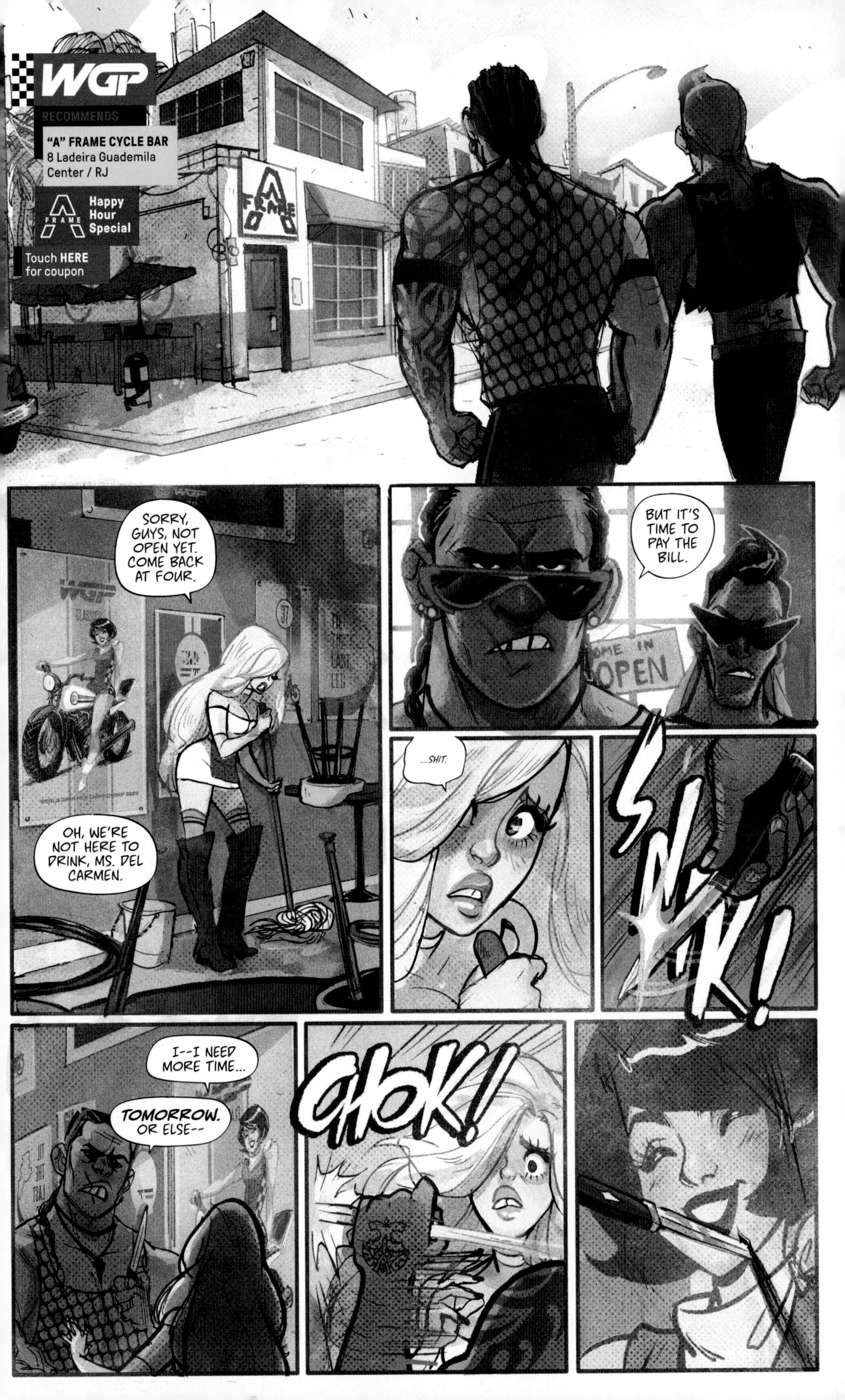
WGP
RECOMMENDS
"A" FRAME CYCLE BAR
8 Ladeira Guademila
Center / RJ
A FRAME
Happy Hour Special
Touch HERE for coupon
SORRY, GUYS, NOT OPEN YET. COME BACK AT FOUR.
OH, WE'RE NOT HERE TO DRINK, MS. DEL CARMEN.
BUT IT'S TIME TO PAY THE BILL.
OPEN
...SHIT.
SNIK!
I--I NEED MORE TIME...
TOMORROW. OR ELSE--
CHOK!

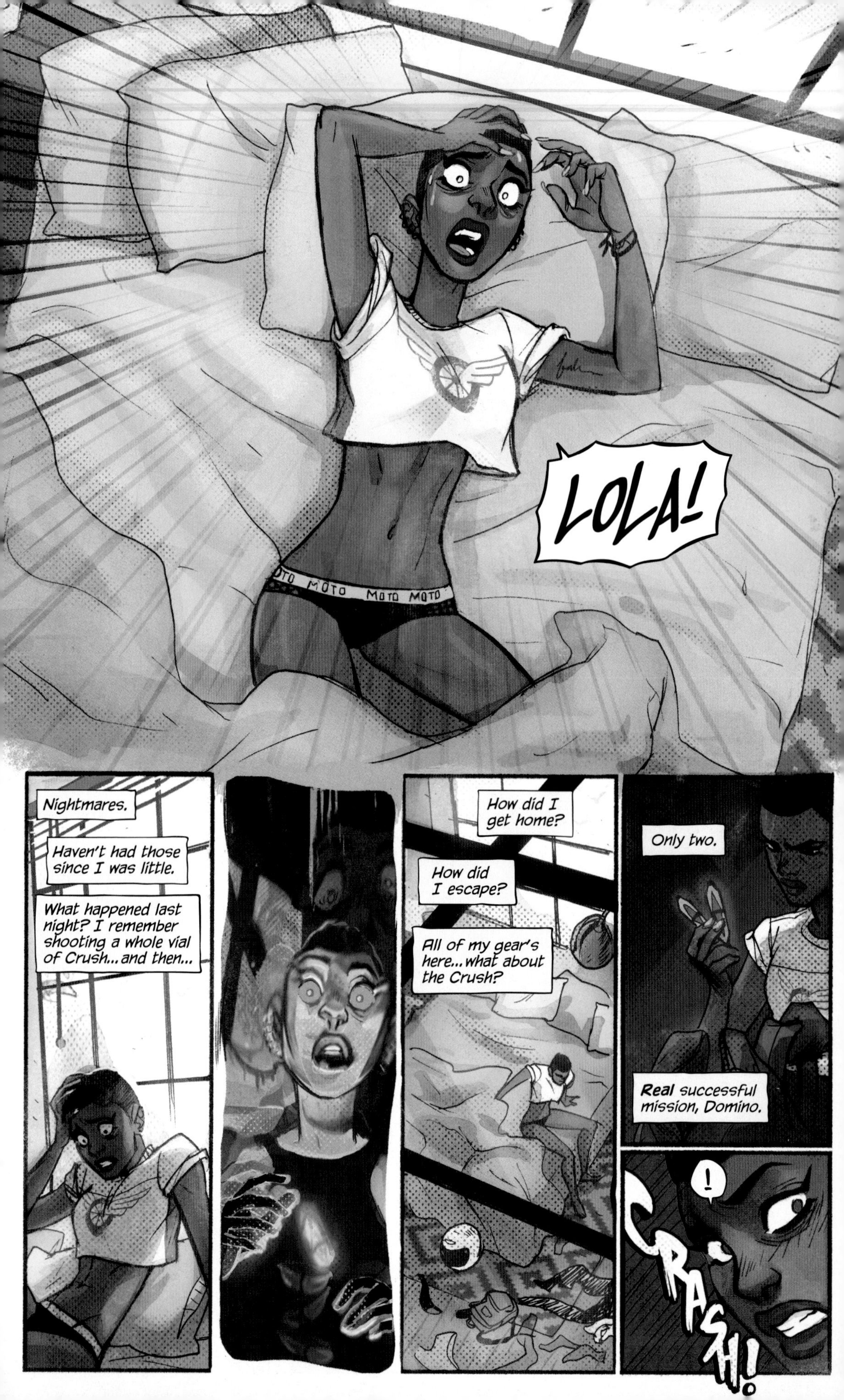
LOLA!
Nightmares.
Haven't had those since I was little.
What happened last night? I remember shooting a whole vial of Crush...and then...
How did I get home?
How did I escape?
All of my gear's here...what about the Crush?
MOTO MOTO MOTO
Only two.
Real successful mission, Domino.
!
CRASH!

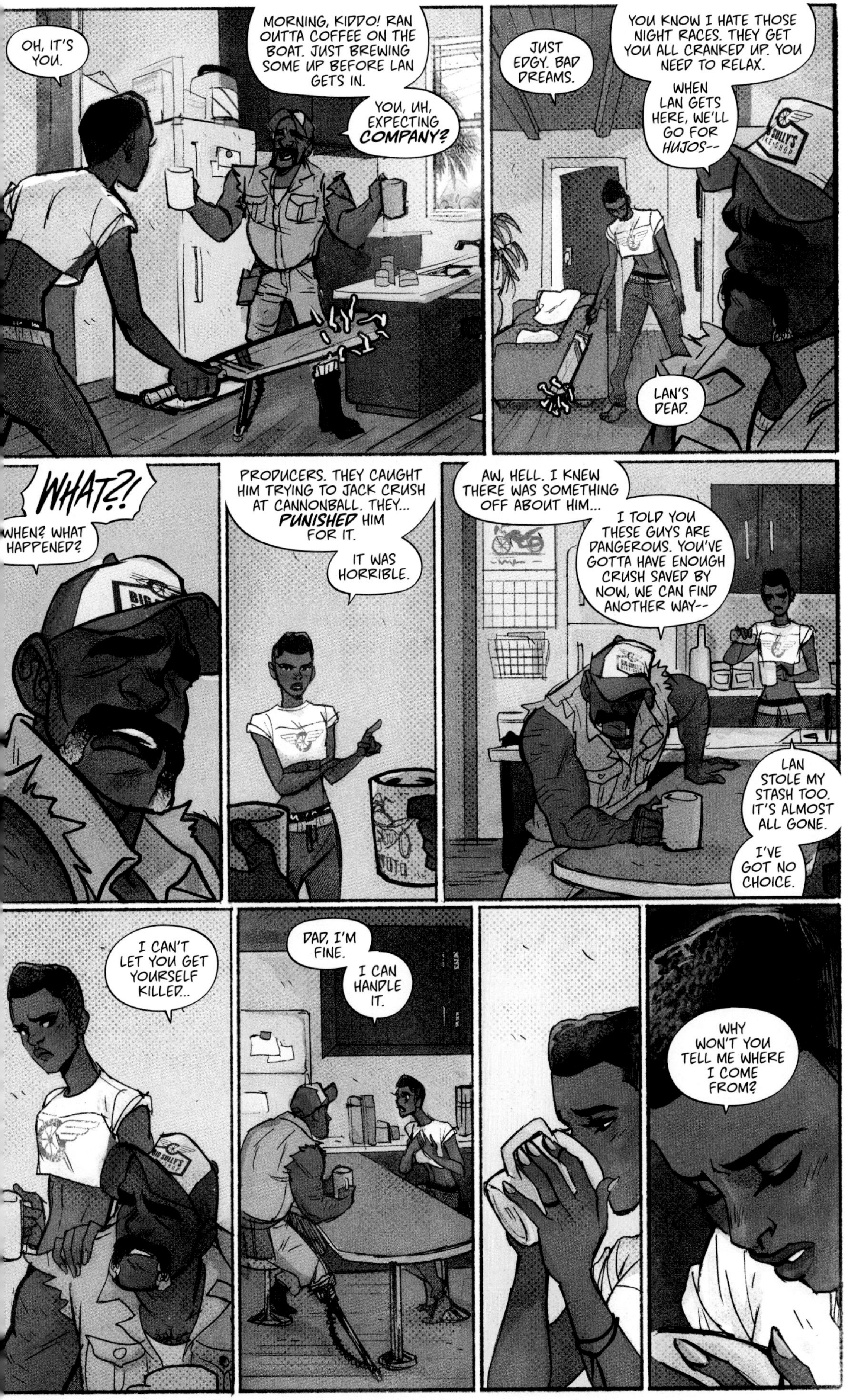

OH, IT'S YOU.
MORNING, KIDDO! RAN OUTTA COFFEE ON THE BOAT. JUST BREWING SOME UP BEFORE LAN GETS IN.
YOU, UH, EXPECTING COMPANY?
JUST EDGY. BAD DREAMS.
YOU KNOW I HATE THOSE NIGHT RACES. THEY GET YOU ALL CRANKED UP. YOU NEED TO RELAX.
WHEN LAN GETS HERE, WE'LL GO FOR HUJOS--
LAN'S DEAD.
WHAT?!
WHEN? WHAT HAPPENED?
PRODUCERS. THEY CAUGHT HIM TRYING TO JACK CRUSH AT CANNONBALL. THEY... PUNISHED HIM FOR IT.
IT WAS HORRIBLE.
AW, HELL. I KNEW THERE WAS SOMETHING OFF ABOUT HIM...
I TOLD YOU THESE GUYS ARE DANGEROUS. YOU'VE GOTTA HAVE ENOUGH CRUSH SAVED BY NOW, WE CAN FIND ANOTHER WAY--
LAN STOLE MY STASH TOO. IT'S ALMOST ALL GONE.
I'VE GOT NO CHOICE.
I CAN'T LET YOU GET YOURSELF KILLED...
DAD, I'M FINE.
I CAN HANDLE IT.
WHY WON'T YOU TELL ME WHERE I COME FROM?

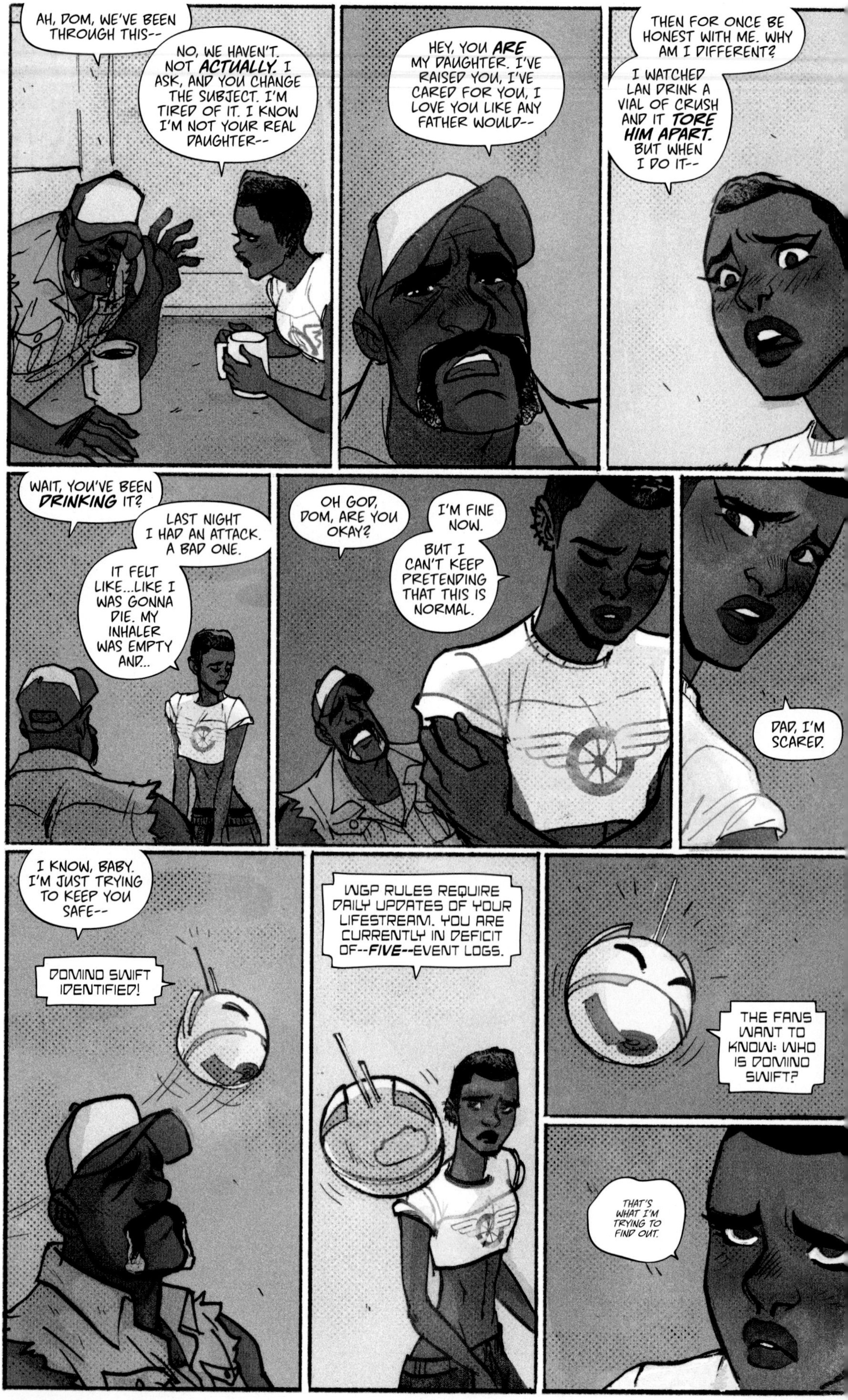
AH, DOM, WE'VE BEEN THROUGH THIS--
NO, WE HAVEN'T. NOT ACTUALLY. I ASK, AND YOU CHANGE THE SUBJECT. I'M TIRED OF IT. I KNOW I'M NOT YOUR REAL DAUGHTER--
HEY, YOU ARE MY DAUGHTER. I'VE RAISED YOU, I'VE CARED FOR YOU, I LOVE YOU LIKE ANY FATHER WOULD--
THEN FOR ONCE BE HONEST WITH ME. WHY AM I DIFFERENT?
I WATCHED LAN DRINK A VIAL OF CRUSH AND IT TORE HIM APART. BUT WHEN I DO IT--
WAIT, YOU'VE BEEN DRINKING IT?
LAST NIGHT I HAD AN ATTACK. A BAD ONE.
IT FELT LIKE...LIKE I WAS GONNA DIE. MY INHALER WAS EMPTY AND...
OH GOD, DOM, ARE YOU OKAY?
I'M FINE NOW.
BUT I CAN'T KEEP PRETENDING THAT THIS IS NORMAL.
DAD, I'M SCARED.
I KNOW, BABY. I'M JUST TRYING TO KEEP YOU SAFE--
DOMINO SWIFT IDENTIFIED!
WGP RULES REQUIRE DAILY UPDATES OF YOUR LIFESTREAM. YOU ARE CURRENTLY IN DEFICIT OF--FIVE--EVENT LOGS.
THE FANS WANT TO KNOW: WHO IS DOMINO SWIFT?
THAT'S WHAT I'M TRYING TO FIND OUT.

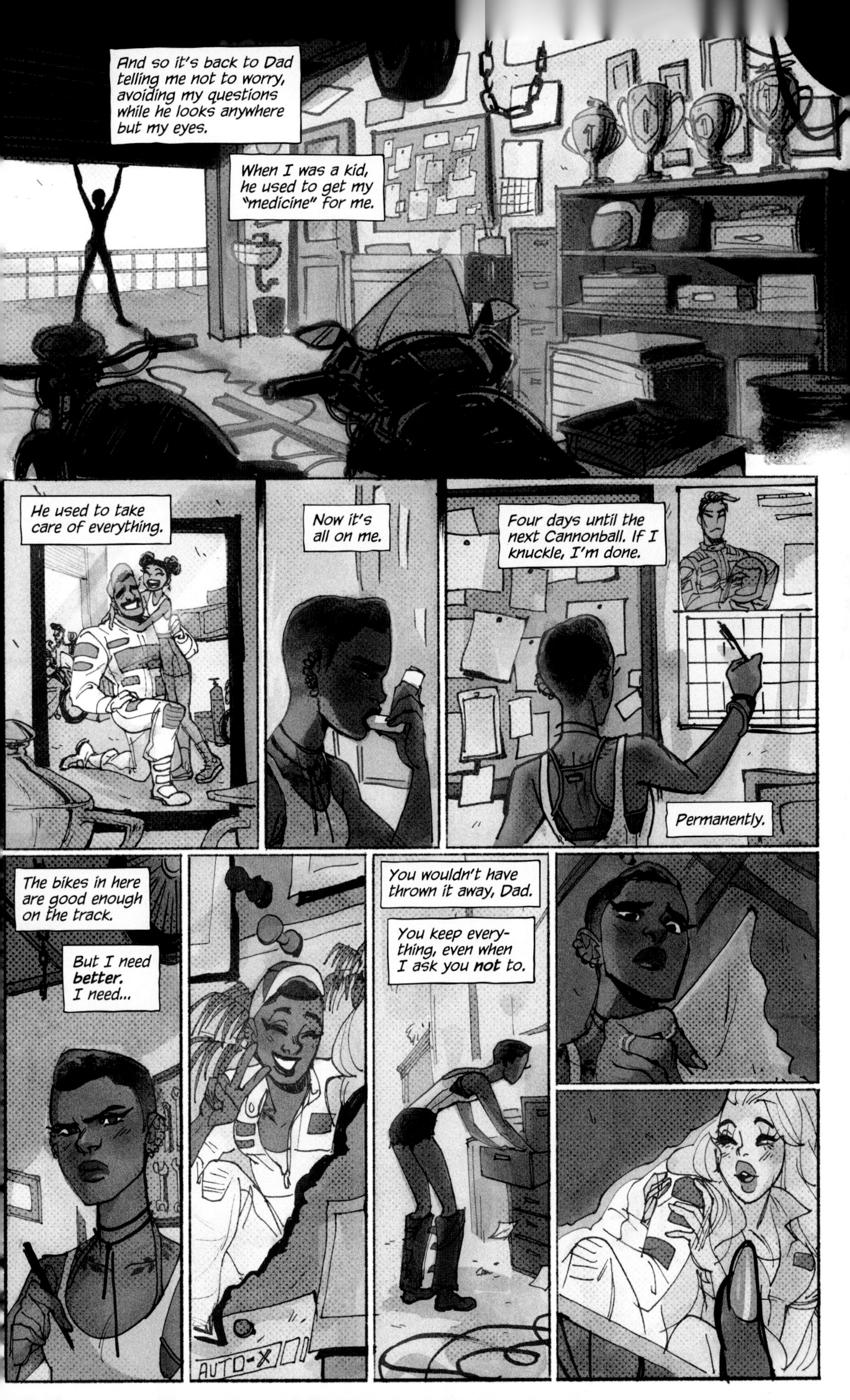
And so it's back to Dad telling me not to worry, avoiding my questions while he looks anywhere but my eyes.
When I was a kid, he used to get my "medicine" for me.
He used to take care of everything.
Now it's all on me.
Four days until the next Cannonball. If I knuckle, I'm done.
Permanently.
The bikes in here are good enough on the track.
But I need **better.** I need...
AUTO-X
You wouldn't have thrown it away, Dad.
You keep every-thing, even when I ask you **not** to.

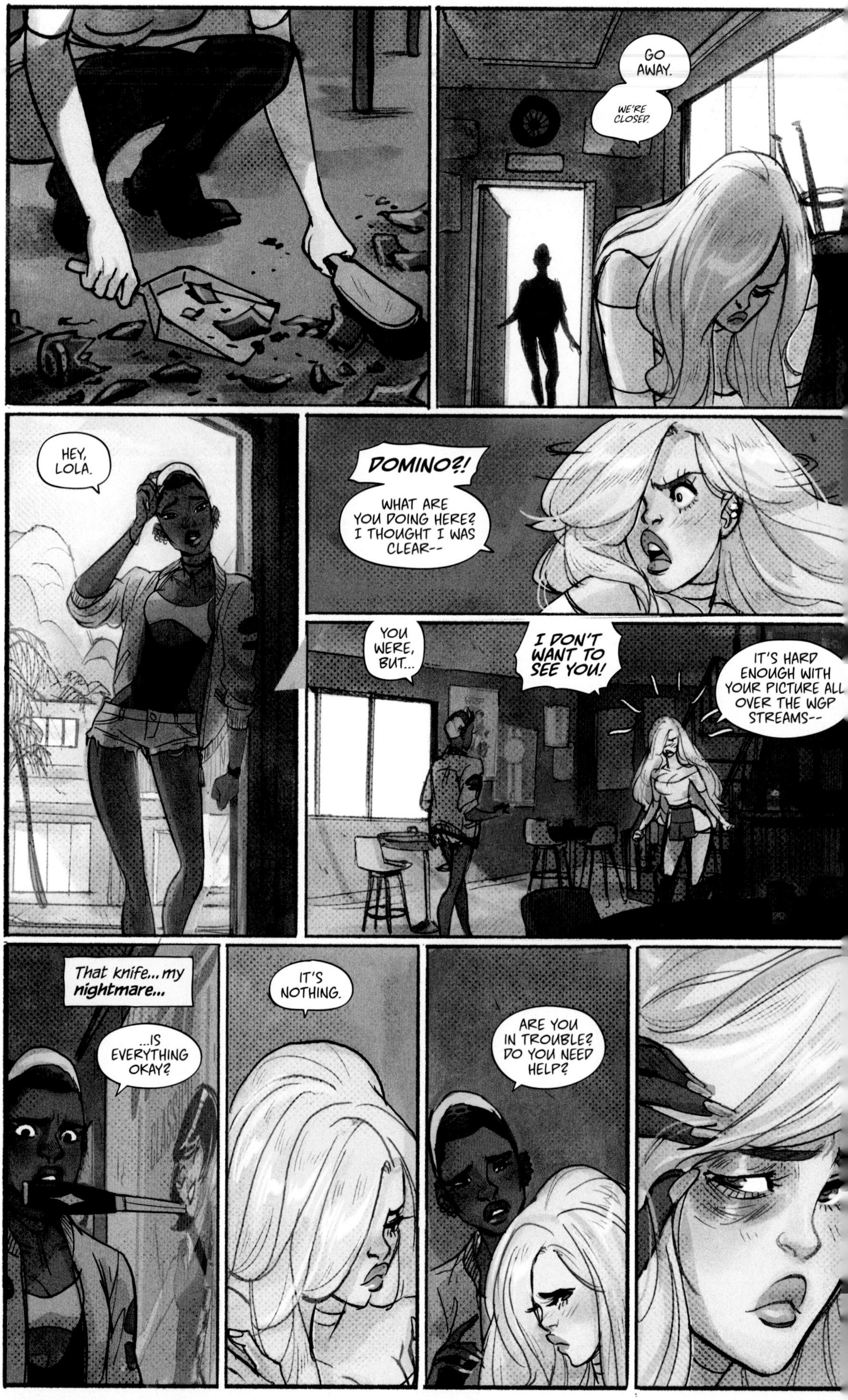
GO AWAY.
WE'RE CLOSED.
HEY, LOLA.
DOMINO?!
WHAT ARE YOU DOING HERE? I THOUGHT I WAS CLEAR--
YOU WERE, BUT...
I DON'T WANT TO SEE YOU!
IT'S HARD ENOUGH WITH YOUR PICTURE ALL OVER THE WGP STREAMS--
That knife... my nightmare...
...IS EVERYTHING OKAY?
IT'S NOTHING.
ARE YOU IN TROUBLE? DO YOU NEED HELP?

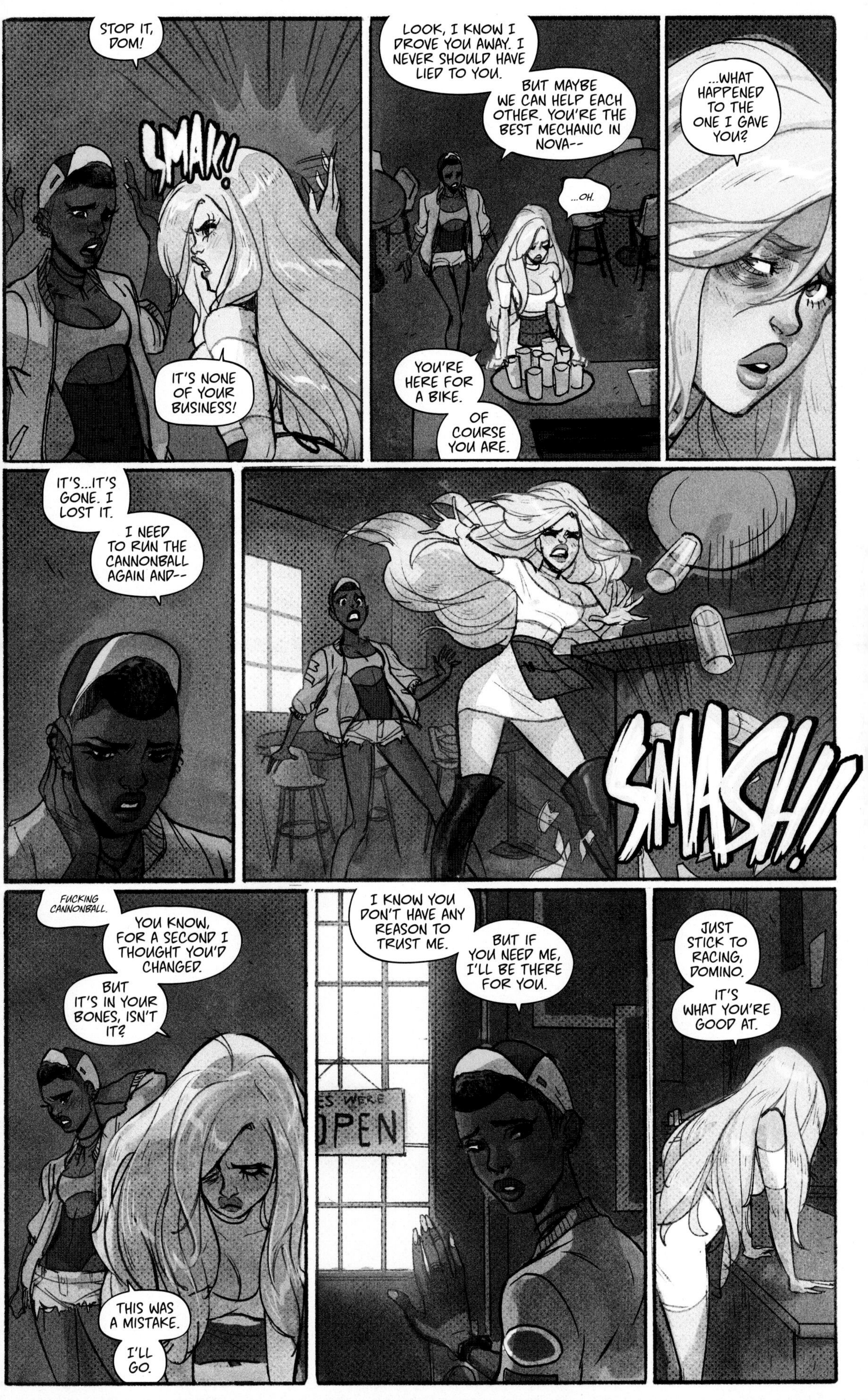
STOP IT, DOM!
SMAK!
IT'S NONE OF YOUR BUSINESS!
LOOK, I KNOW I DROVE YOU AWAY. I NEVER SHOULD HAVE LIED TO YOU.
BUT MAYBE WE CAN HELP EACH OTHER. YOU'RE THE BEST MECHANIC IN NOVA--
...OH.
YOU'RE HERE FOR A BIKE.
OF COURSE YOU ARE.
...WHAT HAPPENED TO THE ONE I GAVE YOU?
IT'S...IT'S GONE. I LOST IT.
I NEED TO RUN THE CANNONBALL AGAIN AND--
SMASH!!
FUCKING CANNONBALL.
YOU KNOW, FOR A SECOND I THOUGHT YOU'D CHANGED.
BUT IT'S IN YOUR BONES, ISN'T IT?
THIS WAS A MISTAKE.
I'LL GO.
I KNOW YOU DON'T HAVE ANY REASON TO TRUST ME.
BUT IF YOU NEED ME, I'LL BE THERE FOR YOU.
OPEN
JUST STICK TO RACING, DOMINO.
IT'S WHAT YOU'RE GOOD AT.

WORLD GRAND PRIX

WGP

INFOPOP

11:52 BZ
87°V / SUNNY

COUNTDOWN TO RACE:
6:06:22:05

Touch **HERE** for
media updates

I promised I'd walk out
of that bar for good.

But that weird nightmare kept
itching at the back of my mind.

It didn't feel like
a dream anymore,
but a **vision**.

I had to see
if it was true.

And if it is,
those goons
should be
showing
up any
time now--

... Shit.

I don't know if
I'm relieved or even
more freaked out.

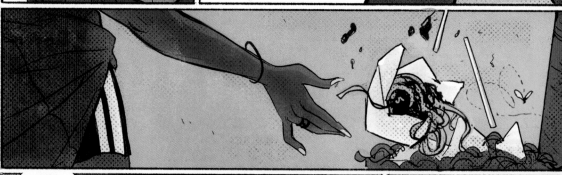

TIME'S
UP, LADY.
WE WARNED
YOU.

NOW WE
GOTTA HURT
YOU.

PLEASE,
NO...!

LEAVE HER
ALONE.

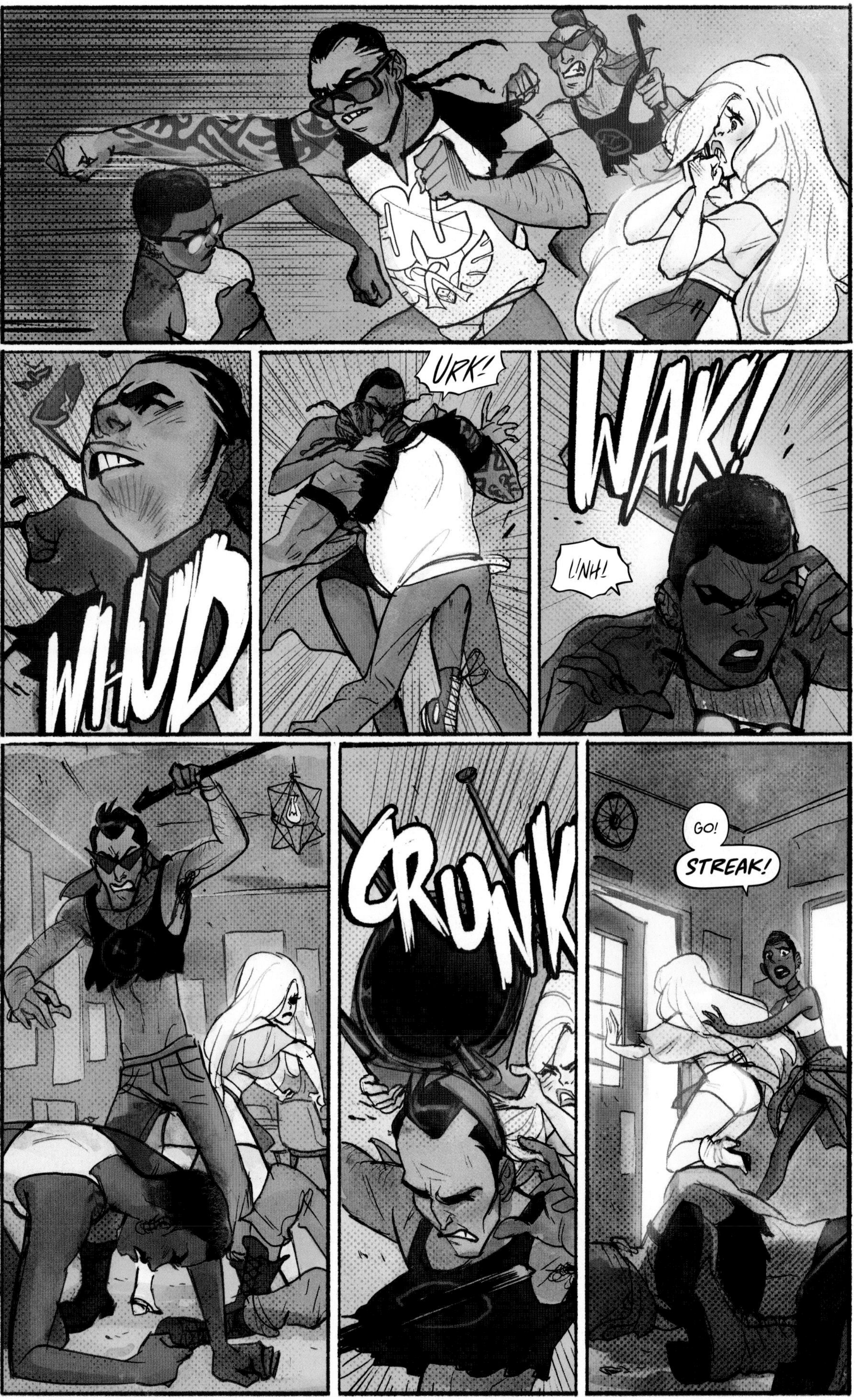
WHUD
URK!
WAK!
UNH!
CRUNK
GO!
STREAK!

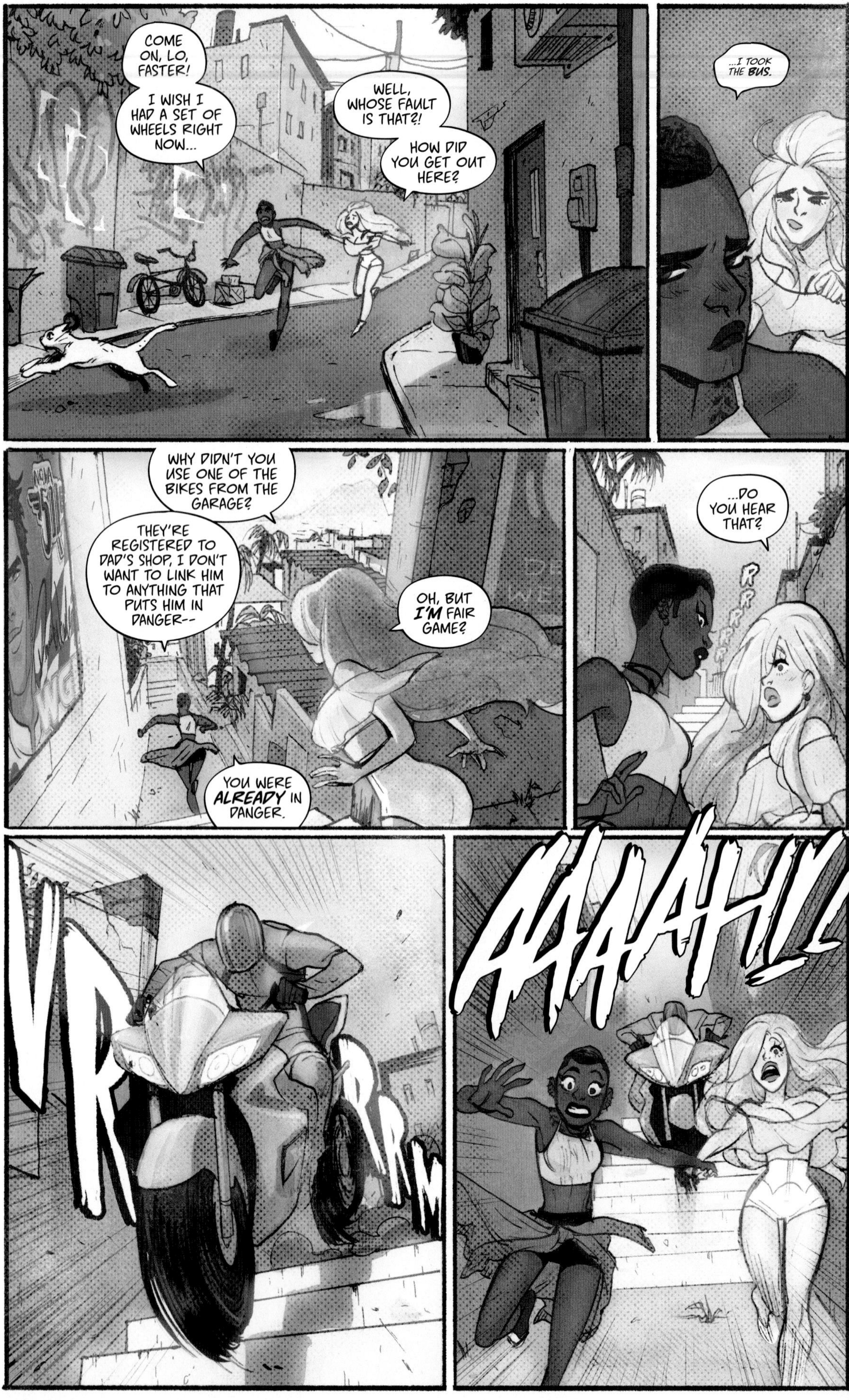
COME ON, LO, FASTER!
I WISH I HAD A SET OF WHEELS RIGHT NOW...
WELL, WHOSE FAULT IS THAT?!
HOW DID YOU GET OUT HERE?
...I TOOK THE BUS.
WHY DIDN'T YOU USE ONE OF THE BIKES FROM THE GARAGE?
THEY'RE REGISTERED TO DAD'S SHOP, I DON'T WANT TO LINK HIM TO ANYTHING THAT PUTS HIM IN DANGER--
OH, BUT I'M FAIR GAME?
YOU WERE ALREADY IN DANGER.
...DO YOU HEAR THAT?
RRRRRRR
VRRRM
AAAAH!!

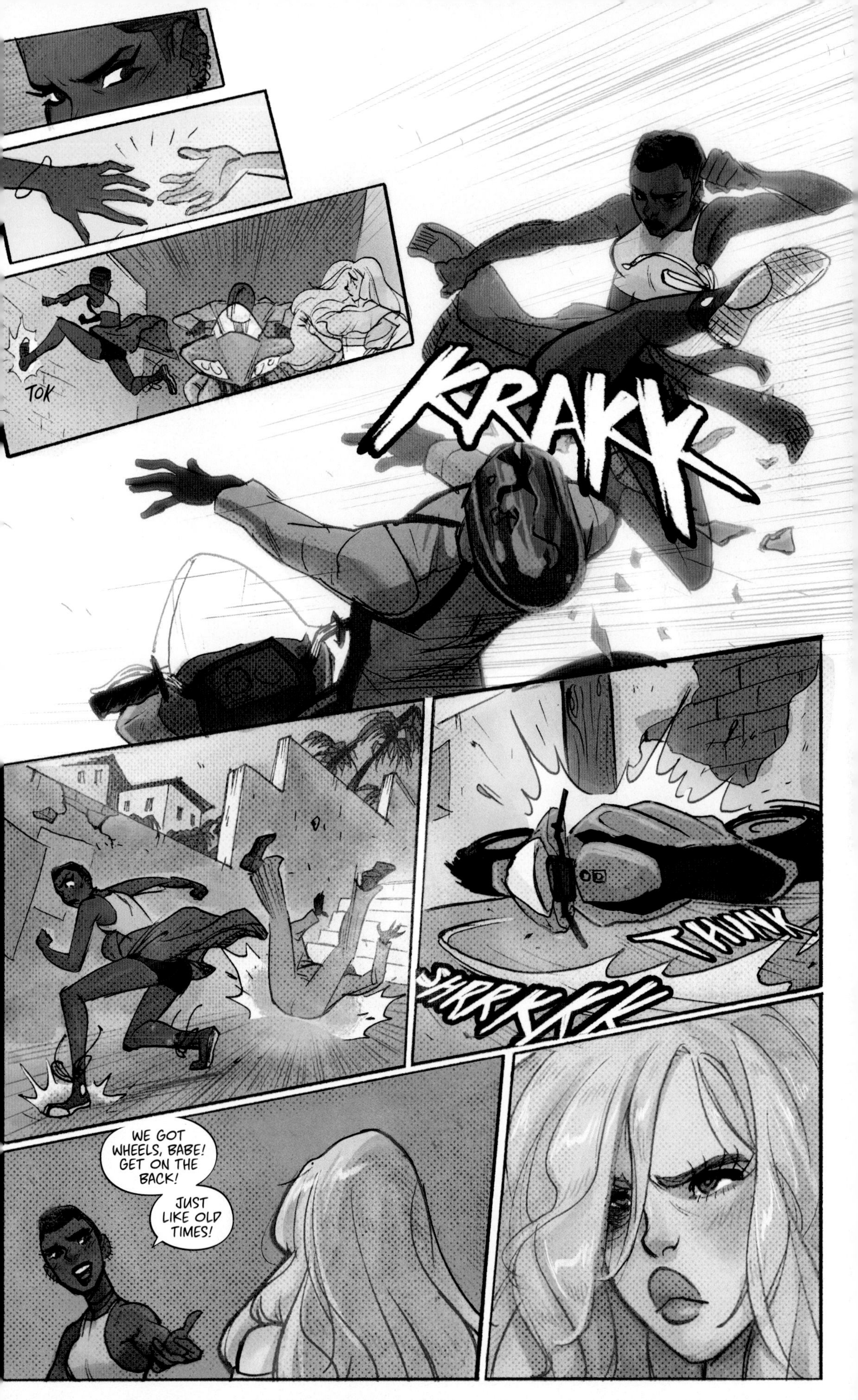
TOK
KRAKK
THUNK
SHRRKKKK
WE GOT WHEELS, BABE! GET ON THE BACK!
JUST LIKE OLD TIMES!

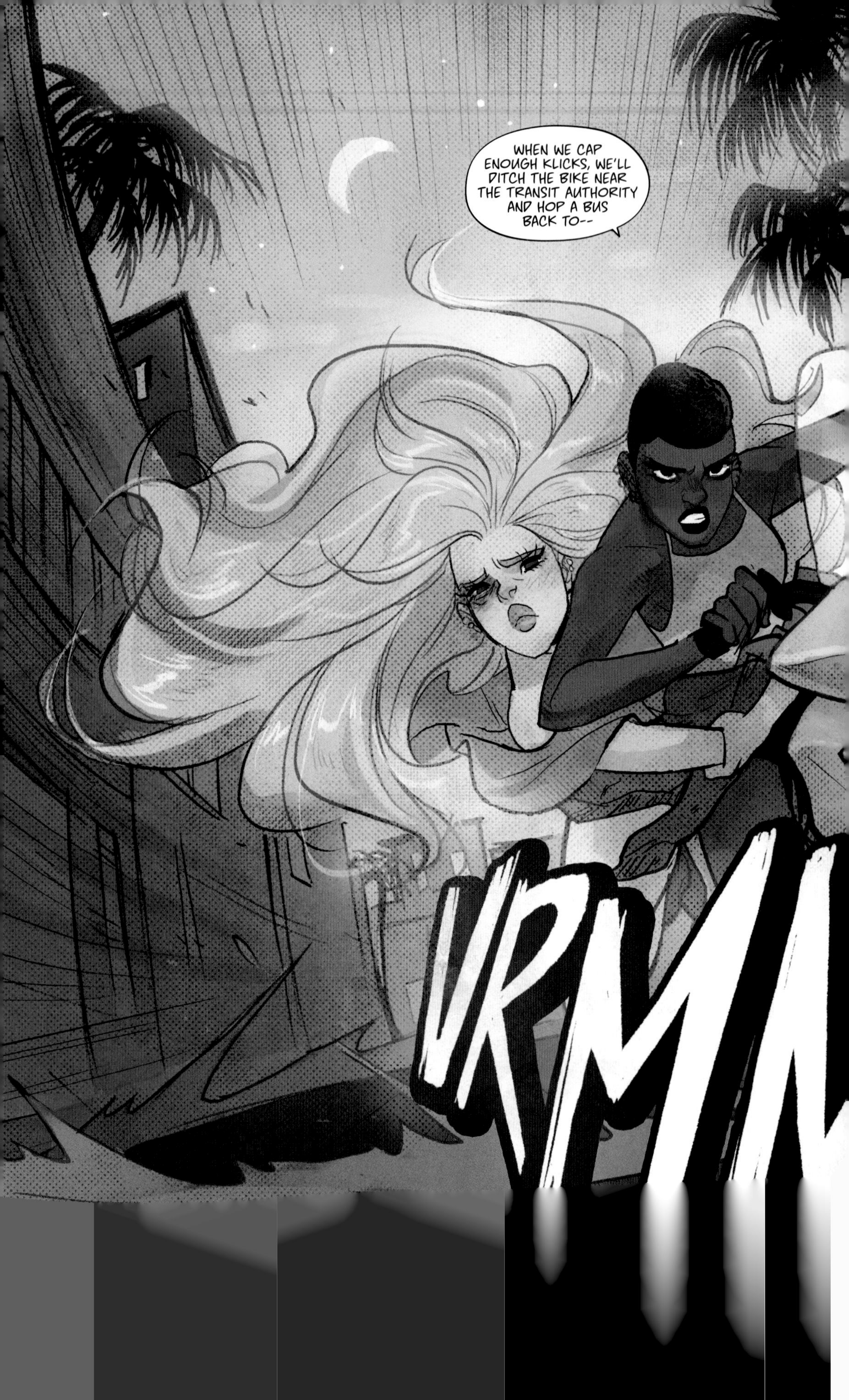
WHEN WE CAP ENOUGH KLICKS, WE'LL DITCH THE BIKE NEAR THE TRANSIT AUTHORITY AND HOP A BUS BACK TO--

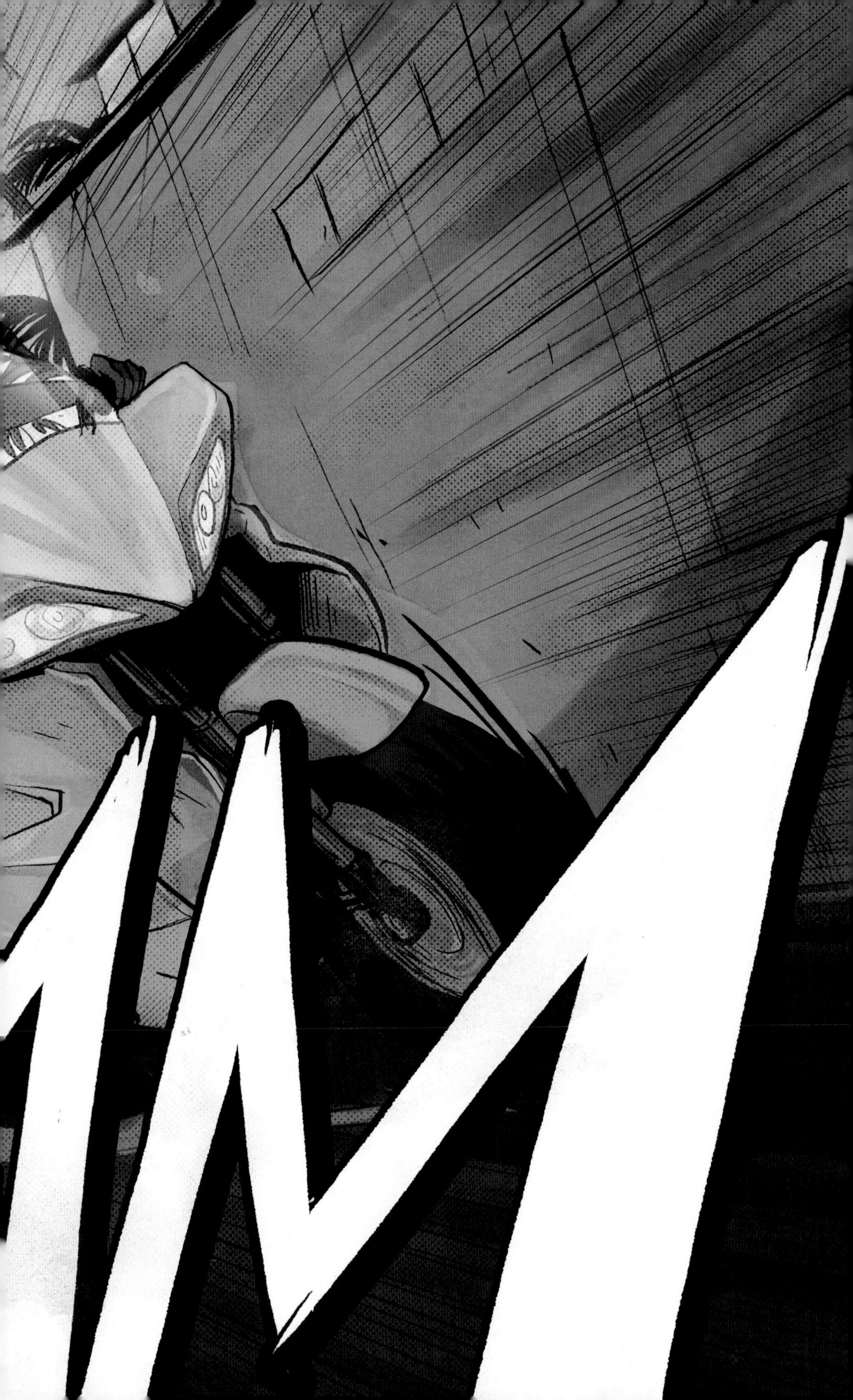
MM

YOU WERE SAYING?
SHIT!
NO SWEAT, I CAN OUTRUN THESE JIMMIES...
KCHK
MAX SPEED
20 40 60 80 100 120 140 160 180
WARNING
MPH
FUEL
185

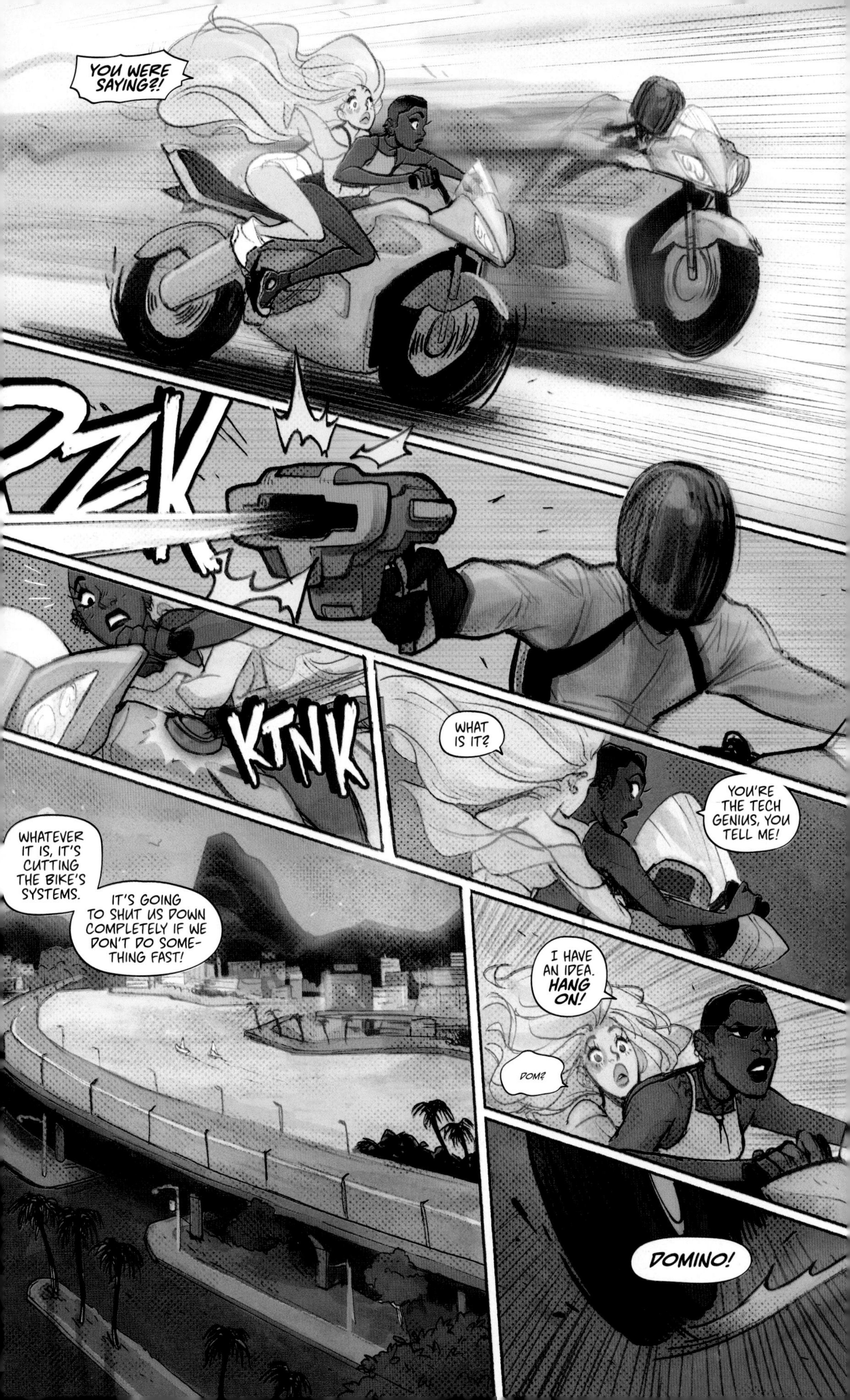
YOU WERE SAYING?!
PZZK
KTNK
WHAT IS IT?
YOU'RE THE TECH GENIUS, YOU TELL ME!
WHATEVER IT IS, IT'S CUTTING THE BIKE'S SYSTEMS.
IT'S GOING TO SHUT US DOWN COMPLETELY IF WE DON'T DO SOME-THING FAST!
I HAVE AN IDEA. HANG ON!
DOM?
DOMINO!

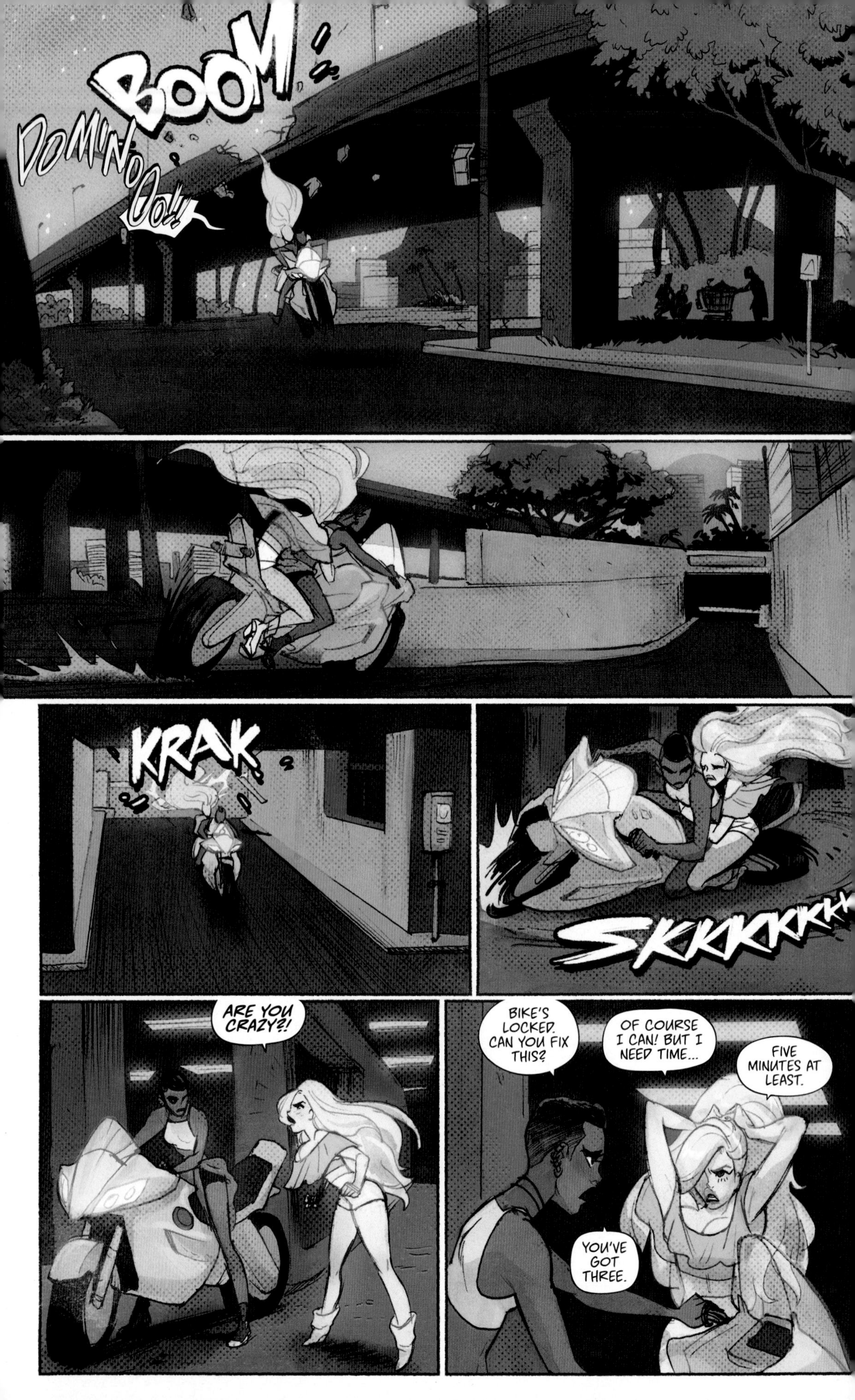
BOOM
DOMINOOOO!!
KRAK
SKKKKKK
ARE YOU CRAZY?!
BIKE'S LOCKED. CAN YOU FIX THIS?
OF COURSE I CAN! BUT I NEED TIME...
FIVE MINUTES AT LEAST.
YOU'VE GOT THREE.

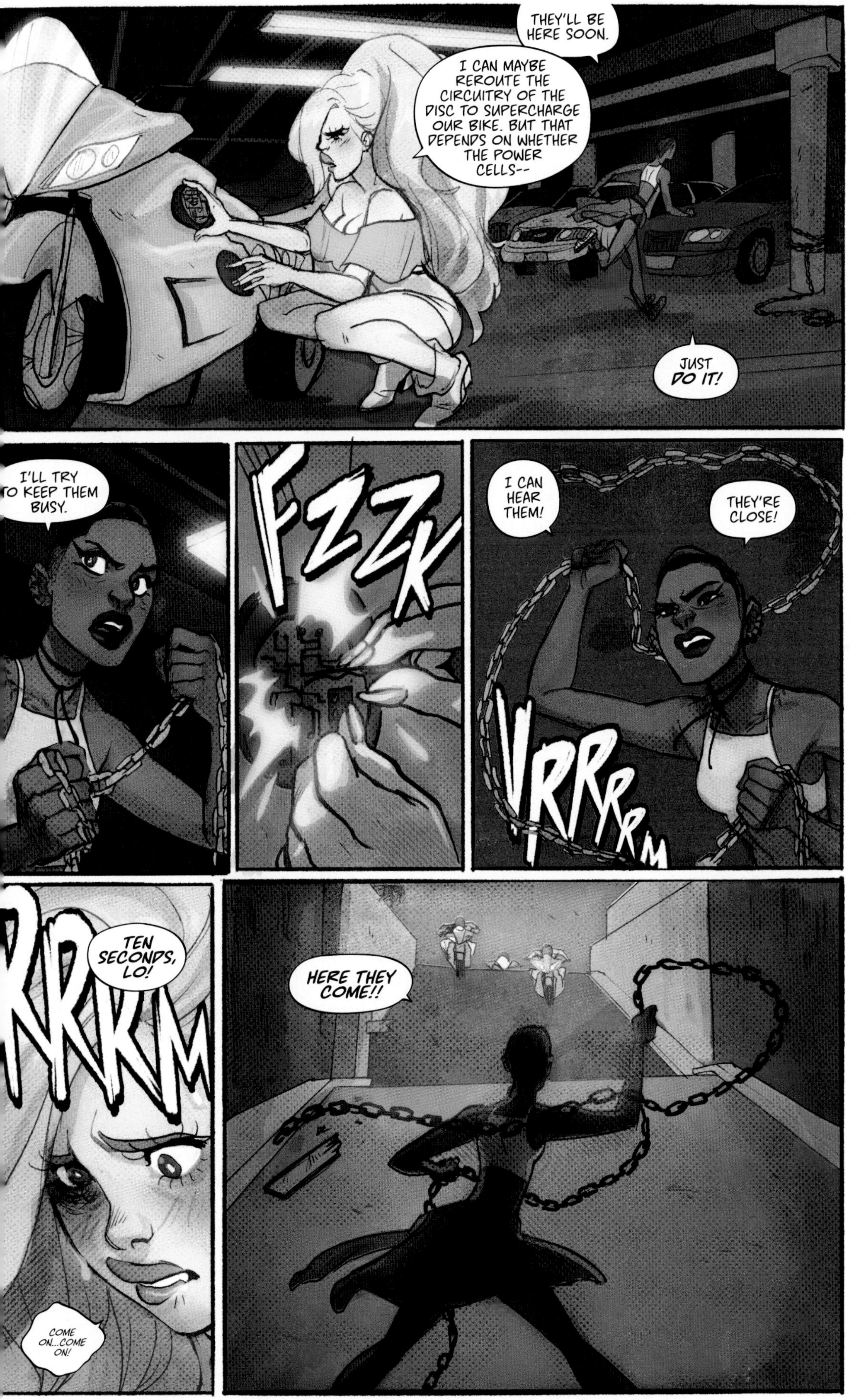
THEY'LL BE HERE SOON.
I CAN MAYBE REROUTE THE CIRCUITRY OF THE DISC TO SUPERCHARGE OUR BIKE. BUT THAT DEPENDS ON WHETHER THE POWER CELLS--
JUST DO IT!
I'LL TRY TO KEEP THEM BUSY.
FZZK
I CAN HEAR THEM!
THEY'RE CLOSE!
VRRRRM
RRRKM
TEN SECONDS, LO!
COME ON...COME ON!
HERE THEY COME!!

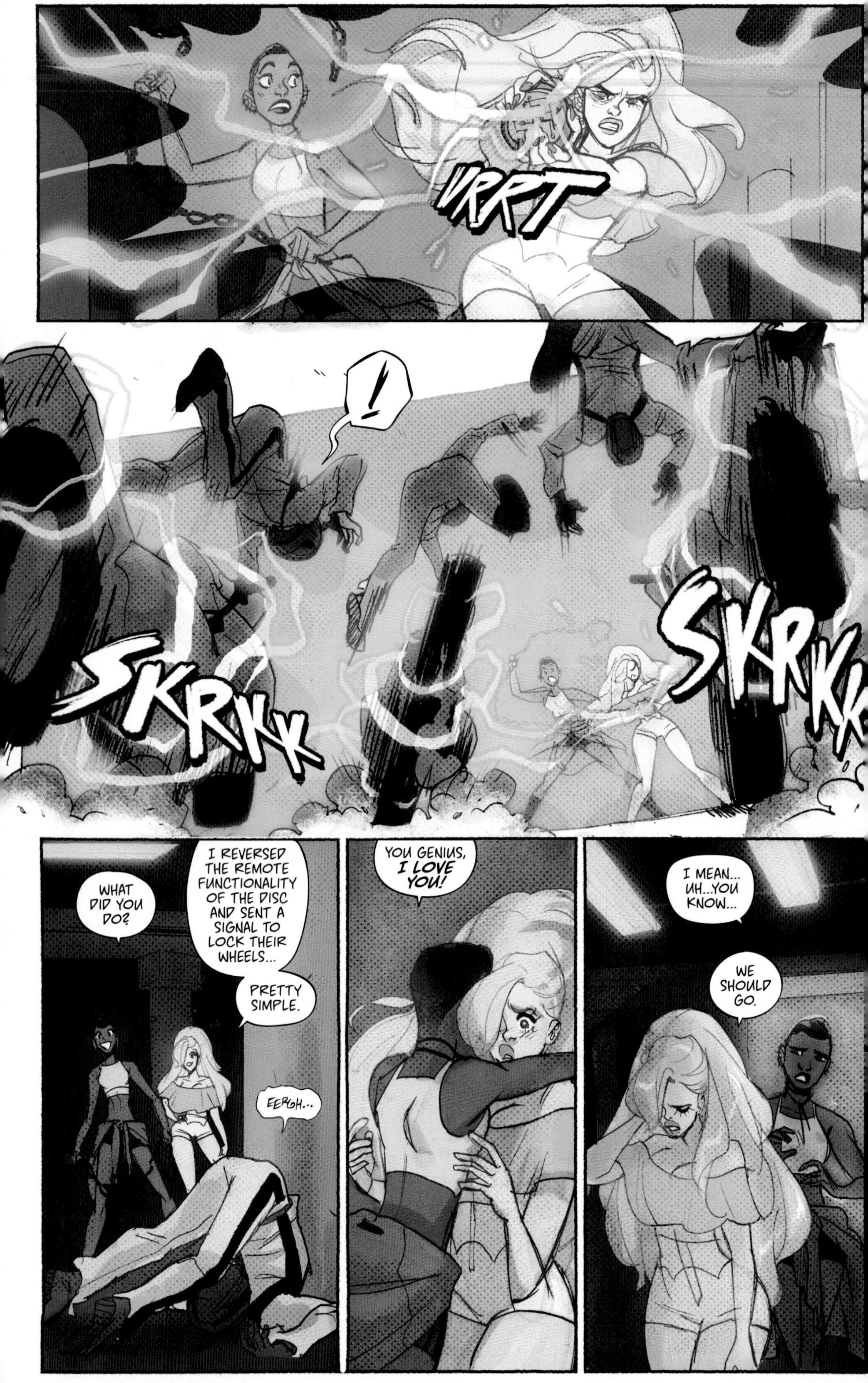
VRRT
!
SKRKK
SKRKK
WHAT DID YOU DO?
I REVERSED THE REMOTE FUNCTIONALITY OF THE DISC AND SENT A SIGNAL TO LOCK THEIR WHEELS...
PRETTY SIMPLE.
EERGH...
YOU GENIUS, I LOVE YOU!
I MEAN... UH...YOU KNOW...
WE SHOULD GO.

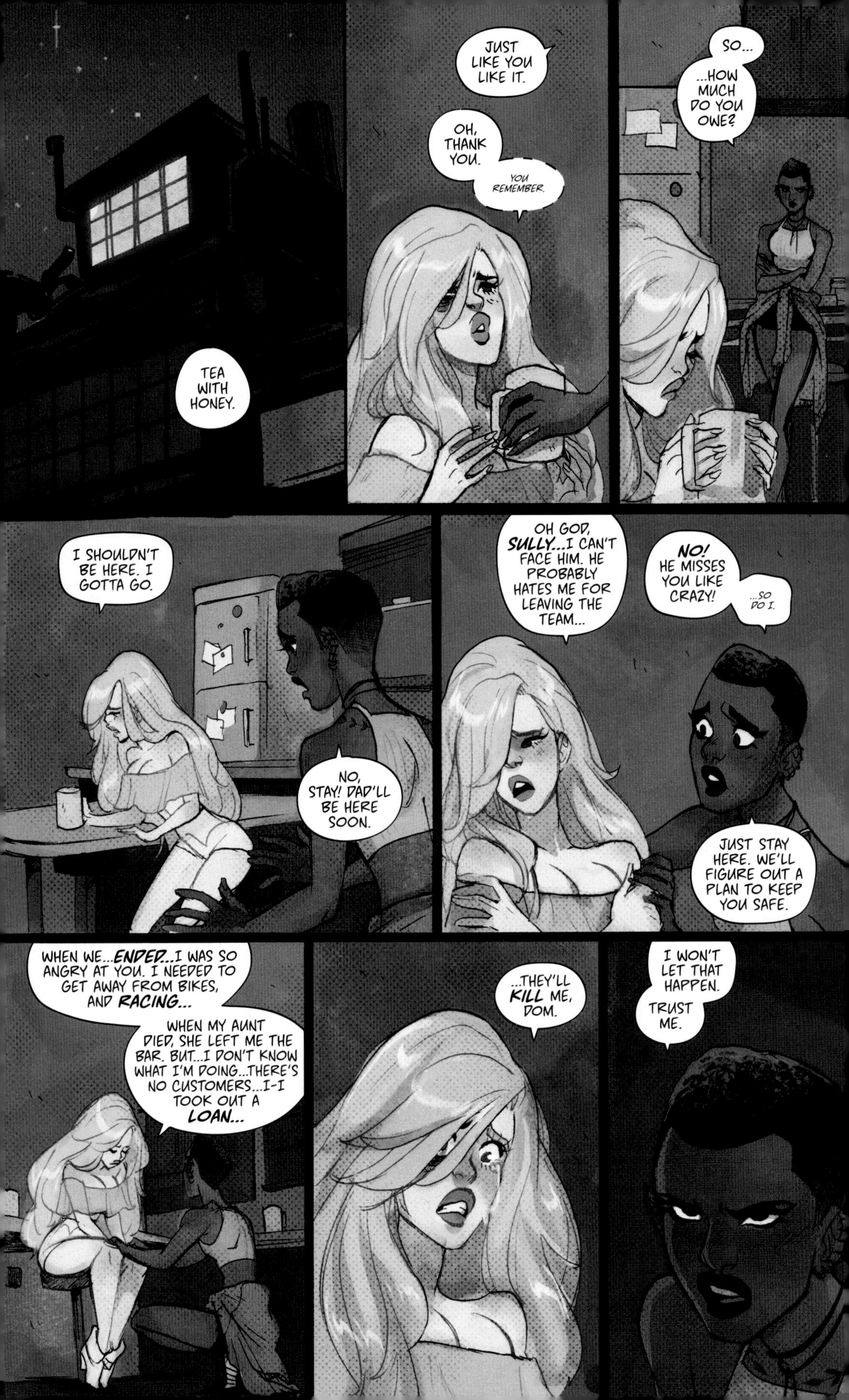
TEA WITH HONEY.
JUST LIKE YOU LIKE IT.
OH, THANK YOU.
YOU REMEMBER.
SO...
...HOW MUCH DO YOU OWE?
I SHOULDN'T BE HERE. I GOTTA GO.
NO, STAY! DAD'LL BE HERE SOON.
OH GOD, SULLY...I CAN'T FACE HIM. HE PROBABLY HATES ME FOR LEAVING THE TEAM...
NO! HE MISSES YOU LIKE CRAZY!
...SO DO I.
JUST STAY HERE. WE'LL FIGURE OUT A PLAN TO KEEP YOU SAFE.
WHEN WE...ENDED...I WAS SO ANGRY AT YOU. I NEEDED TO GET AWAY FROM BIKES, AND RACING...
WHEN MY AUNT DIED, SHE LEFT ME THE BAR. BUT...I DON'T KNOW WHAT I'M DOING...THERE'S NO CUSTOMERS...I-I TOOK OUT A LOAN...
...THEY'LL KILL ME, DOM.
I WON'T LET THAT HAPPEN.
TRUST ME.

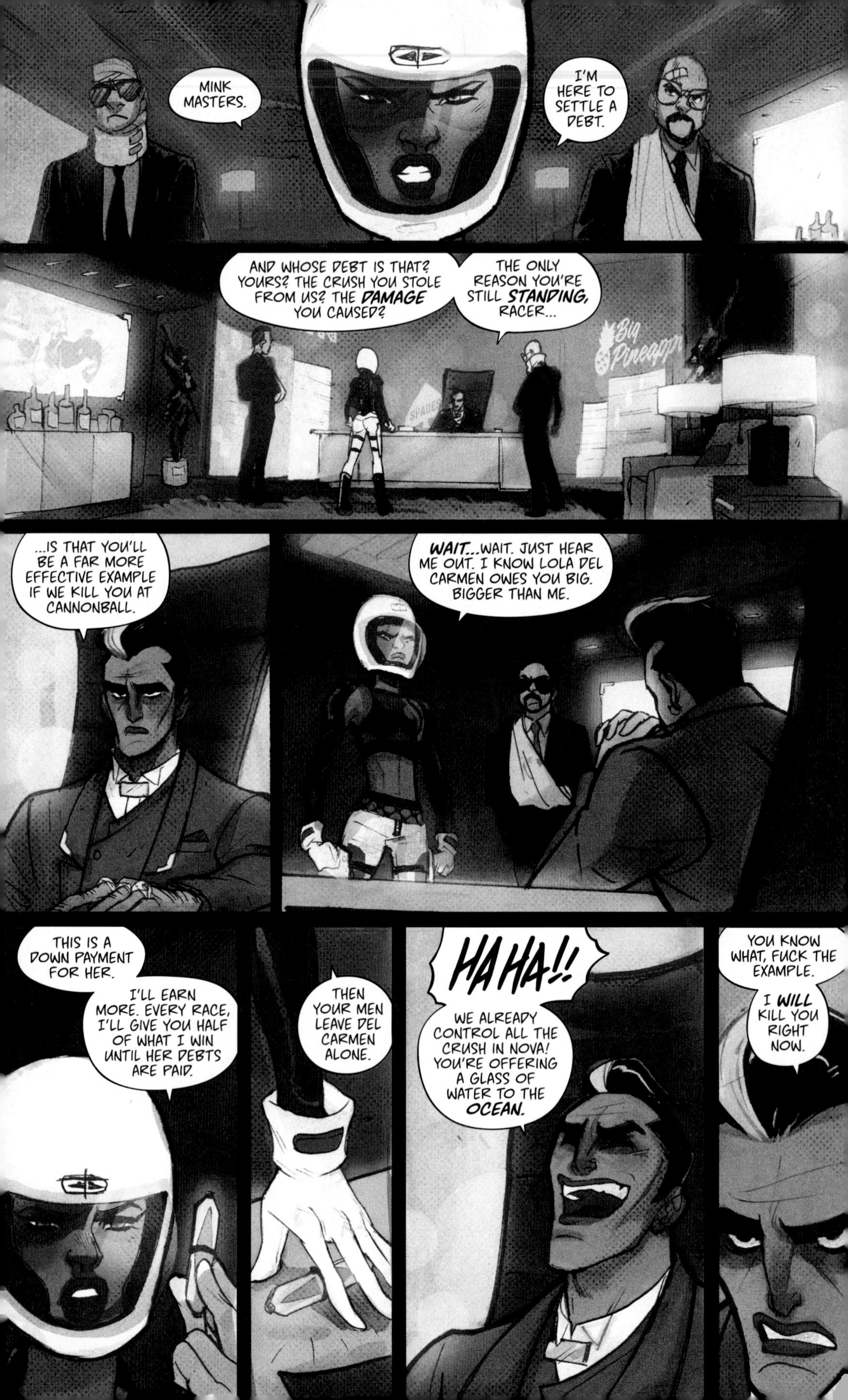
MINK MASTERS.
I'M HERE TO SETTLE A DEBT.
AND WHOSE DEBT IS THAT? YOURS? THE CRUSH YOU STOLE FROM US? THE DAMAGE YOU CAUSED?
THE ONLY REASON YOU'RE STILL STANDING, RACER...
Big Pineapp
SPADES
...IS THAT YOU'LL BE A FAR MORE EFFECTIVE EXAMPLE IF WE KILL YOU AT CANNONBALL.
WAIT...WAIT. JUST HEAR ME OUT. I KNOW LOLA DEL CARMEN OWES YOU BIG. BIGGER THAN ME.
THIS IS A DOWN PAYMENT FOR HER.
I'LL EARN MORE. EVERY RACE, I'LL GIVE YOU HALF OF WHAT I WIN UNTIL HER DEBTS ARE PAID.
THEN YOUR MEN LEAVE DEL CARMEN ALONE.
HAHA!!
WE ALREADY CONTROL ALL THE CRUSH IN NOVA! YOU'RE OFFERING A GLASS OF WATER TO THE OCEAN.
YOU KNOW WHAT, FUCK THE EXAMPLE.
I WILL KILL YOU RIGHT NOW.

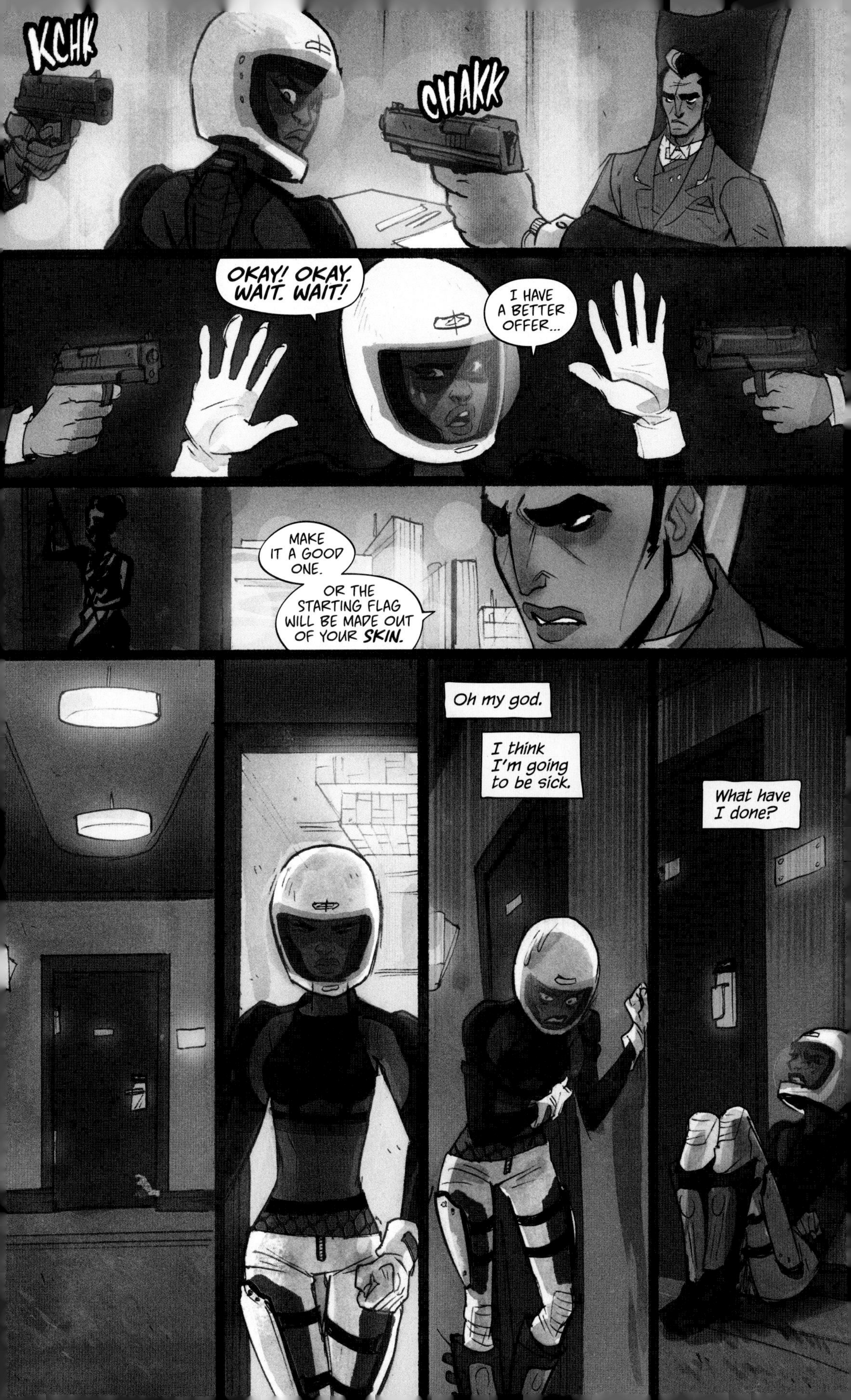
KCHK
CHAKK
OKAY! OKAY. WAIT. WAIT!
I HAVE A BETTER OFFER...
MAKE IT A GOOD ONE.
OR THE STARTING FLAG WILL BE MADE OUT OF YOUR SKIN.
Oh my god.
I think I'm going to be sick.
What have I done?

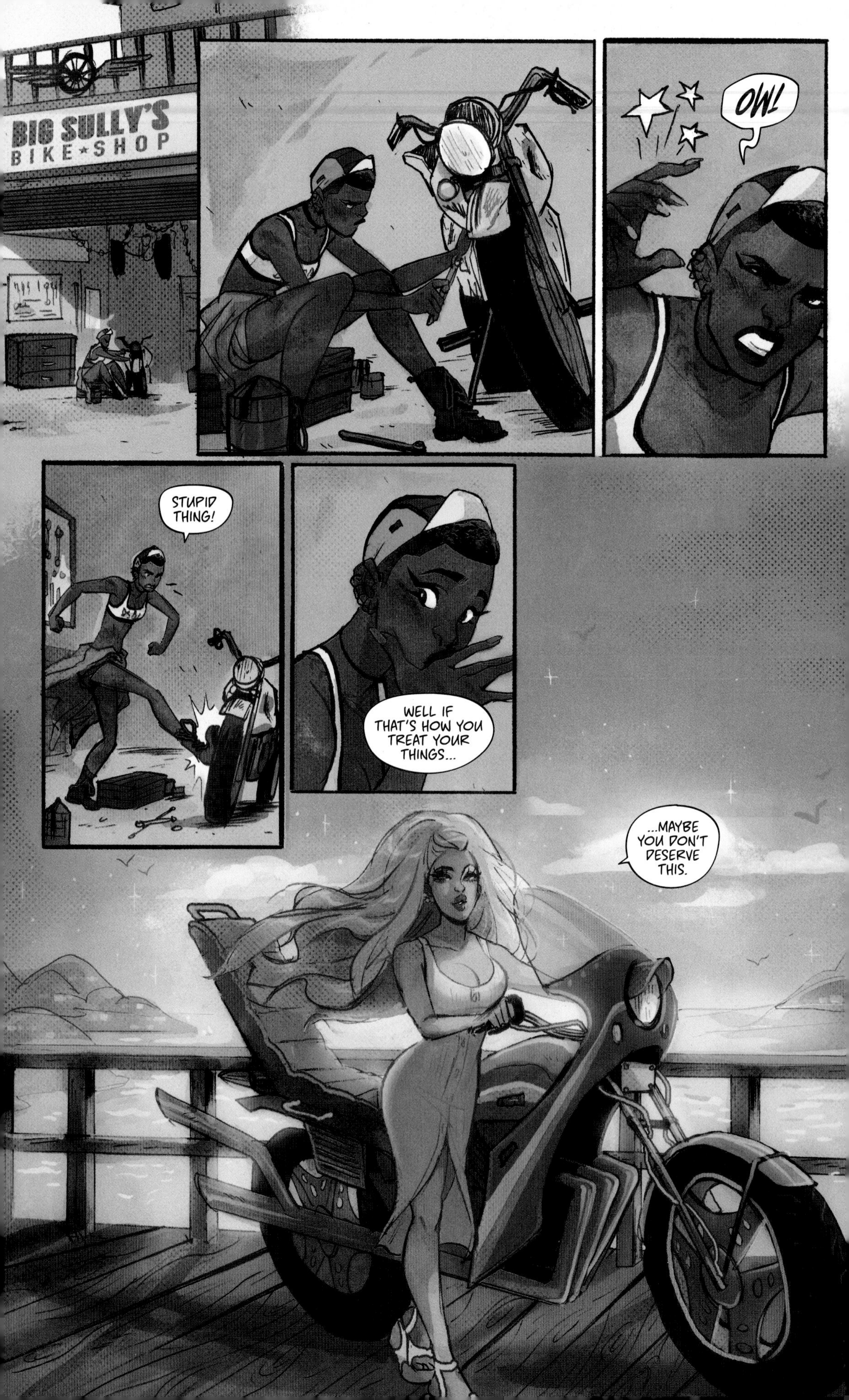
BIG SULLY'S
BIKE★SHOP
OW!
STUPID THING!
WELL IF THAT'S HOW YOU TREAT YOUR THINGS...
...MAYBE YOU DON'T DESERVE THIS.

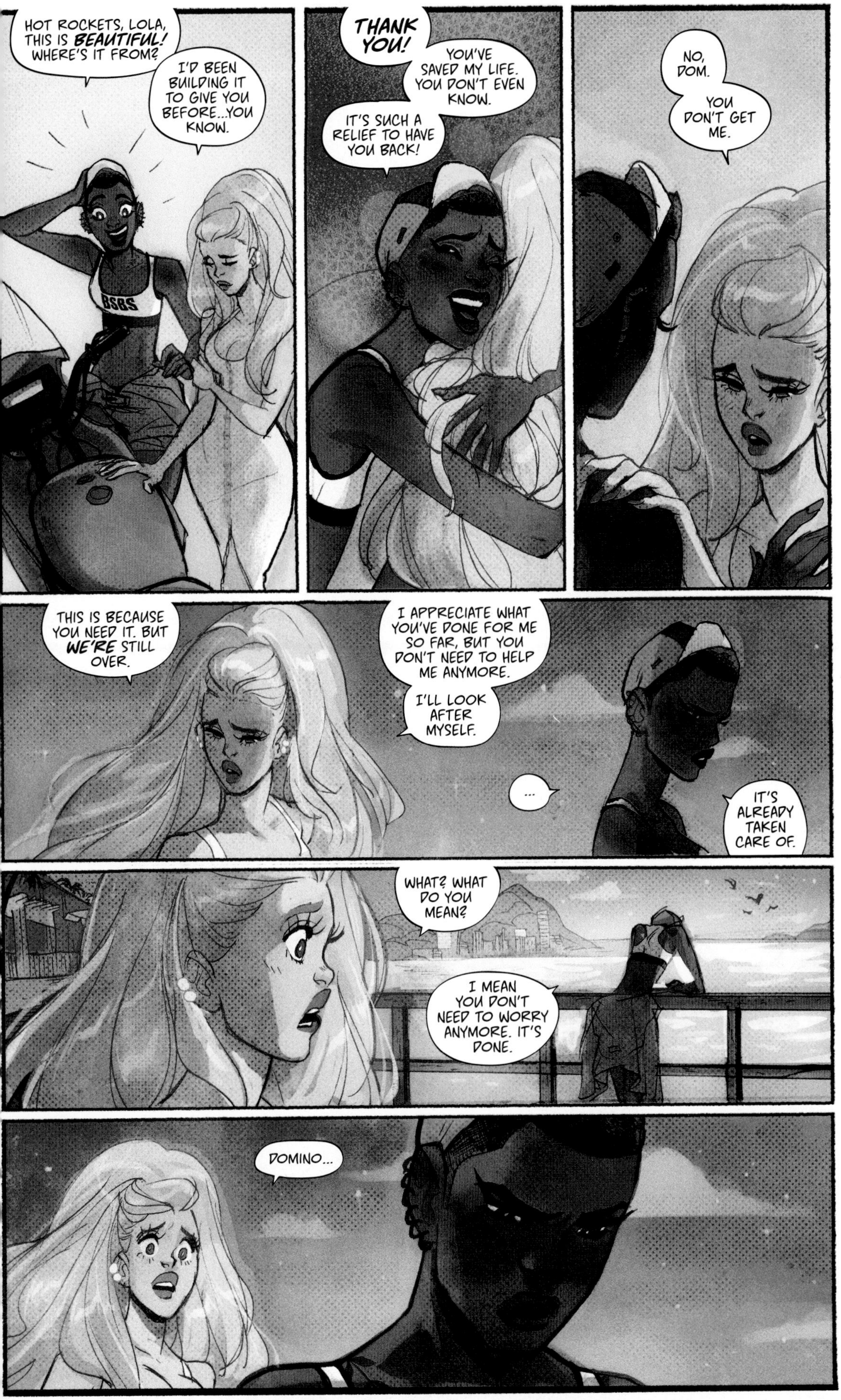
HOT ROCKETS, LOLA, THIS IS BEAUTIFUL! WHERE'S IT FROM?
I'D BEEN BUILDING IT TO GIVE YOU BEFORE...YOU KNOW.
BSBS
THANK YOU!
YOU'VE SAVED MY LIFE. YOU DON'T EVEN KNOW.
IT'S SUCH A RELIEF TO HAVE YOU BACK!
NO, DOM.
YOU DON'T GET ME.
THIS IS BECAUSE YOU NEED IT. BUT WE'RE STILL OVER.
I APPRECIATE WHAT YOU'VE DONE FOR ME SO FAR, BUT YOU DON'T NEED TO HELP ME ANYMORE.
I'LL LOOK AFTER MYSELF.
...
IT'S ALREADY TAKEN CARE OF.
WHAT? WHAT DO YOU MEAN?
I MEAN YOU DON'T NEED TO WORRY ANYMORE. IT'S DONE.
DOMINO...

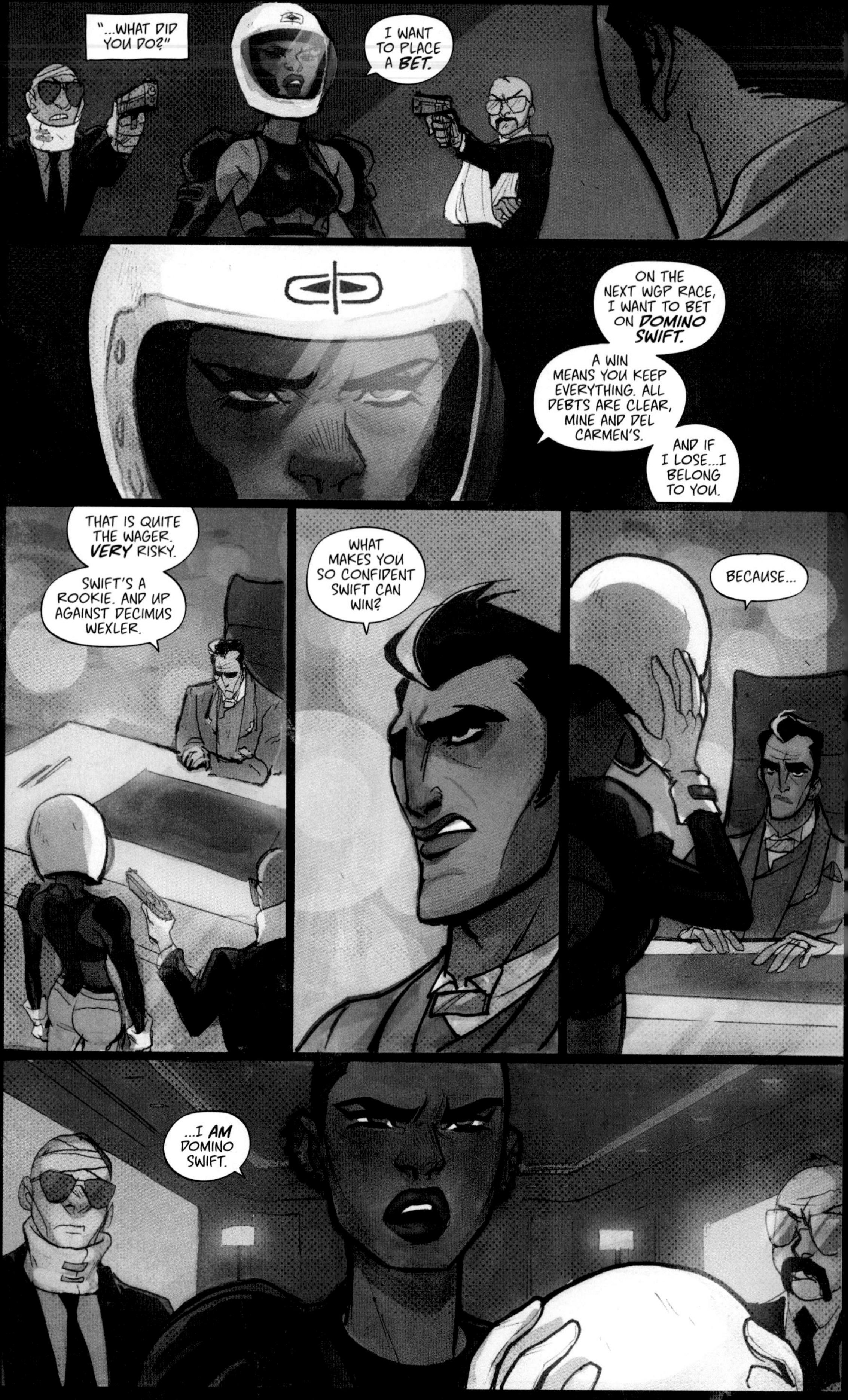
"...WHAT DID YOU DO?"
I WANT TO PLACE A **BET.**
ON THE NEXT WGP RACE, I WANT TO BET ON ***DOMINO SWIFT.***
A WIN MEANS YOU KEEP EVERYTHING. ALL DEBTS ARE CLEAR, MINE AND DEL CARMEN'S.
AND IF I LOSE...I BELONG TO YOU.
THAT IS QUITE THE WAGER. ***VERY*** RISKY.
SWIFT'S A ROOKIE. AND UP AGAINST DECIMUS WEXLER.
WHAT MAKES YOU SO CONFIDENT SWIFT CAN WIN?
BECAUSE...
...I ***AM*** DOMINO SWIFT.

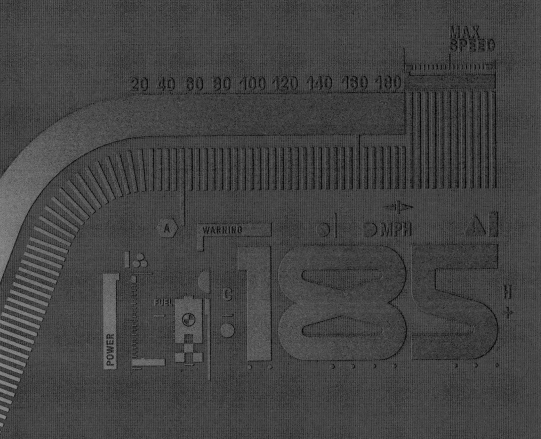

MAX
SPEED

20 40 60 80 100 120 140 160 180

A   WARNING   MPH

185

POWER   FUEL

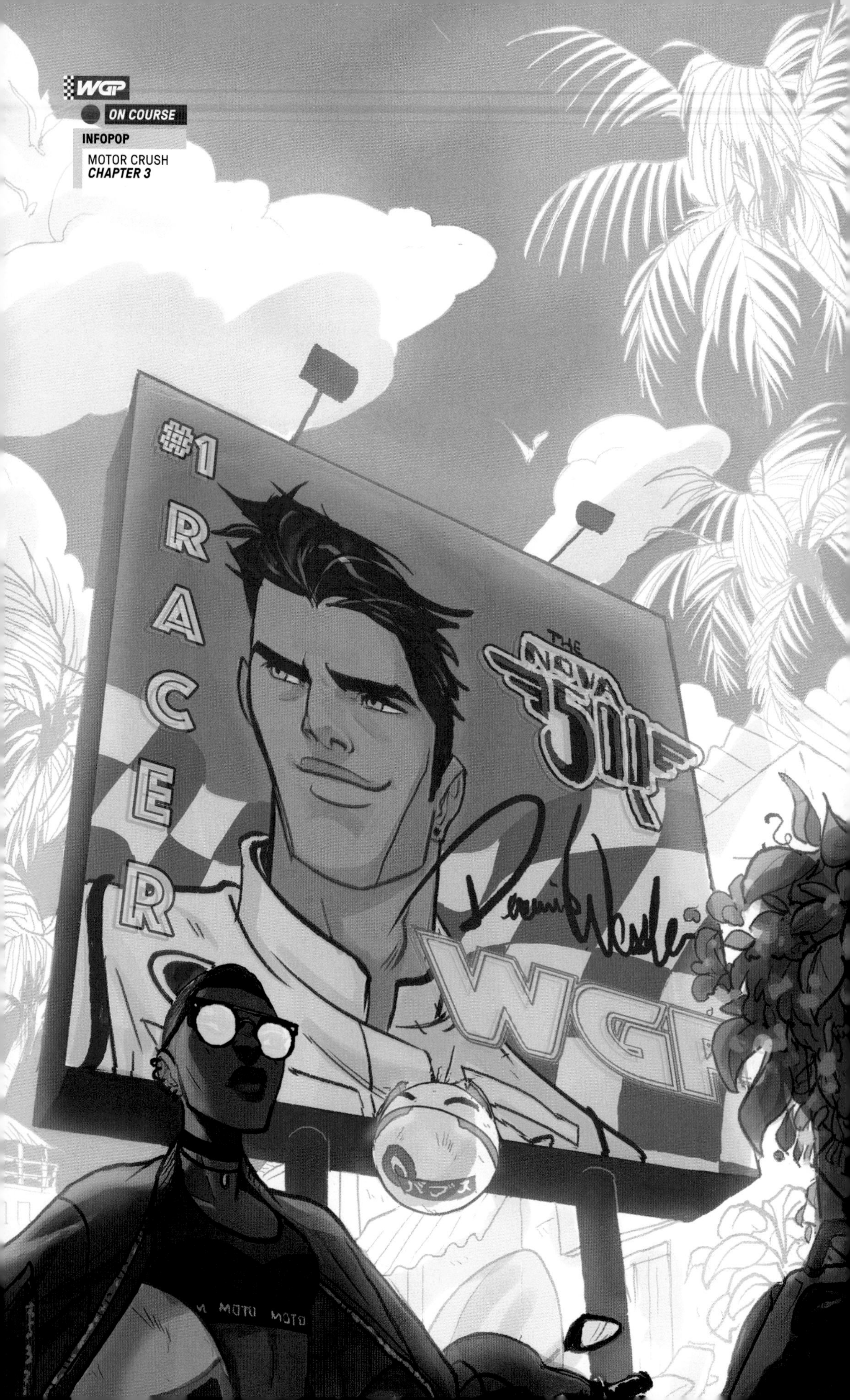
WGP
ON COURSE
INFOPOP
MOTOR CRUSH
CHAPTER 3
#1 RACER
THE NOVA 500
WGP
MOTO MOTO

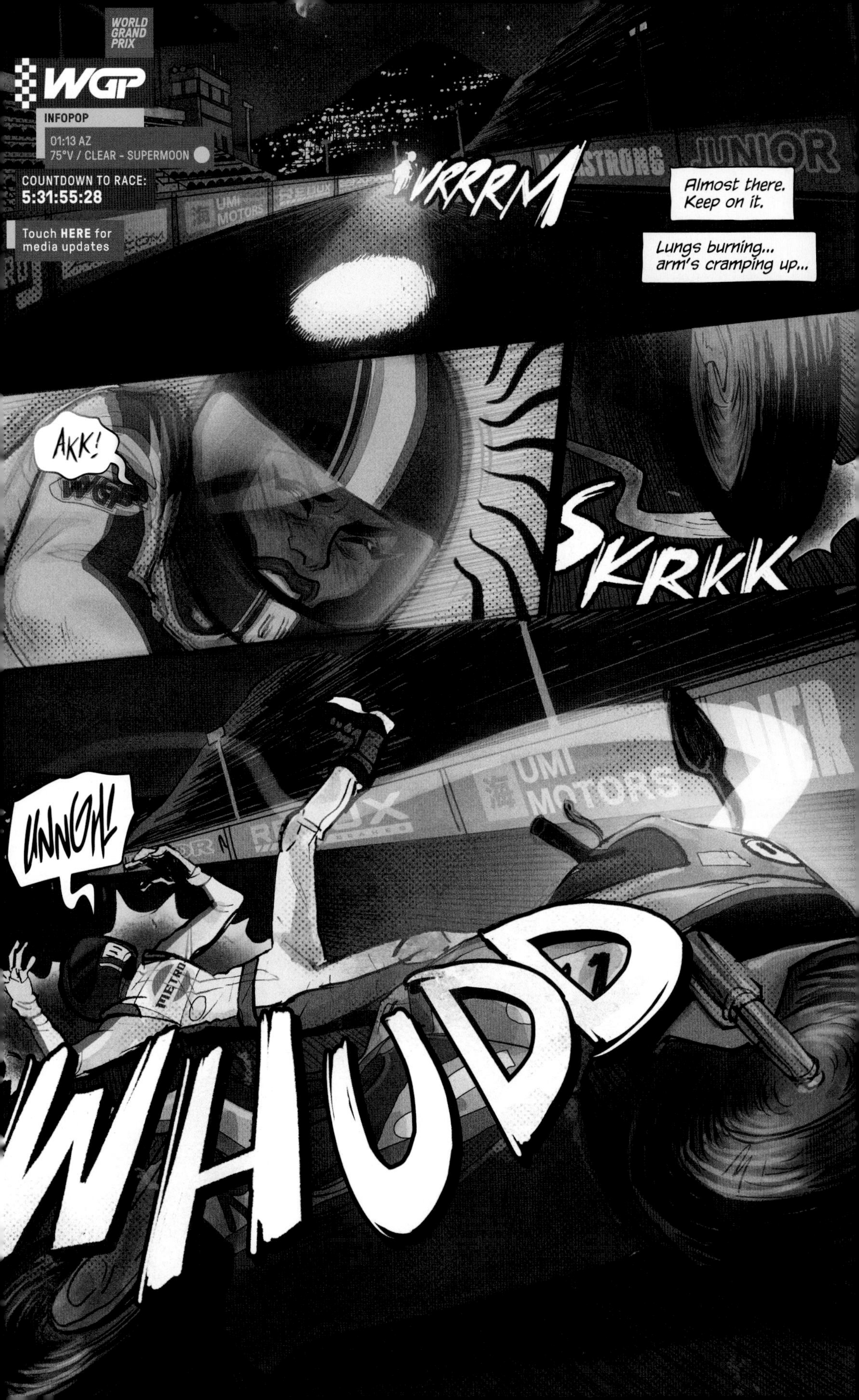
WORLD GRAND PRIX
WGP
INFOPOP
01:13 AZ
75°V / CLEAR - SUPERMOON
COUNTDOWN TO RACE:
5:31:55:28
Touch HERE for media updates
VRRRM
Almost there. Keep on it.
Lungs burning... arm's cramping up...
AKK!
SKRKK
UNNGH!
WHUDD

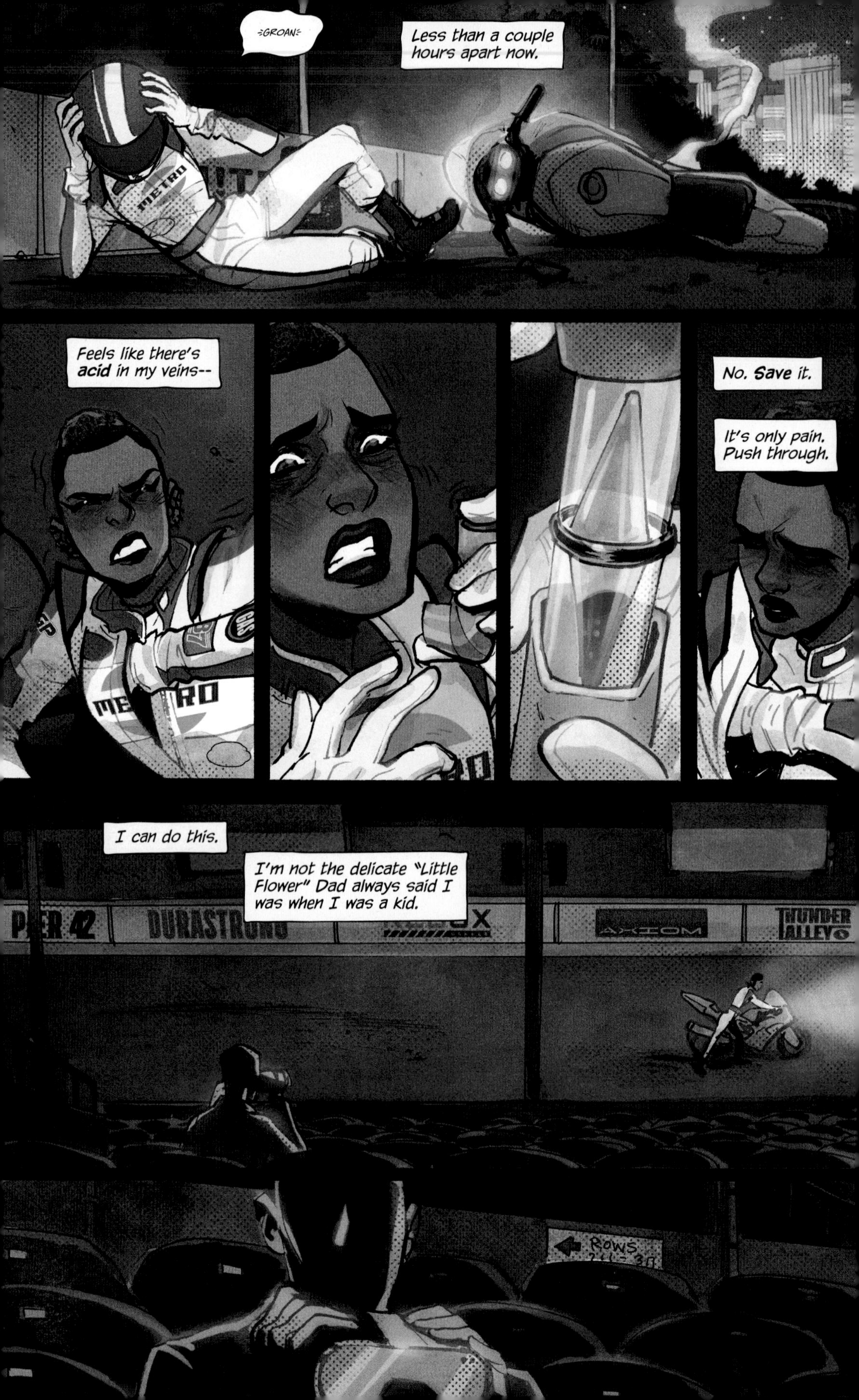

GROAN
Less than a couple hours apart now.
Feels like there's acid in my veins--
No. Save it.
It's only pain. Push through.
I can do this.
I'm not the delicate "Little Flower" Dad always said I was when I was a kid.
PIER 42
DURASTRONG
AXIOM
THUNDER ALLEY
ROWS

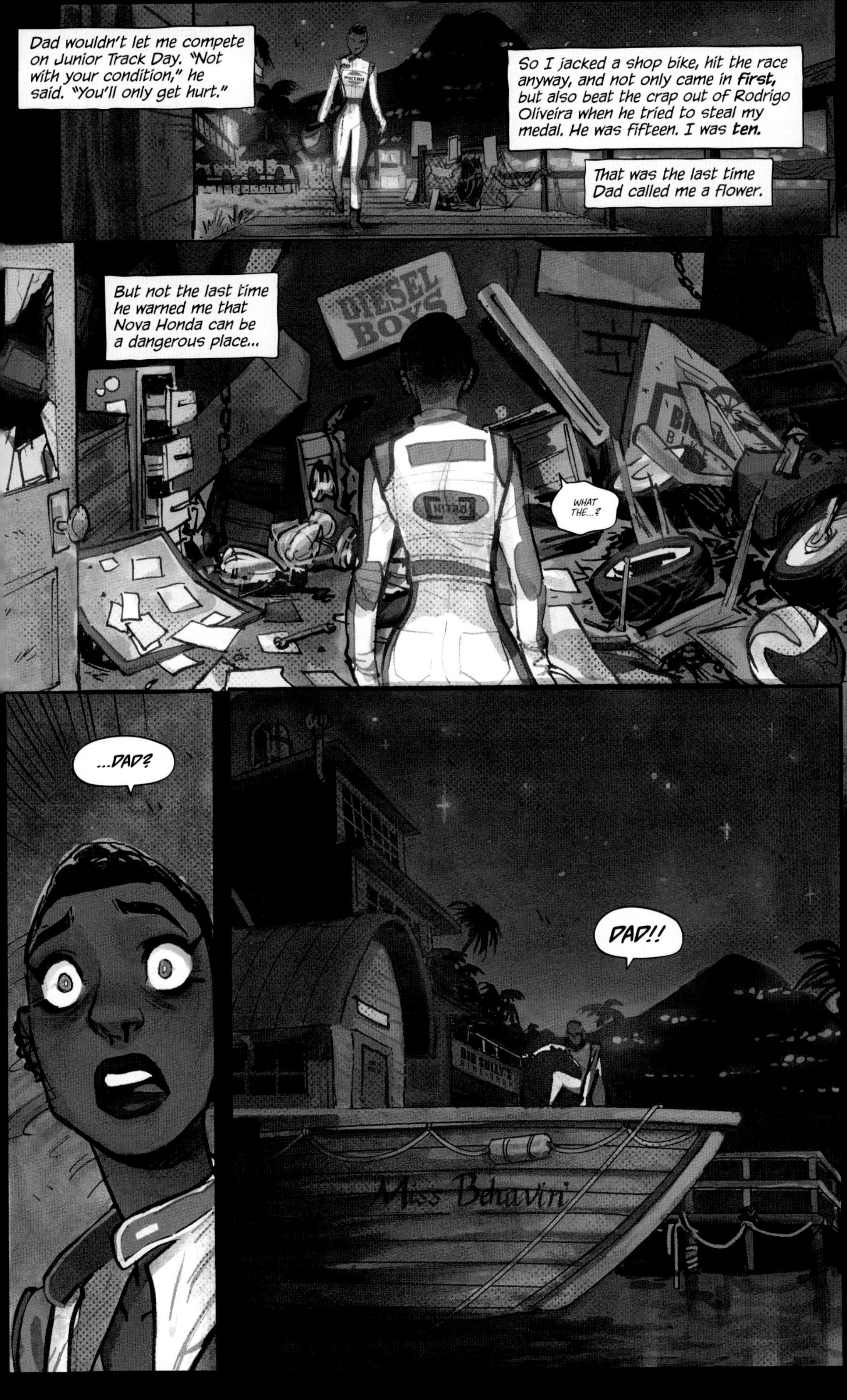
Dad wouldn't let me compete on Junior Track Day. "Not with your condition," he said. "You'll only get hurt."
So I jacked a shop bike, hit the race anyway, and not only came in **first,** but also beat the crap out of Rodrigo Oliveira when he tried to steal my medal. He was fifteen. I was **ten.**
That was the last time Dad called me a flower.
But not the last time he warned me that Nova Honda can be a dangerous place...
DIESEL BOYS
NITRO
WHAT THE...?
...DAD?
DAD!!
BIG SULLY'S BIKE SHOP
Miss Behavin'

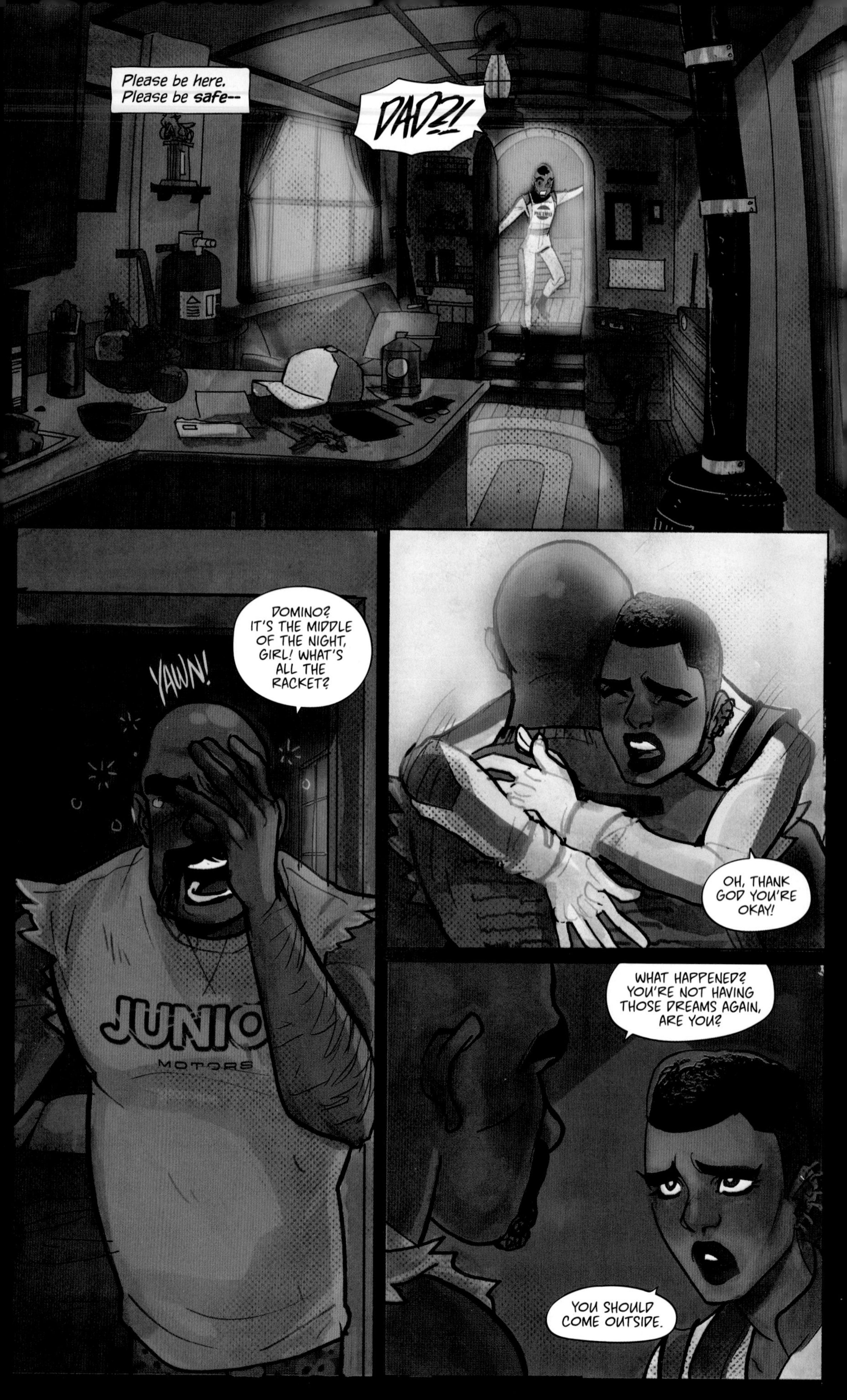
Please be here. Please be *safe*--
DAD?!
YAWN!
DOMINO? IT'S THE MIDDLE OF THE NIGHT, GIRL! WHAT'S ALL THE RACKET?
JUNIO
MOTORS
OH, THANK GOD YOU'RE OKAY!
WHAT HAPPENED? YOU'RE NOT HAVING THOSE DREAMS AGAIN, ARE YOU?
YOU SHOULD COME OUTSIDE.

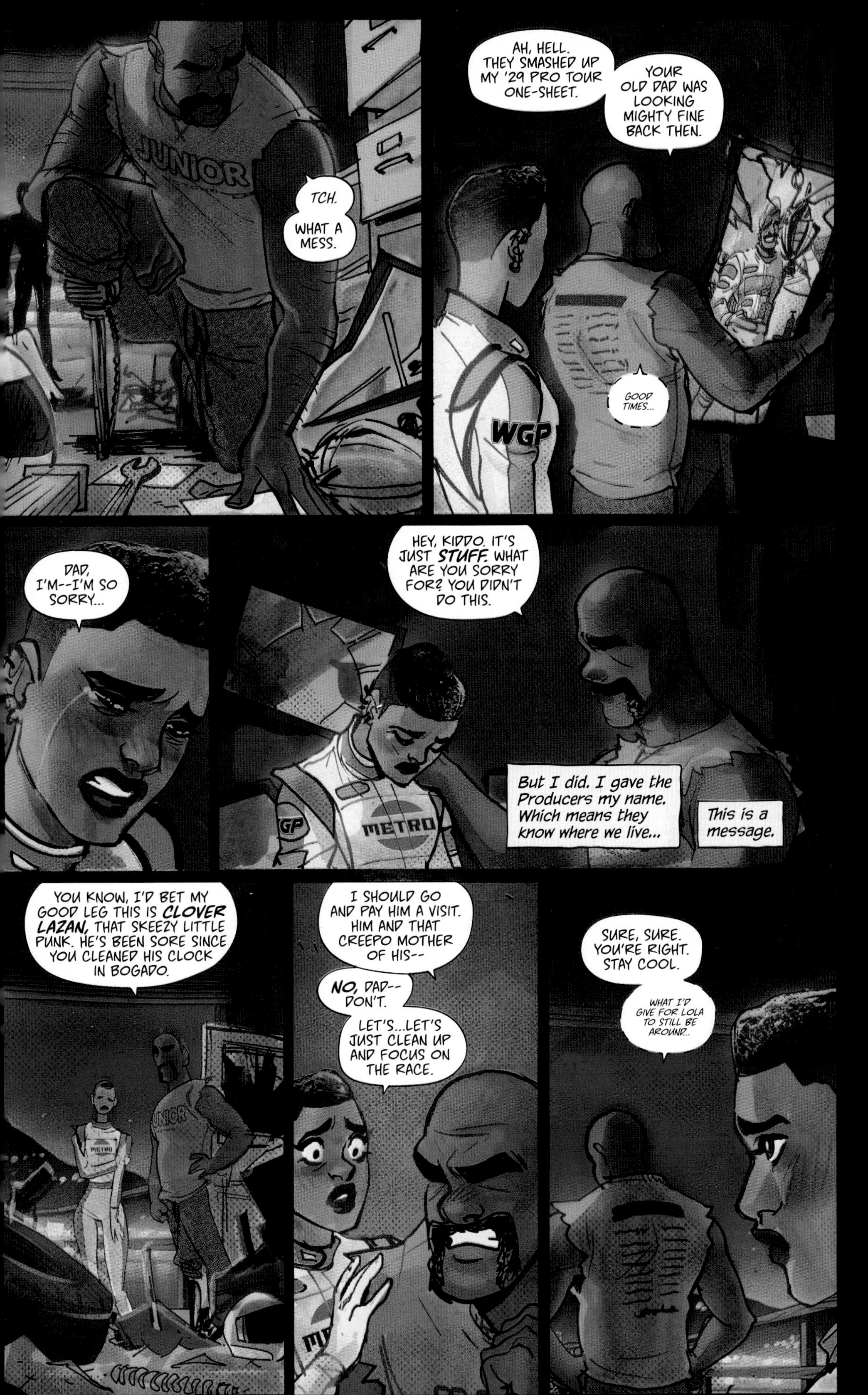
TCH.
WHAT A MESS.
AH, HELL. THEY SMASHED UP MY '29 PRO TOUR ONE-SHEET.
YOUR OLD DAD WAS LOOKING MIGHTY FINE BACK THEN.
GOOD TIMES...
WGP
DAD, I'M--I'M SO SORRY...
HEY, KIDDO. IT'S JUST STUFF. WHAT ARE YOU SORRY FOR? YOU DIDN'T DO THIS.
But I did. I gave the Producers my name. Which means they know where we live...
This is a message.
METRO
YOU KNOW, I'D BET MY GOOD LEG THIS IS CLOVER LAZAN, THAT SKEEZY LITTLE PUNK. HE'S BEEN SORE SINCE YOU CLEANED HIS CLOCK IN BOGADO.
I SHOULD GO AND PAY HIM A VISIT. HIM AND THAT CREEPO MOTHER OF HIS--
NO, DAD-- DON'T.
LET'S...LET'S JUST CLEAN UP AND FOCUS ON THE RACE.
SURE, SURE. YOU'RE RIGHT. STAY COOL.
WHAT I'D GIVE FOR LOLA TO STILL BE AROUND...

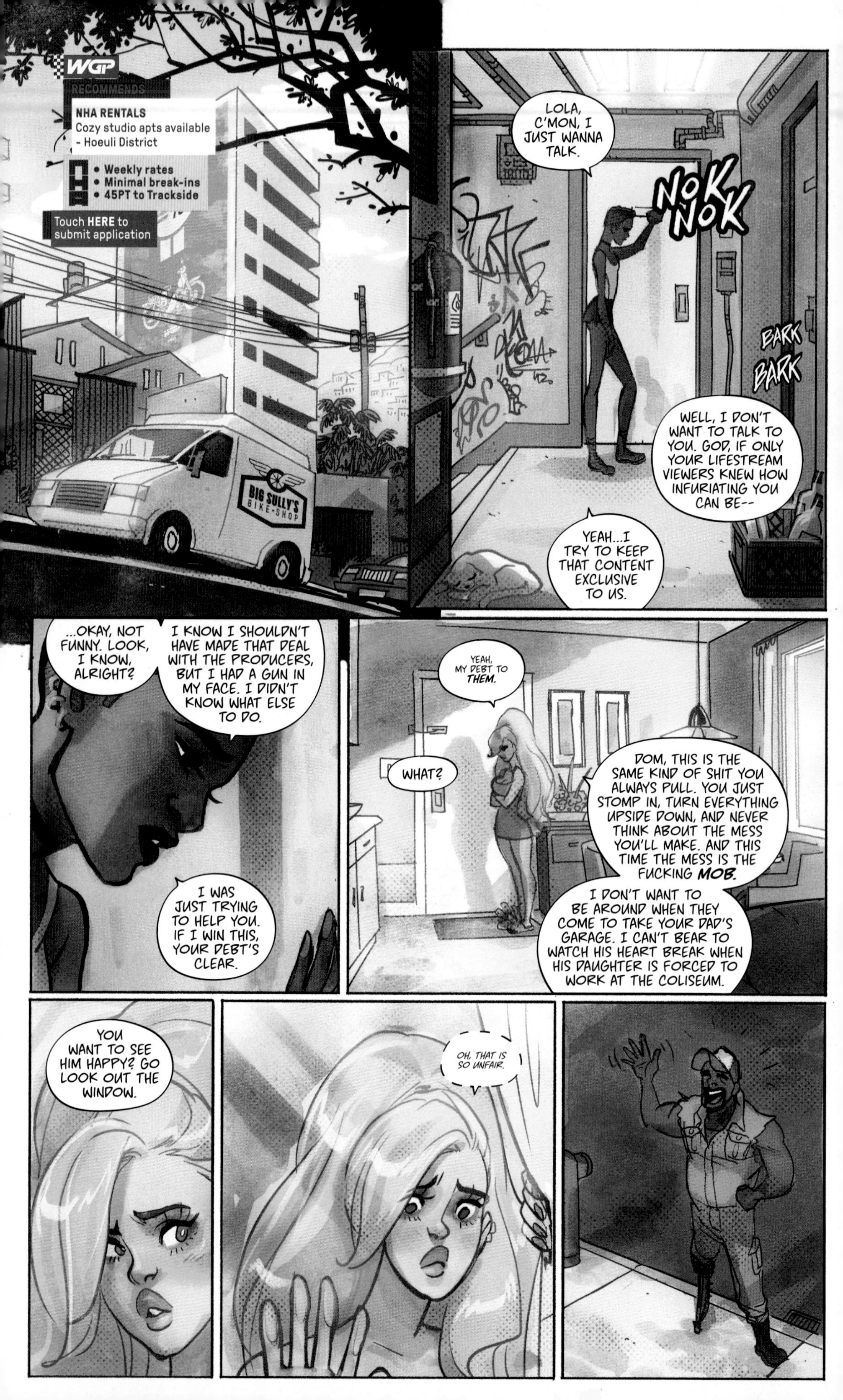
WGP
RECOMMENDS
NHA RENTALS
Cozy studio apts available
- Hoeuli District
• Weekly rates
• Minimal break-ins
• 45PT to Trackside
Touch HERE to submit application
BIG SULLY'S BIKE-SHOP
LOLA, C'MON, I JUST WANNA TALK.
NOK NOK
BARK BARK
WELL, I DON'T WANT TO TALK TO YOU. GOD, IF ONLY YOUR LIFESTREAM VIEWERS KNEW HOW INFURIATING YOU CAN BE--
YEAH...I TRY TO KEEP THAT CONTENT EXCLUSIVE TO US.
...OKAY, NOT FUNNY. LOOK, I KNOW, ALRIGHT?
I KNOW I SHOULDN'T HAVE MADE THAT DEAL WITH THE PRODUCERS, BUT I HAD A GUN IN MY FACE. I DIDN'T KNOW WHAT ELSE TO DO.
I WAS JUST TRYING TO HELP YOU. IF I WIN THIS, YOUR DEBT'S CLEAR.
YEAH, MY DEBT TO THEM.
WHAT?
DOM, THIS IS THE SAME KIND OF SHIT YOU ALWAYS PULL. YOU JUST STOMP IN, TURN EVERYTHING UPSIDE DOWN, AND NEVER THINK ABOUT THE MESS YOU'LL MAKE. AND THIS TIME THE MESS IS THE FUCKING MOB.
I DON'T WANT TO BE AROUND WHEN THEY COME TO TAKE YOUR DAD'S GARAGE. I CAN'T BEAR TO WATCH HIS HEART BREAK WHEN HIS DAUGHTER IS FORCED TO WORK AT THE COLISEUM.
YOU WANT TO SEE HIM HAPPY? GO LOOK OUT THE WINDOW.
OH, THAT IS SO UNFAIR.

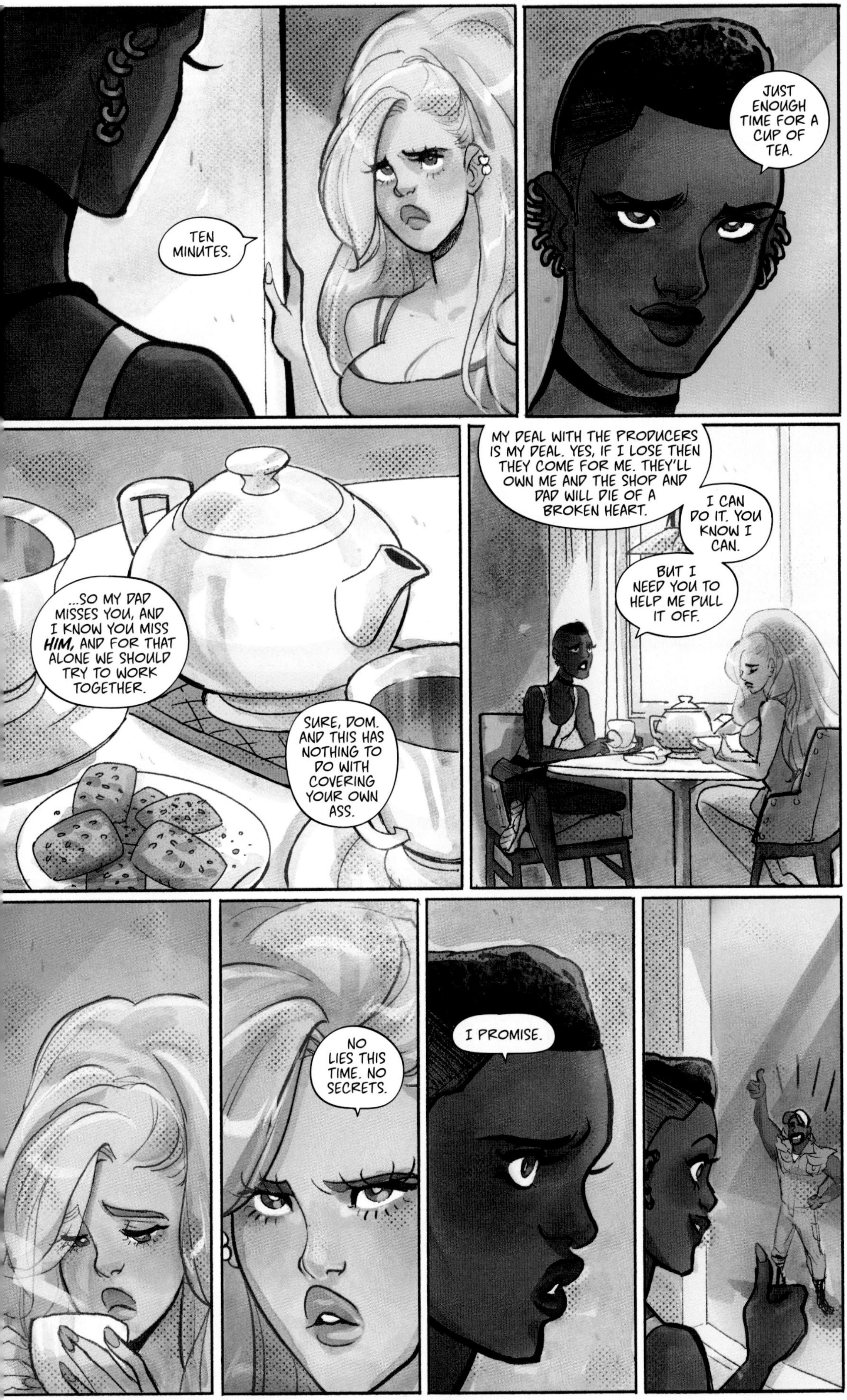
TEN MINUTES.
JUST ENOUGH TIME FOR A CUP OF TEA.
...SO MY DAD MISSES YOU, AND I KNOW YOU MISS **HIM,** AND FOR THAT ALONE WE SHOULD TRY TO WORK TOGETHER.
SURE, DOM. AND THIS HAS NOTHING TO DO WITH COVERING YOUR OWN ASS.
MY DEAL WITH THE PRODUCERS IS MY DEAL. YES, IF I LOSE THEN THEY COME FOR ME. THEY'LL OWN ME AND THE SHOP AND DAD WILL DIE OF A BROKEN HEART.
I CAN DO IT. YOU KNOW I CAN.
BUT I NEED YOU TO HELP ME PULL IT OFF.
NO LIES THIS TIME. NO SECRETS.
I PROMISE.

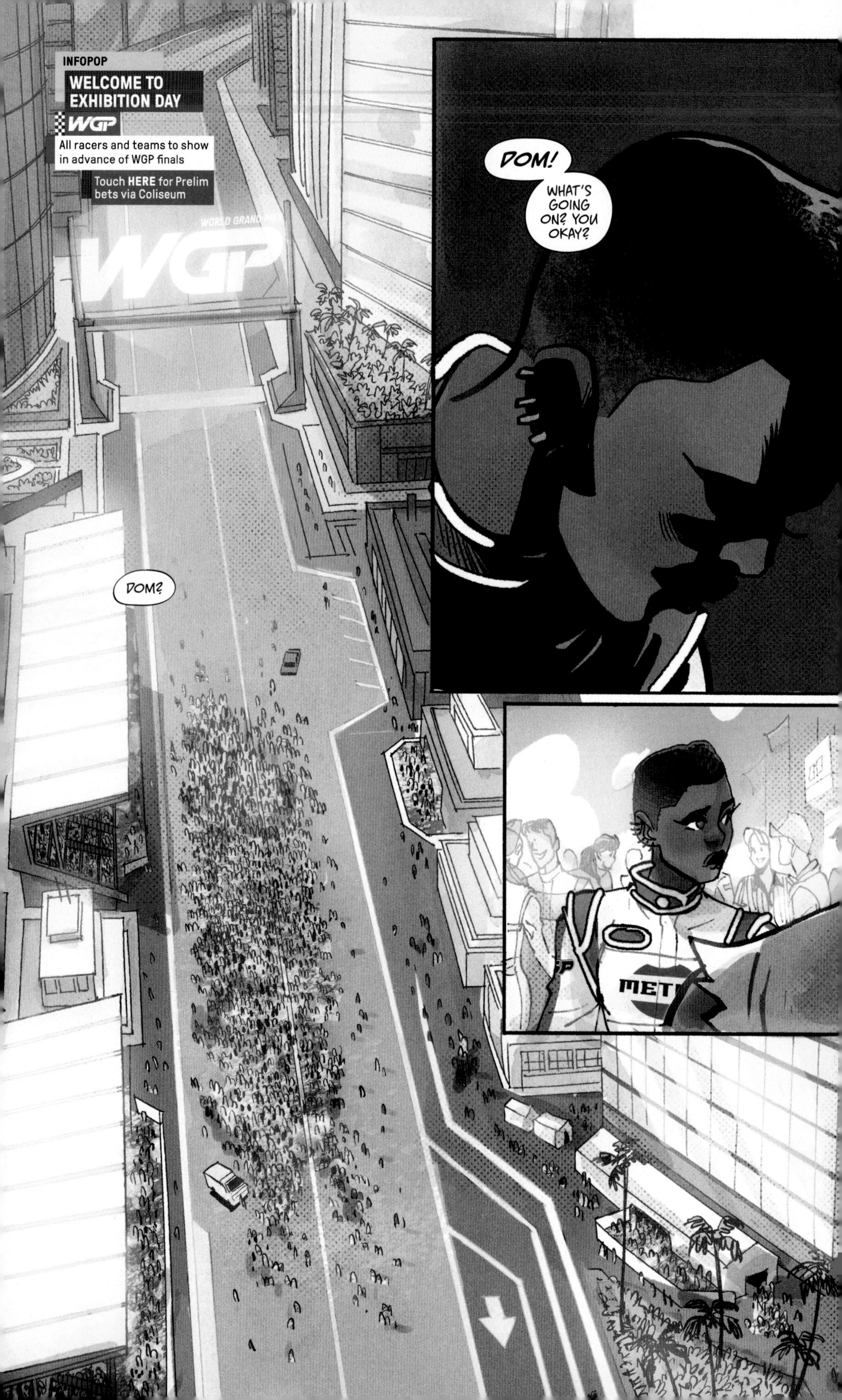
INFOPOP
WELCOME TO EXHIBITION DAY
WGP
All racers and teams to show in advance of WGP finals
Touch HERE for Prelim bets via Coliseum
WORLD GRAND PRIX
WGP
DOM?
DOM!
WHAT'S GOING ON? YOU OKAY?
METI

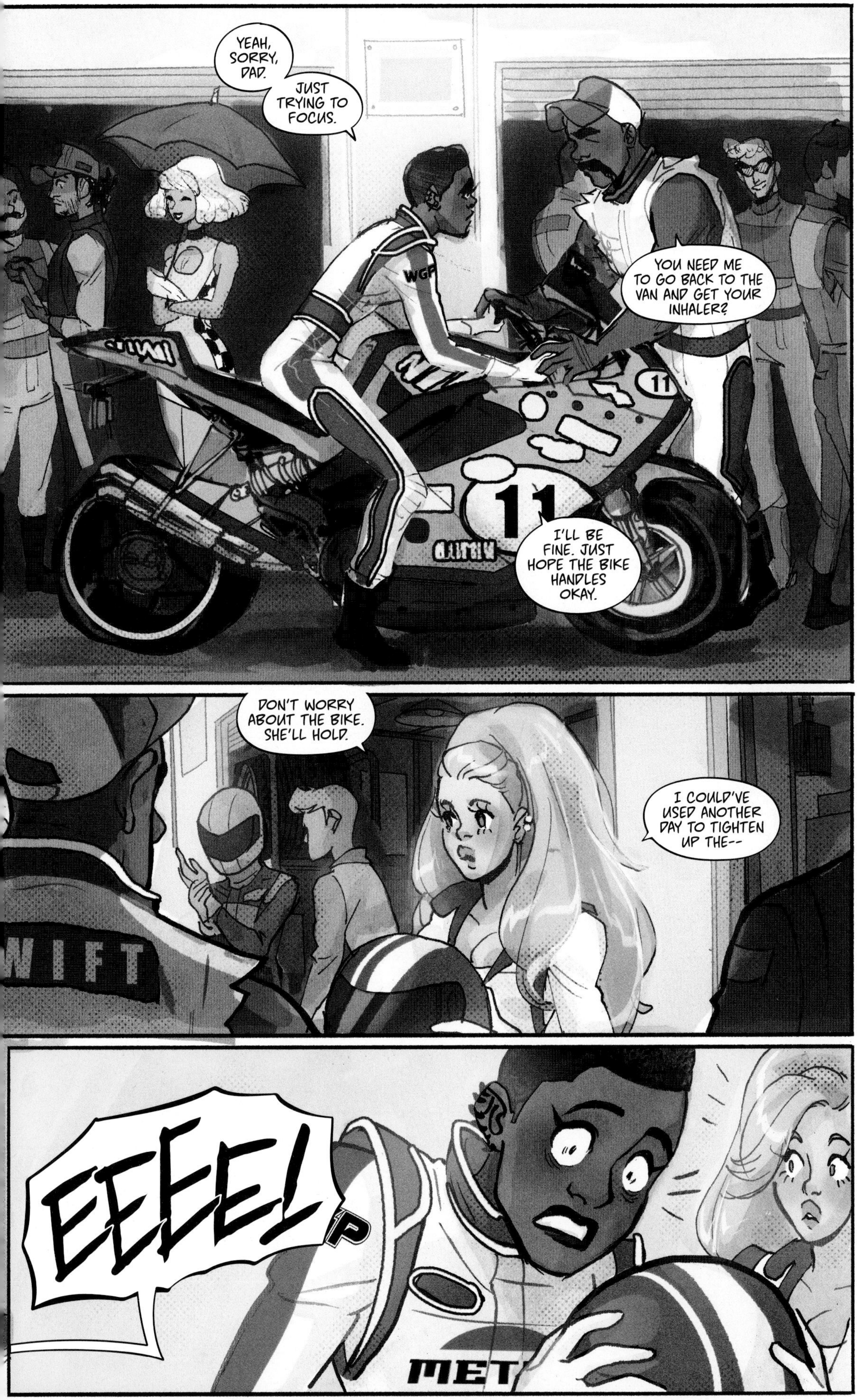
YEAH, SORRY, DAD.
JUST TRYING TO FOCUS.
WGP
YOU NEED ME TO GO BACK TO THE VAN AND GET YOUR INHALER?
11
11
I'LL BE FINE. JUST HOPE THE BIKE HANDLES OKAY.
DON'T WORRY ABOUT THE BIKE. SHE'LL HOLD.
I COULD'VE USED ANOTHER DAY TO TIGHTEN UP THE--
WIFT
EEEEL
MET

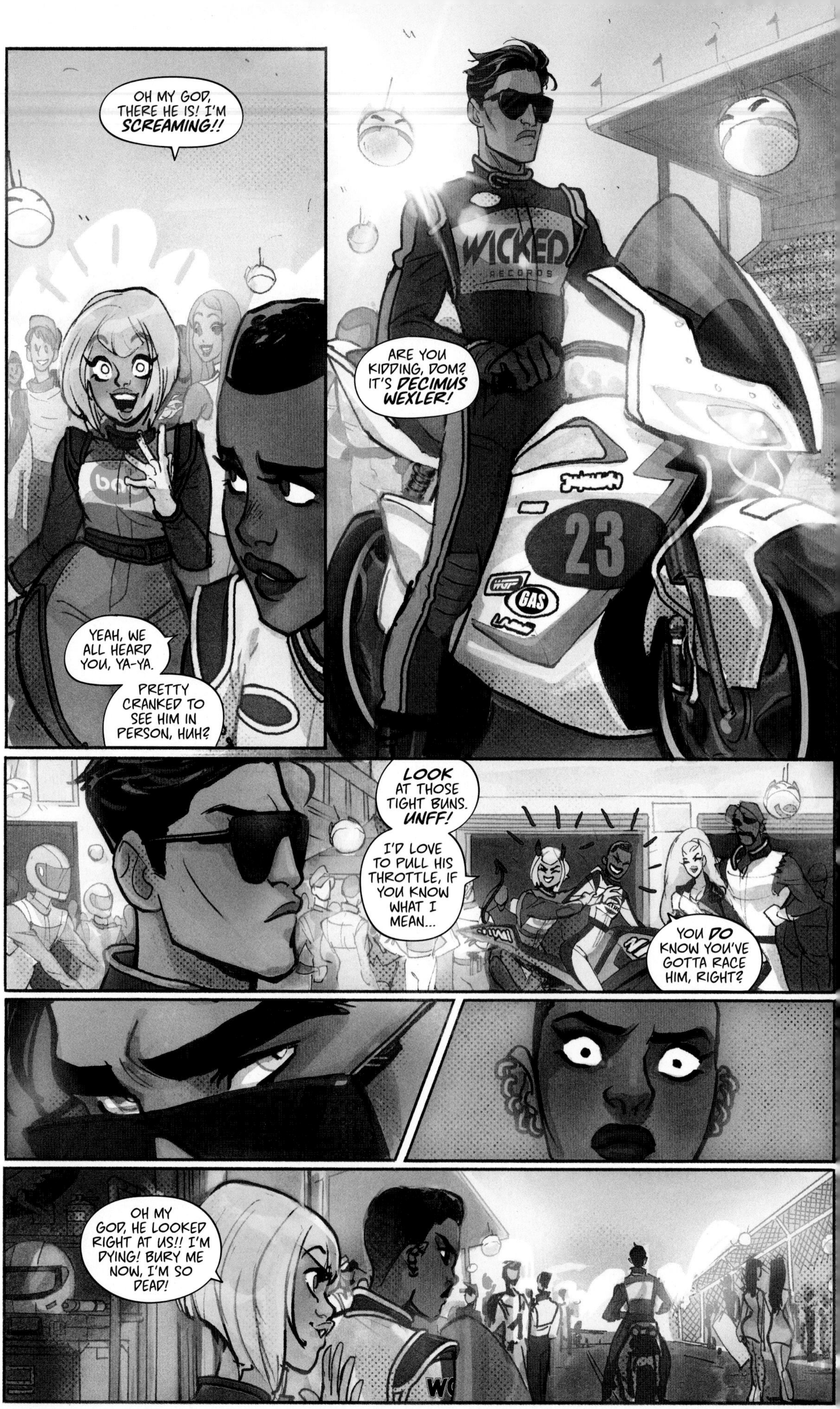
OH MY GOD, THERE HE IS! I'M SCREAMING!!
ARE YOU KIDDING, DOM? IT'S DECIMUS WEXLER!
YEAH, WE ALL HEARD YOU, YA-YA.
PRETTY CRANKED TO SEE HIM IN PERSON, HUH?
WICKED RECORDS
23
GAS
LOOK AT THOSE TIGHT BUNS. UNFF!
I'D LOVE TO PULL HIS THROTTLE, IF YOU KNOW WHAT I MEAN...
YOU DO KNOW YOU'VE GOTTA RACE HIM, RIGHT?
OH MY GOD, HE LOOKED RIGHT AT US!! I'M DYING! BURY ME NOW, I'M SO DEAD!

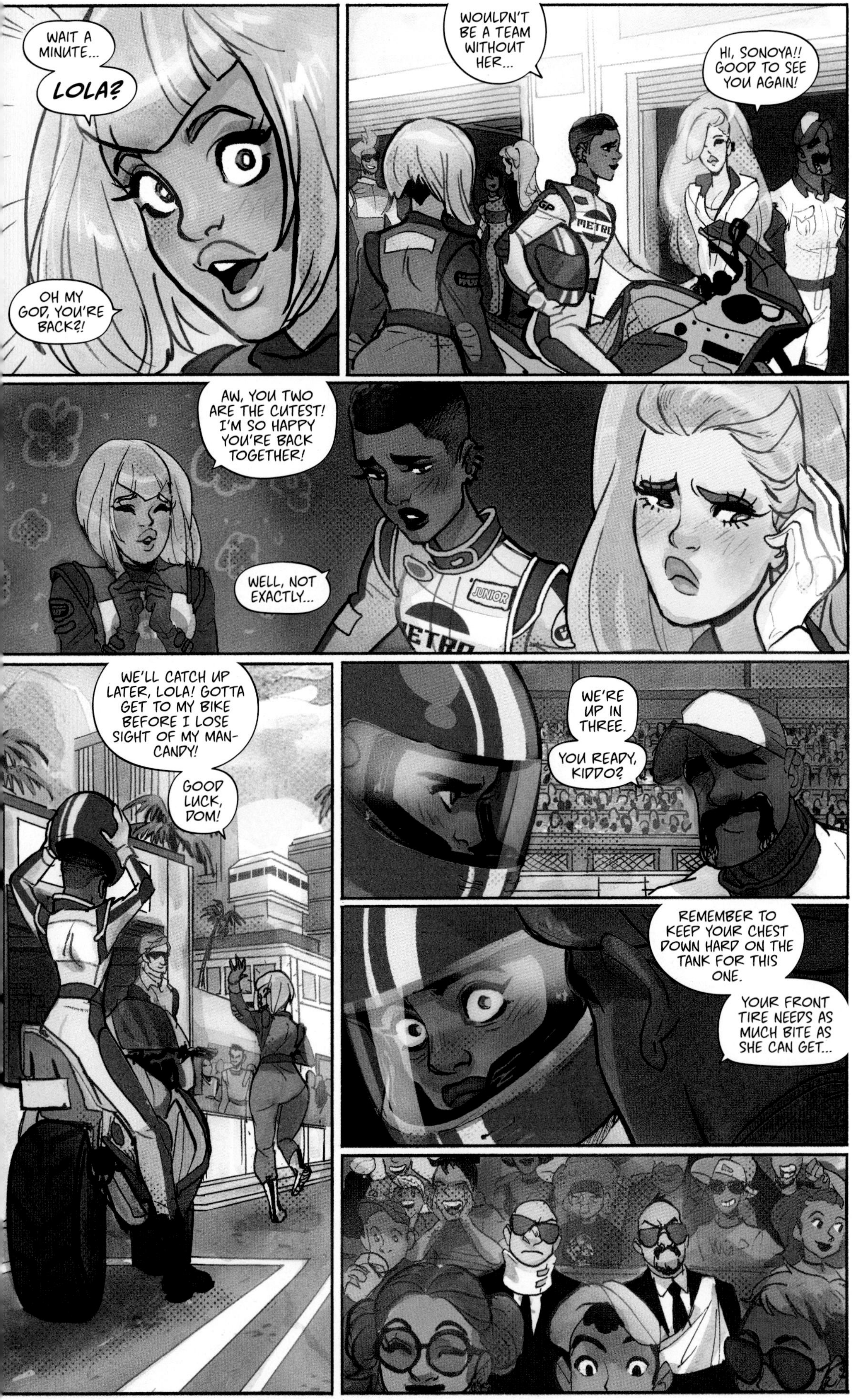
WAIT A MINUTE...
LOLA?
OH MY GOD, YOU'RE BACK?!
WOULDN'T BE A TEAM WITHOUT HER...
HI, SONOYA!! GOOD TO SEE YOU AGAIN!
AW, YOU TWO ARE THE CUTEST! I'M SO HAPPY YOU'RE BACK TOGETHER!
WELL, NOT EXACTLY...
METRO
JUNIOR
WE'LL CATCH UP LATER, LOLA! GOTTA GET TO MY BIKE BEFORE I LOSE SIGHT OF MY MAN-CANDY!
GOOD LUCK, DOM!
WE'RE UP IN THREE.
YOU READY, KIDDO?
REMEMBER TO KEEP YOUR CHEST DOWN HARD ON THE TANK FOR THIS ONE.
YOUR FRONT TIRE NEEDS AS MUCH BITE AS SHE CAN GET...

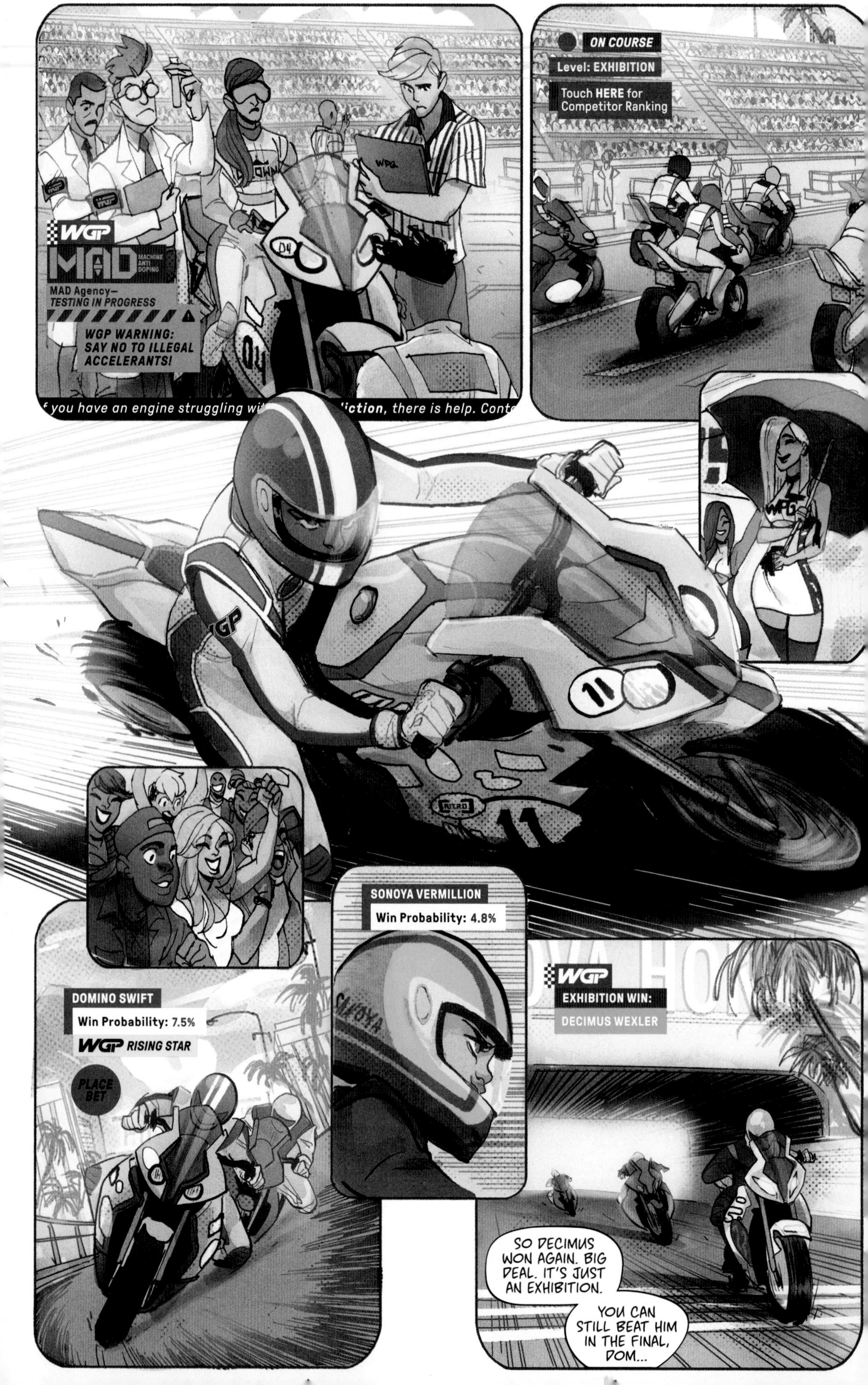
WGP
MAD
MACHINE ANTI DOPING
MAD Agency—
TESTING IN PROGRESS
WGP WARNING:
SAY NO TO ILLEGAL
ACCELERANTS!
ON COURSE
Level: EXHIBITION
Touch HERE for
Competitor Ranking
SONOYA VERMILLION
Win Probability: 4.8%
DOMINO SWIFT
Win Probability: 7.5%
WGP RISING STAR
PLACE BET
WGP
EXHIBITION WIN:
DECIMUS WEXLER
SO DECIMUS WON AGAIN. BIG DEAL. IT'S JUST AN EXHIBITION.
YOU CAN STILL BEAT HIM IN THE FINAL, DOM...

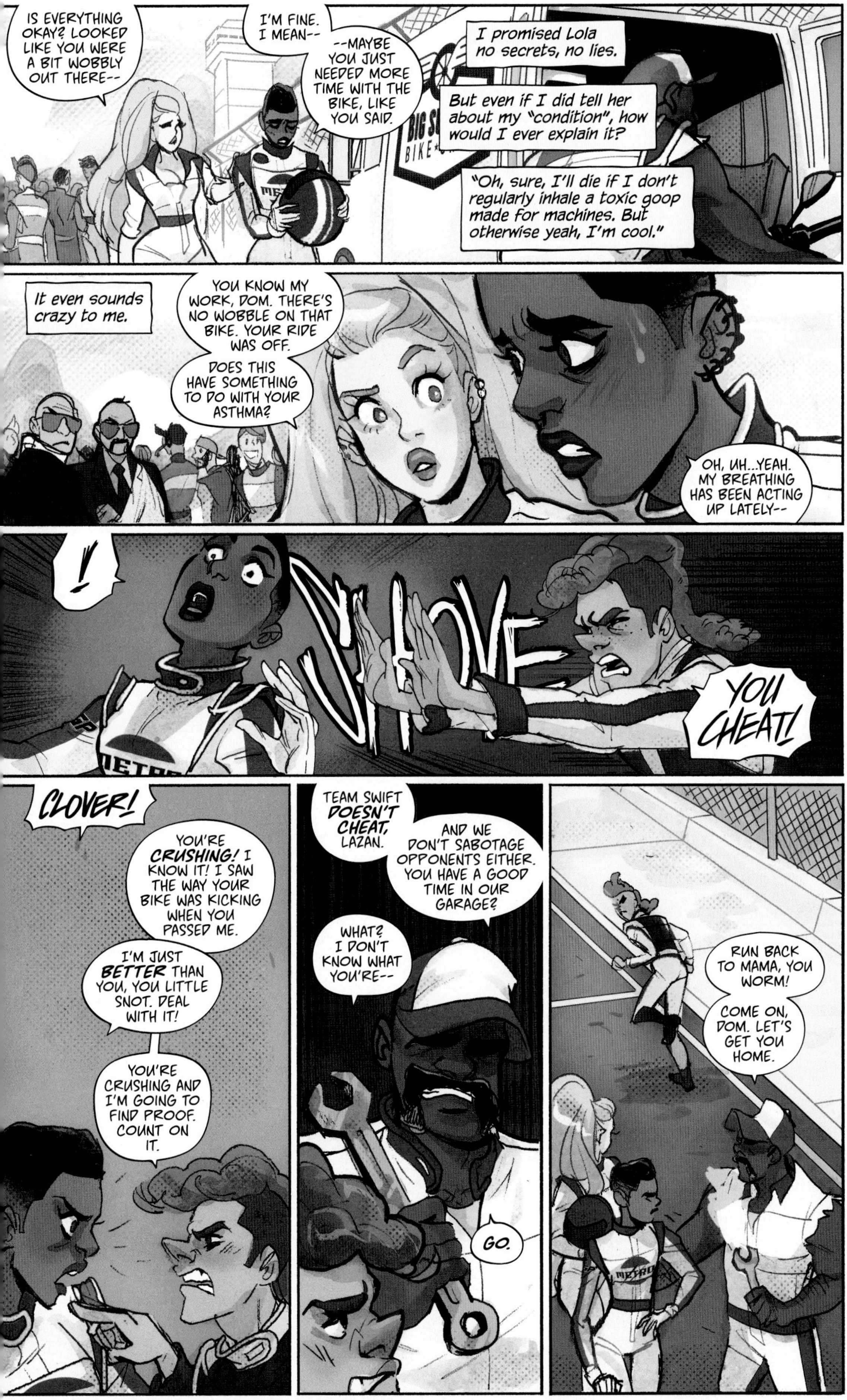

IS EVERYTHING OKAY? LOOKED LIKE YOU WERE A BIT WOBBLY OUT THERE--
I'M FINE. I MEAN--
--MAYBE YOU JUST NEEDED MORE TIME WITH THE BIKE, LIKE YOU SAID.
I promised Lola no secrets, no lies.
But even if I did tell her about my "condition", how would I ever explain it?
"Oh, sure, I'll die if I don't regularly inhale a toxic goop made for machines. But otherwise yeah, I'm cool."
It even sounds crazy to me.
YOU KNOW MY WORK, DOM. THERE'S NO WOBBLE ON THAT BIKE. YOUR RIDE WAS OFF.
DOES THIS HAVE SOMETHING TO DO WITH YOUR ASTHMA?
OH, UH...YEAH. MY BREATHING HAS BEEN ACTING UP LATELY--
!
SHOVE
YOU CHEAT!
CLOVER!
YOU'RE CRUSHING! I KNOW IT! I SAW THE WAY YOUR BIKE WAS KICKING WHEN YOU PASSED ME.
I'M JUST BETTER THAN YOU, YOU LITTLE SNOT. DEAL WITH IT!
YOU'RE CRUSHING AND I'M GOING TO FIND PROOF. COUNT ON IT.
TEAM SWIFT DOESN'T CHEAT, LAZAN.
AND WE DON'T SABOTAGE OPPONENTS EITHER. YOU HAVE A GOOD TIME IN OUR GARAGE?
WHAT? I DON'T KNOW WHAT YOU'RE--
GO.
RUN BACK TO MAMA, YOU WORM!
COME ON, DOM. LET'S GET YOU HOME.

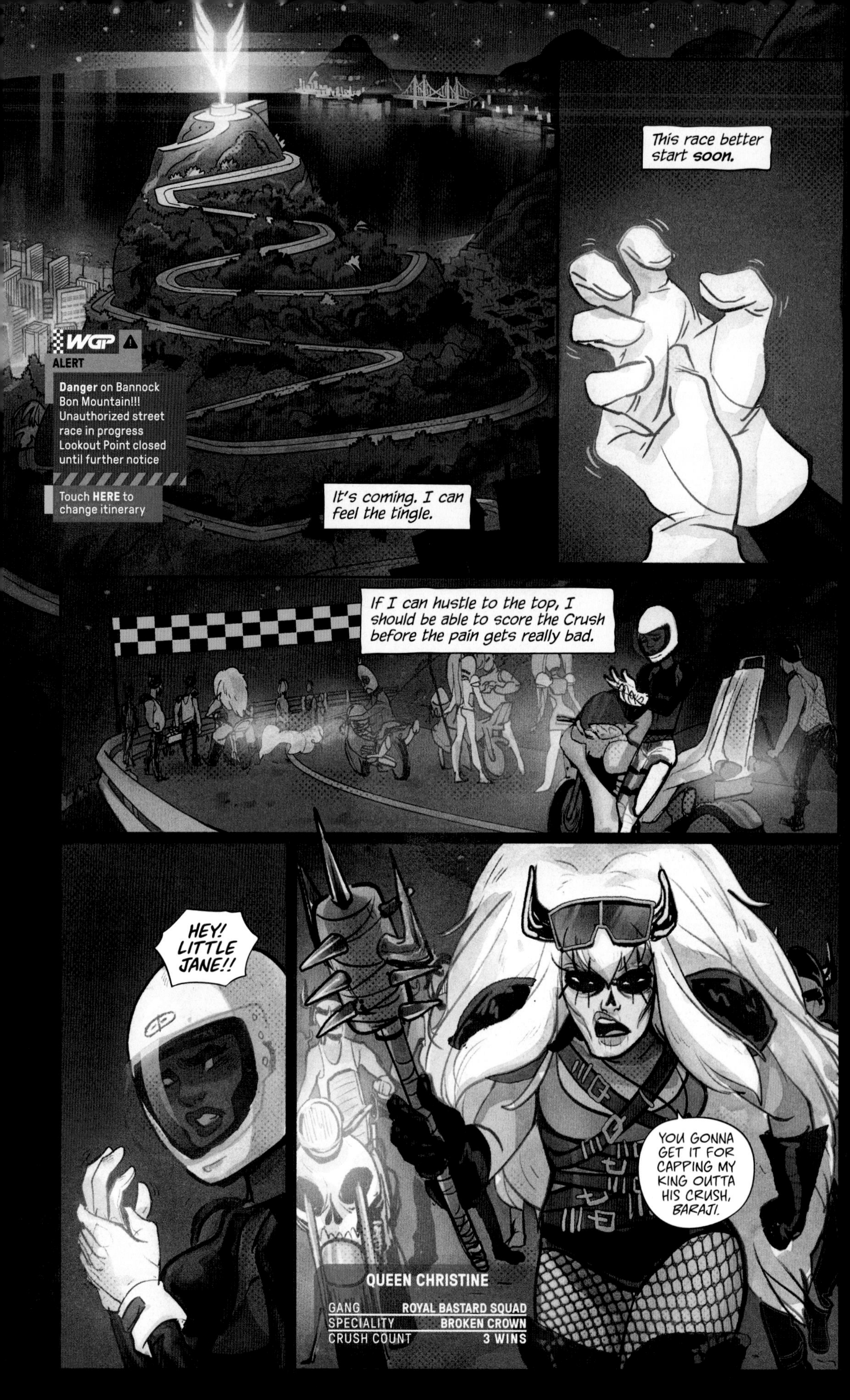
WGP
ALERT
Danger on Bannock Bon Mountain!!! Unauthorized street race in progress Lookout Point closed until further notice
Touch HERE to change itinerary
It's coming. I can feel the tingle.
This race better start soon.
If I can hustle to the top, I should be able to score the Crush before the pain gets really bad.
HEY! LITTLE JANE!!
YOU GONNA GET IT FOR CAPPING MY KING OUTTA HIS CRUSH, BARAJI.
QUEEN CHRISTINE
GANG ROYAL BASTARD SQUAD
SPECIALITY BROKEN CROWN
CRUSH COUNT 3 WINS

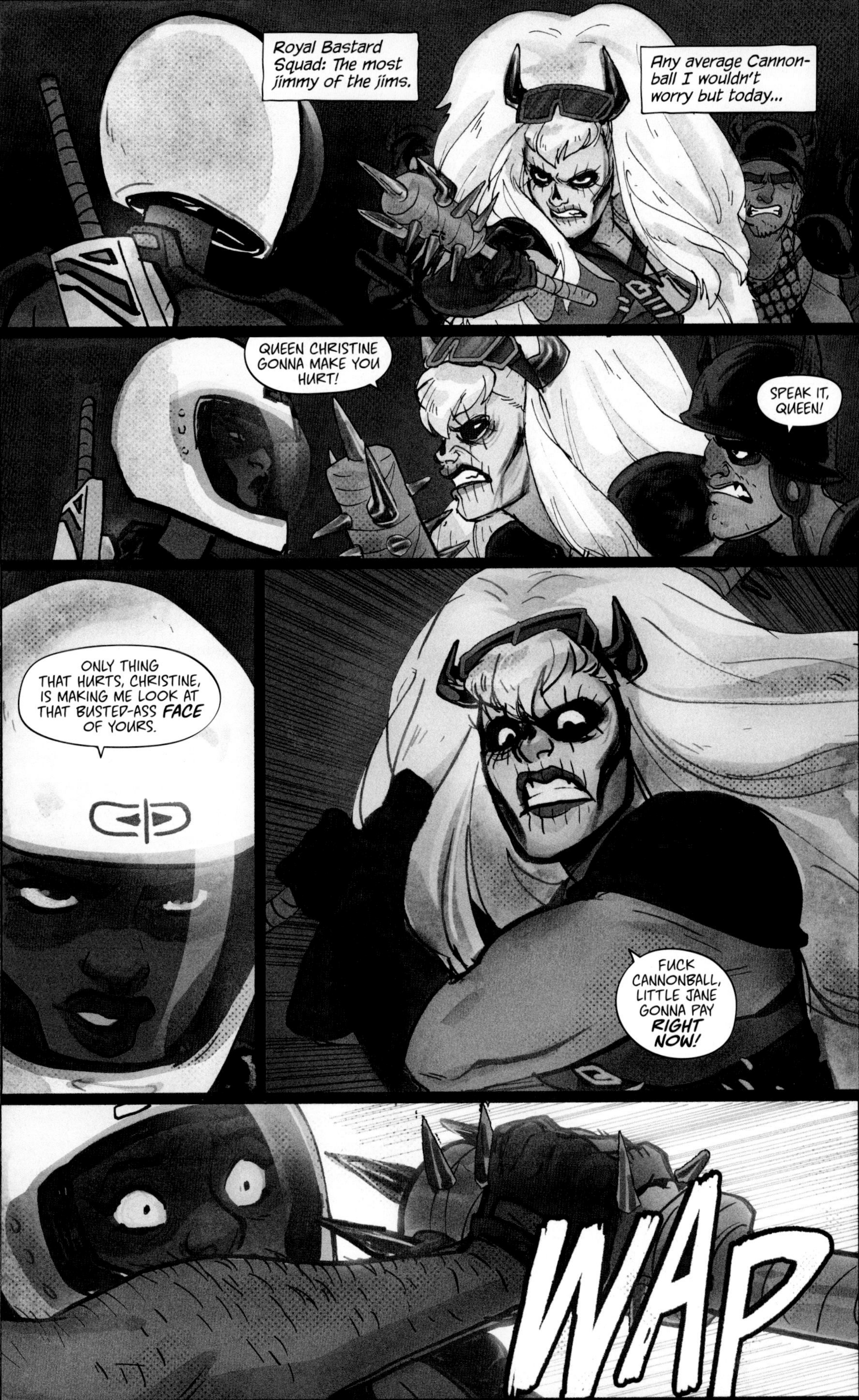
Royal Bastard Squad: The most jimmy of the jims.
Any average Cannonball I wouldn't worry but today...
QUEEN CHRISTINE GONNA MAKE YOU HURT!
SPEAK IT, QUEEN!
ONLY THING THAT HURTS, CHRISTINE, IS MAKING ME LOOK AT THAT BUSTED-ASS FACE OF YOURS.
FUCK CANNONBALL, LITTLE JANE GONNA PAY RIGHT NOW!
WAP

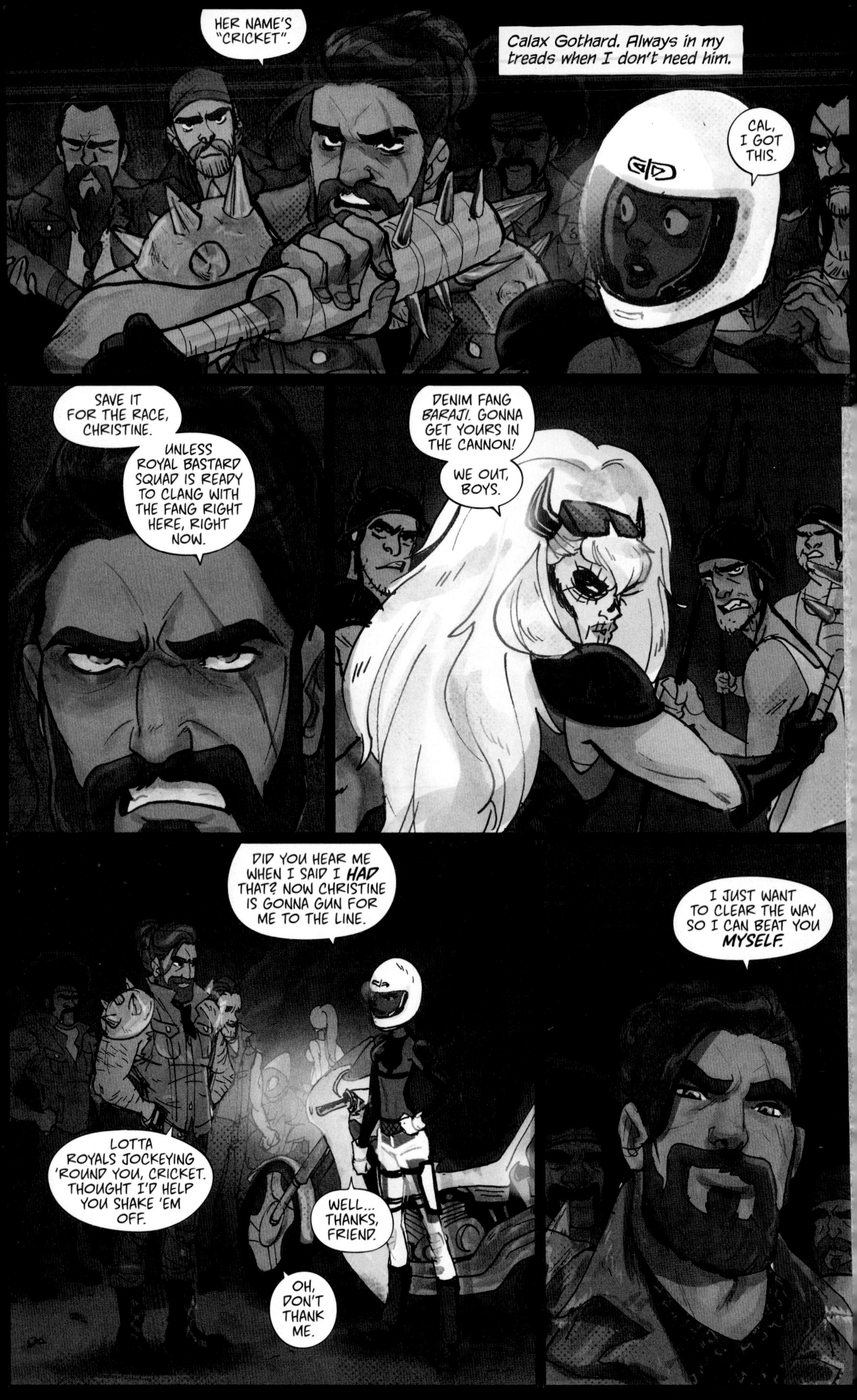
HER NAME'S "CRICKET".
Calax Gothard. Always in my treads when I don't need him.
CAL, I GOT THIS.
SAVE IT FOR THE RACE, CHRISTINE.
UNLESS ROYAL BASTARD SQUAD IS READY TO CLANG WITH THE FANG RIGHT HERE, RIGHT NOW.
DENIM FANG BARAJI. GONNA GET YOURS IN THE CANNON!
WE OUT, BOYS.
LOTTA ROYALS JOCKEYING 'ROUND YOU, CRICKET. THOUGHT I'D HELP YOU SHAKE 'EM OFF.
WELL... THANKS, FRIEND.
OH, DON'T THANK ME.
DID YOU HEAR ME WHEN I SAID I HAD THAT? NOW CHRISTINE IS GONNA GUN FOR ME TO THE LINE.
I JUST WANT TO CLEAR THE WAY SO I CAN BEAT YOU MYSELF.

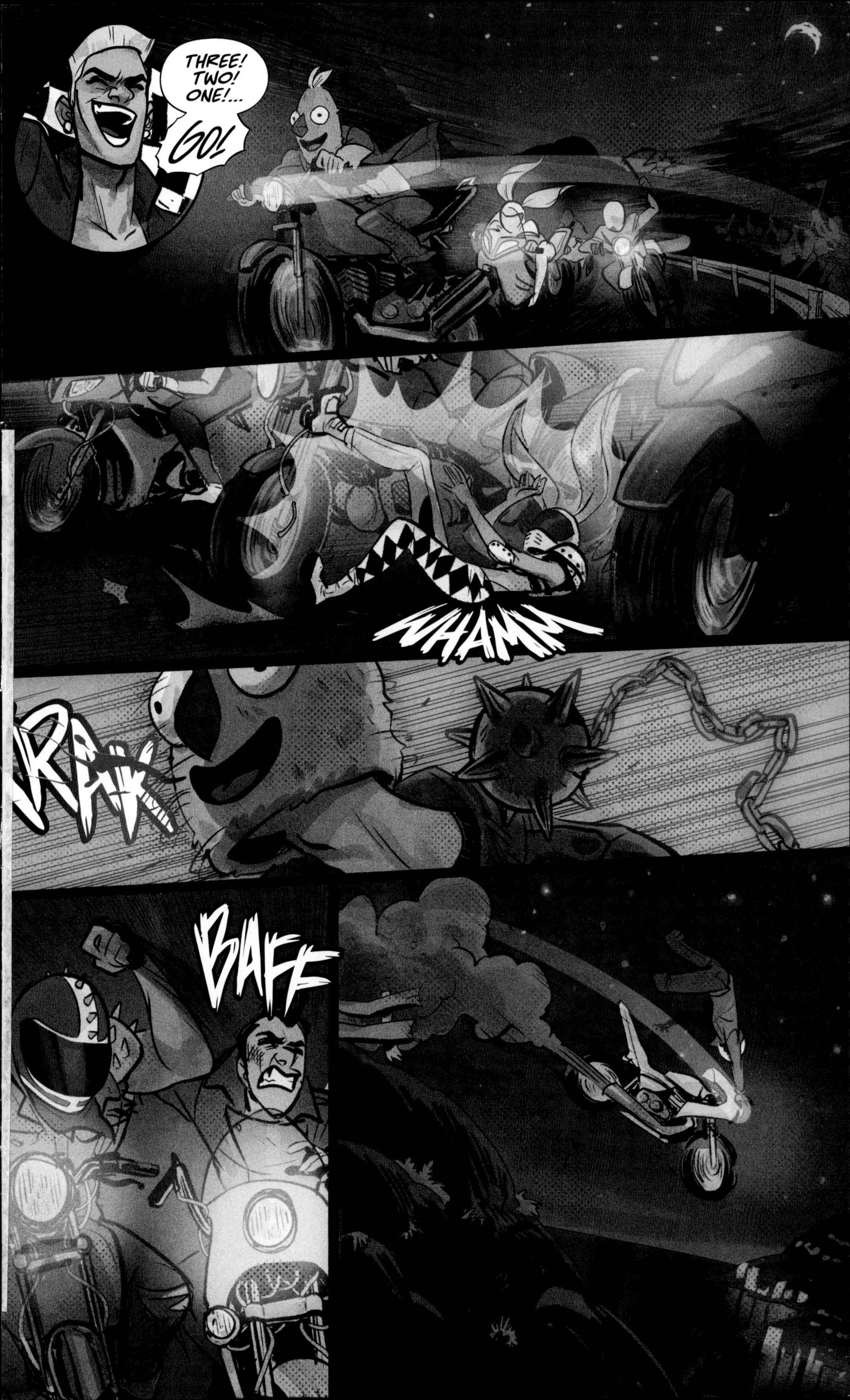
THREE! TWO! ONE!...
GO!
WHAMM
KRAK
BLAFF

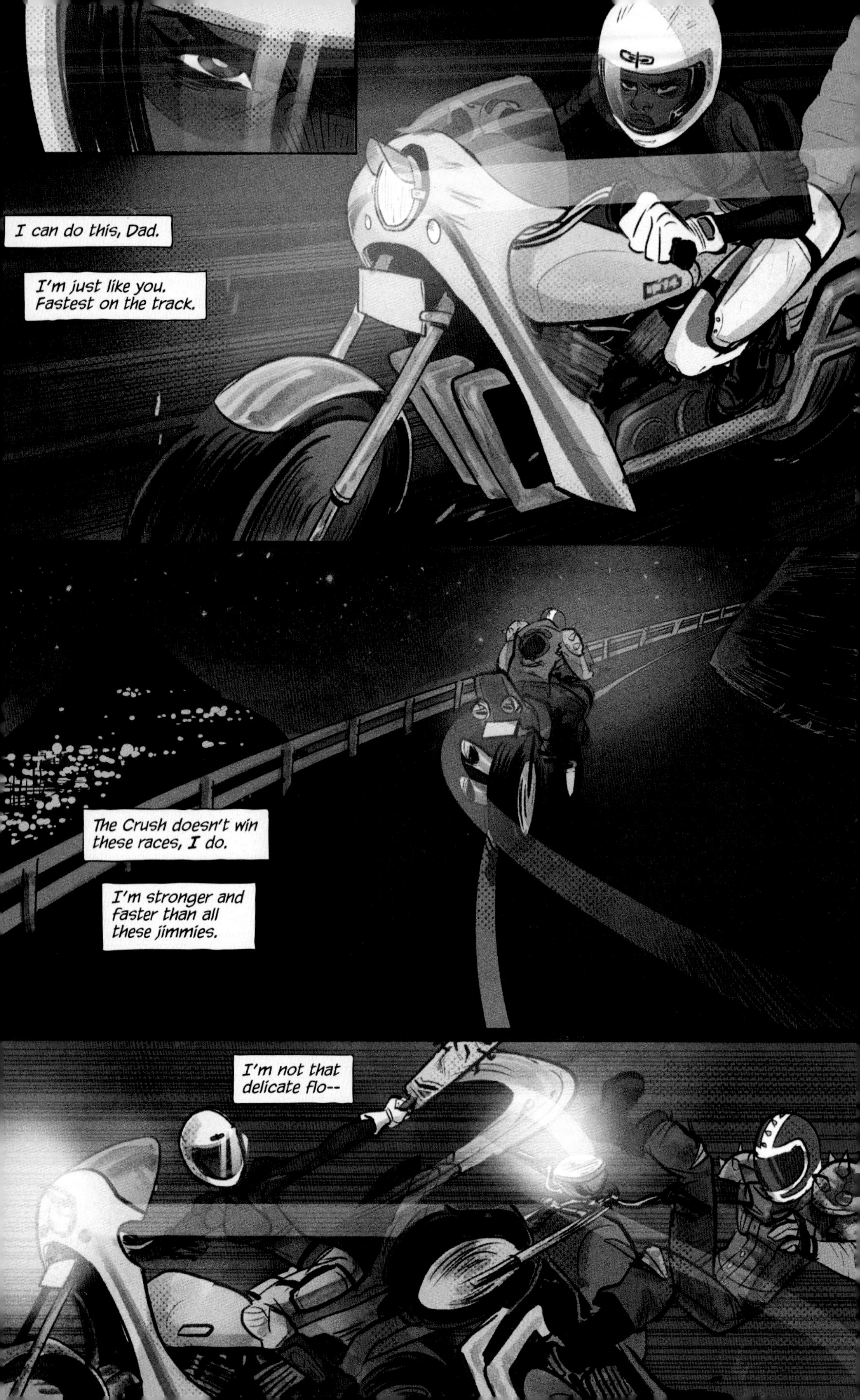
I can do this, Dad.
I'm just like you. Fastest on the track.
The Crush doesn't win these races, I do.
I'm stronger and faster than all these jimmies.
I'm not that delicate flo--

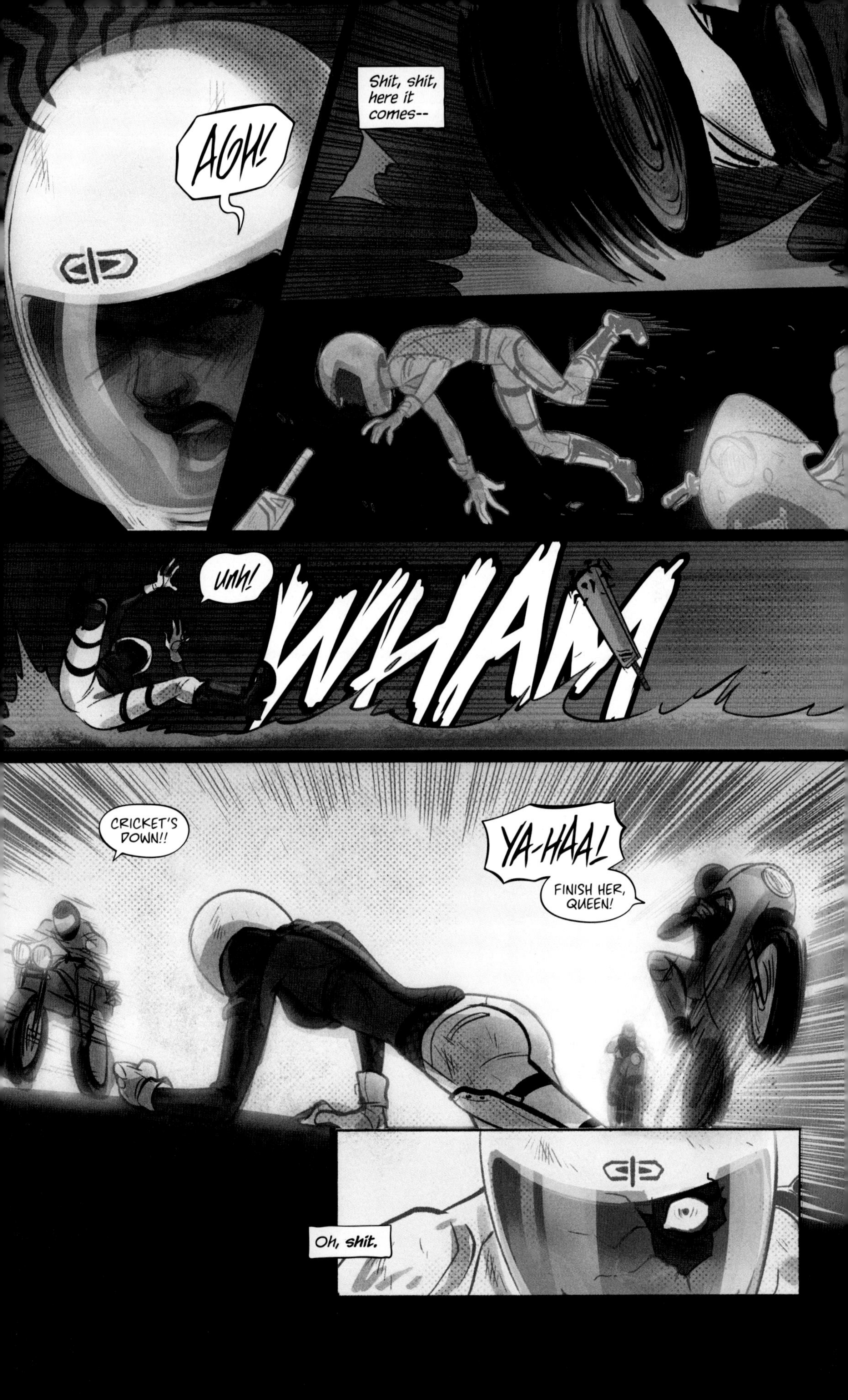

AGH!
Shit, shit, here it comes--
unh!
WHAM
CRICKET'S DOWN!!
YA-HAA!
FINISH HER, QUEEN!
Oh, shit.

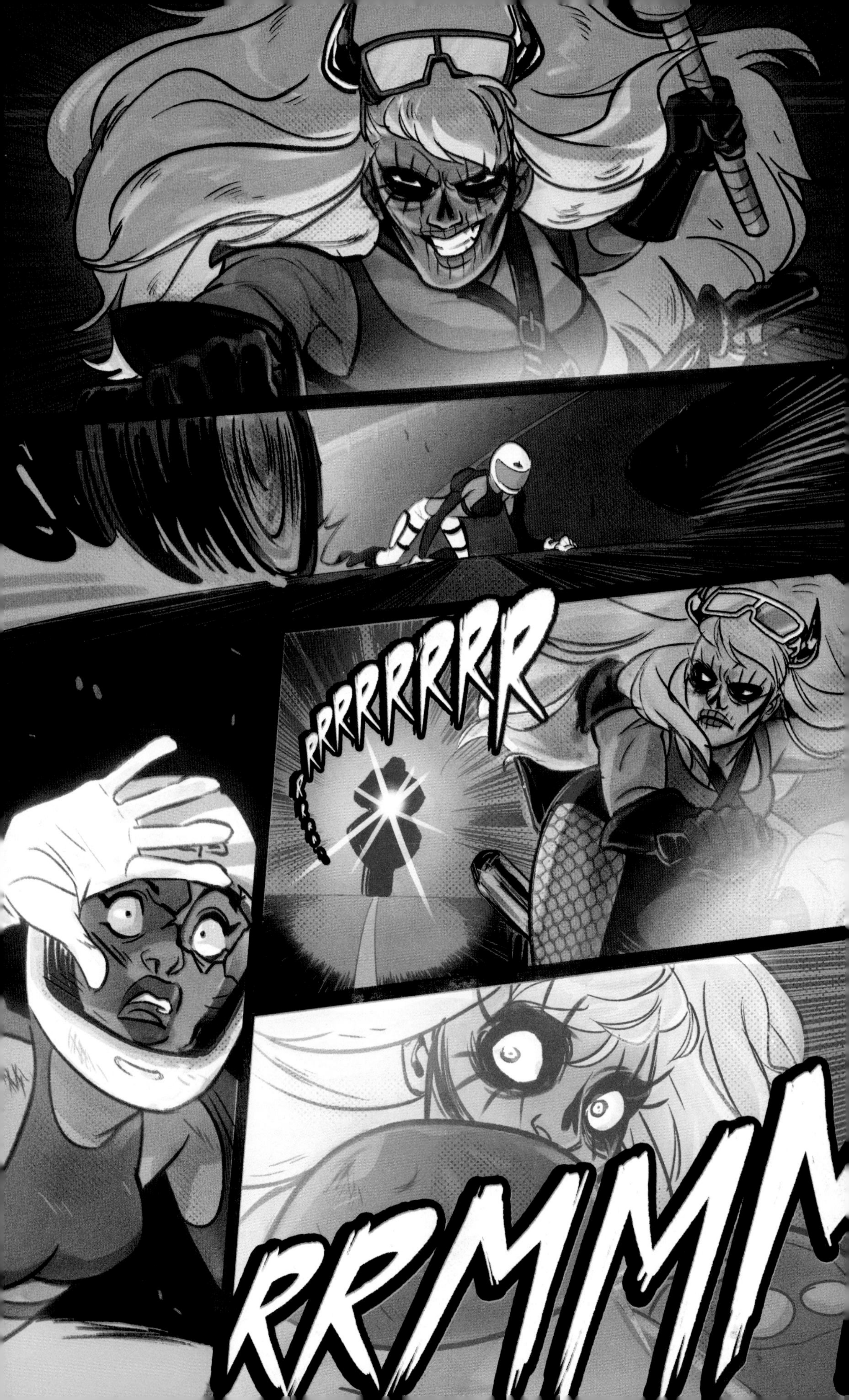
RRRRRRRR
RRRRRRRRR
RRMMM

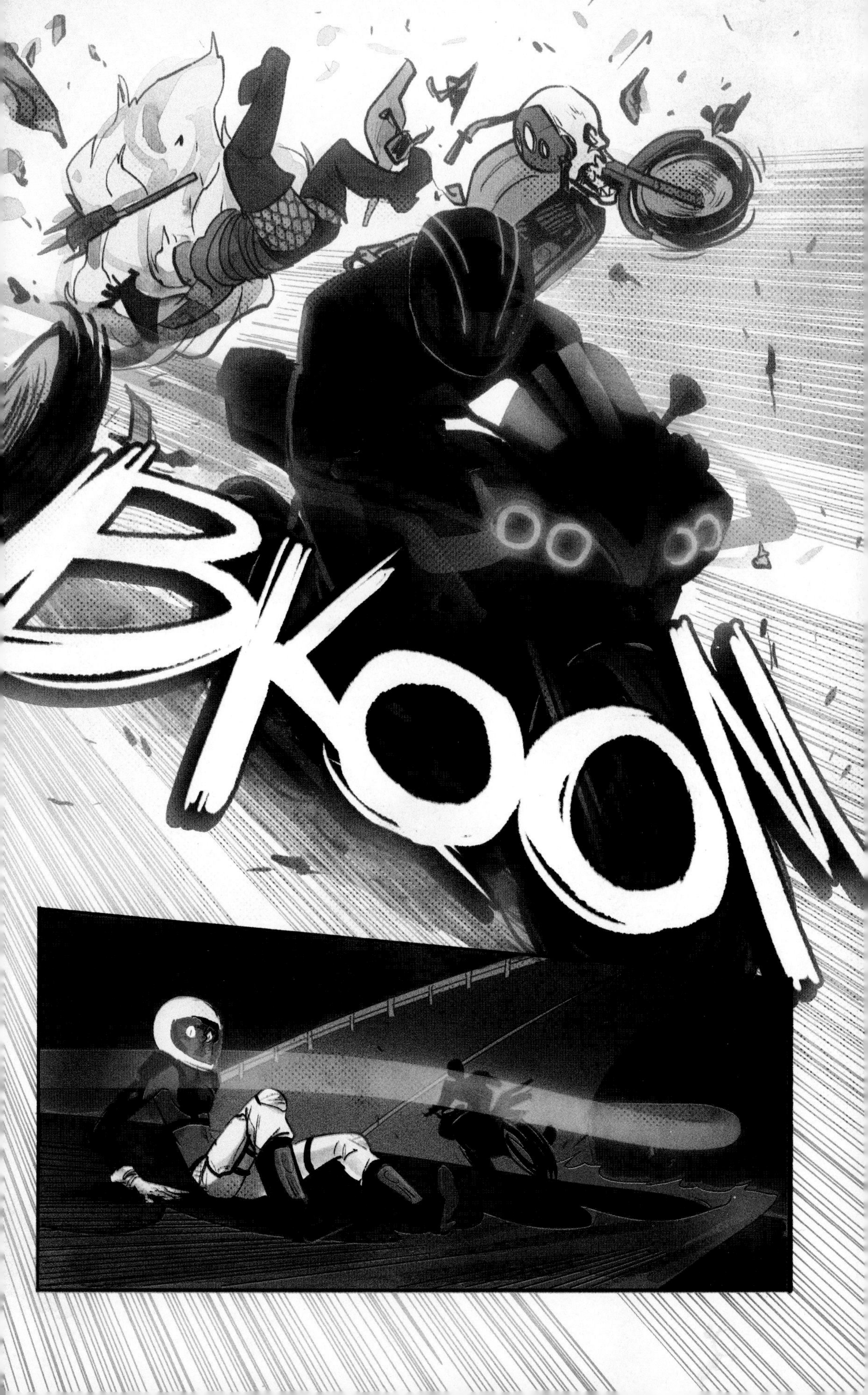
BOOM

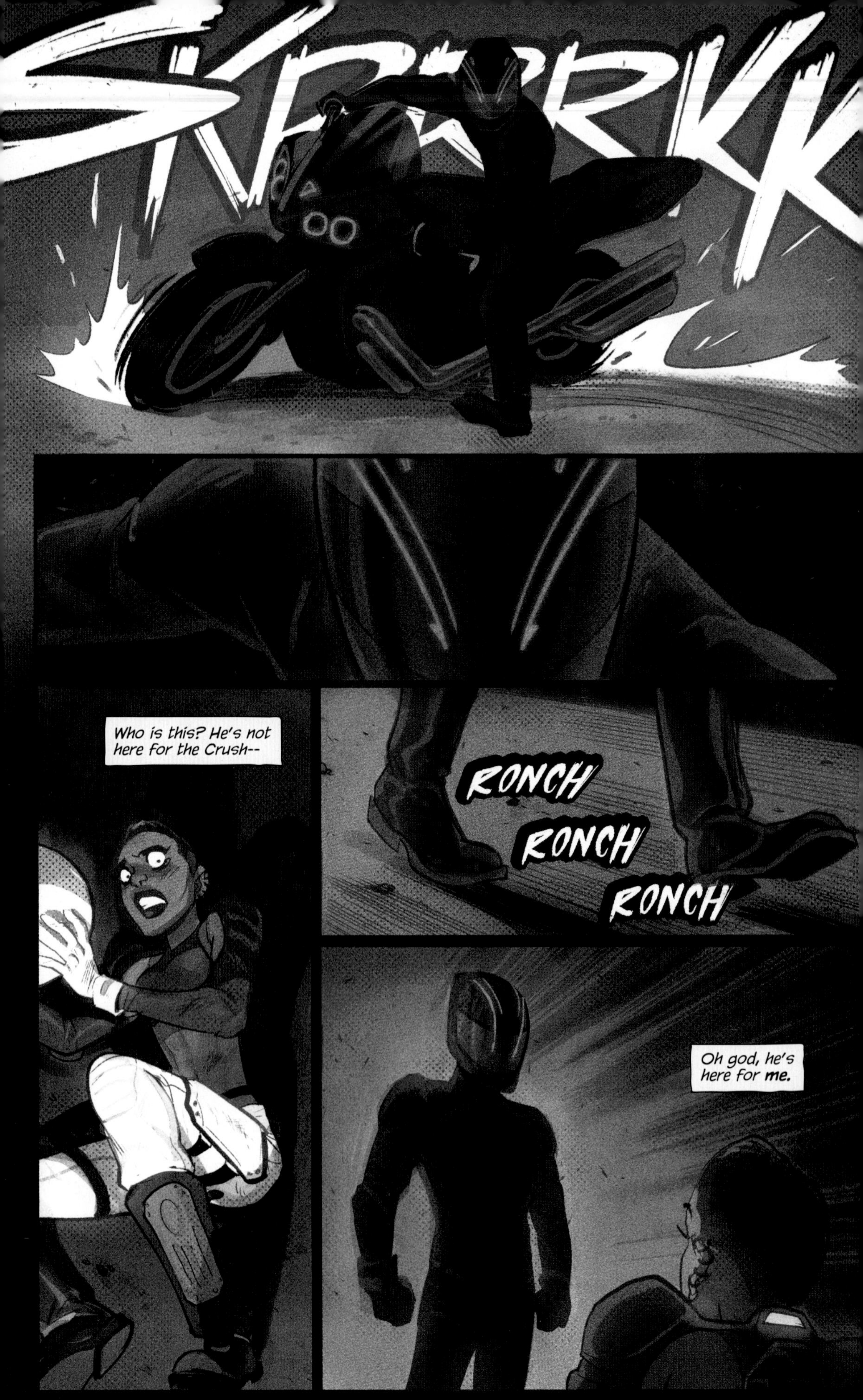
Who is this? He's not here for the Crush--
RONCH
RONCH
RONCH
Oh god, he's here for **me.**

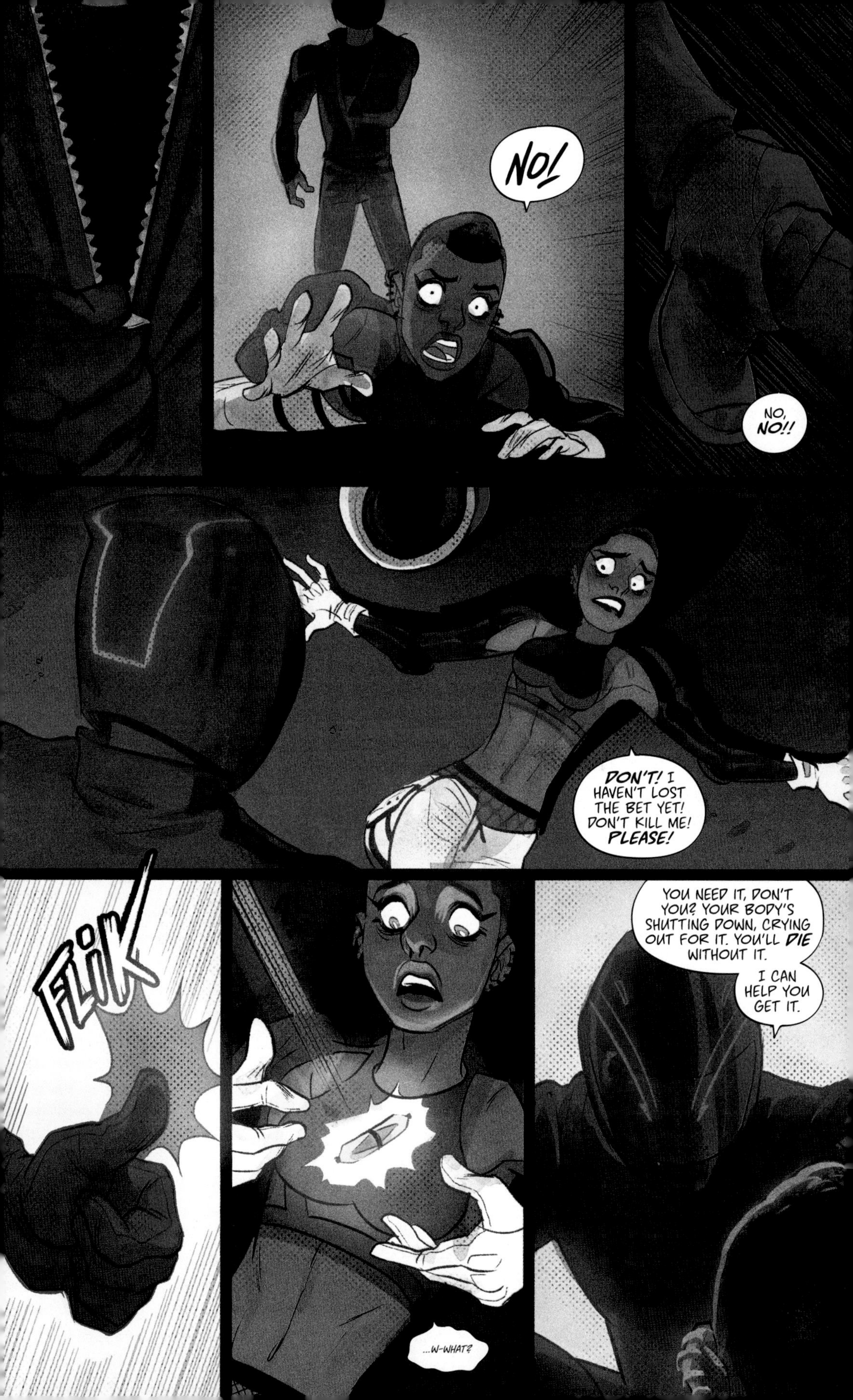
NO!
NO, NO!!
DON'T! I HAVEN'T LOST THE BET YET! DON'T KILL ME! PLEASE!
FLIK
YOU NEED IT, DON'T YOU? YOUR BODY'S SHUTTING DOWN, CRYING OUT FOR IT. YOU'LL DIE WITHOUT IT.
I CAN HELP YOU GET IT.
...W-WHAT?

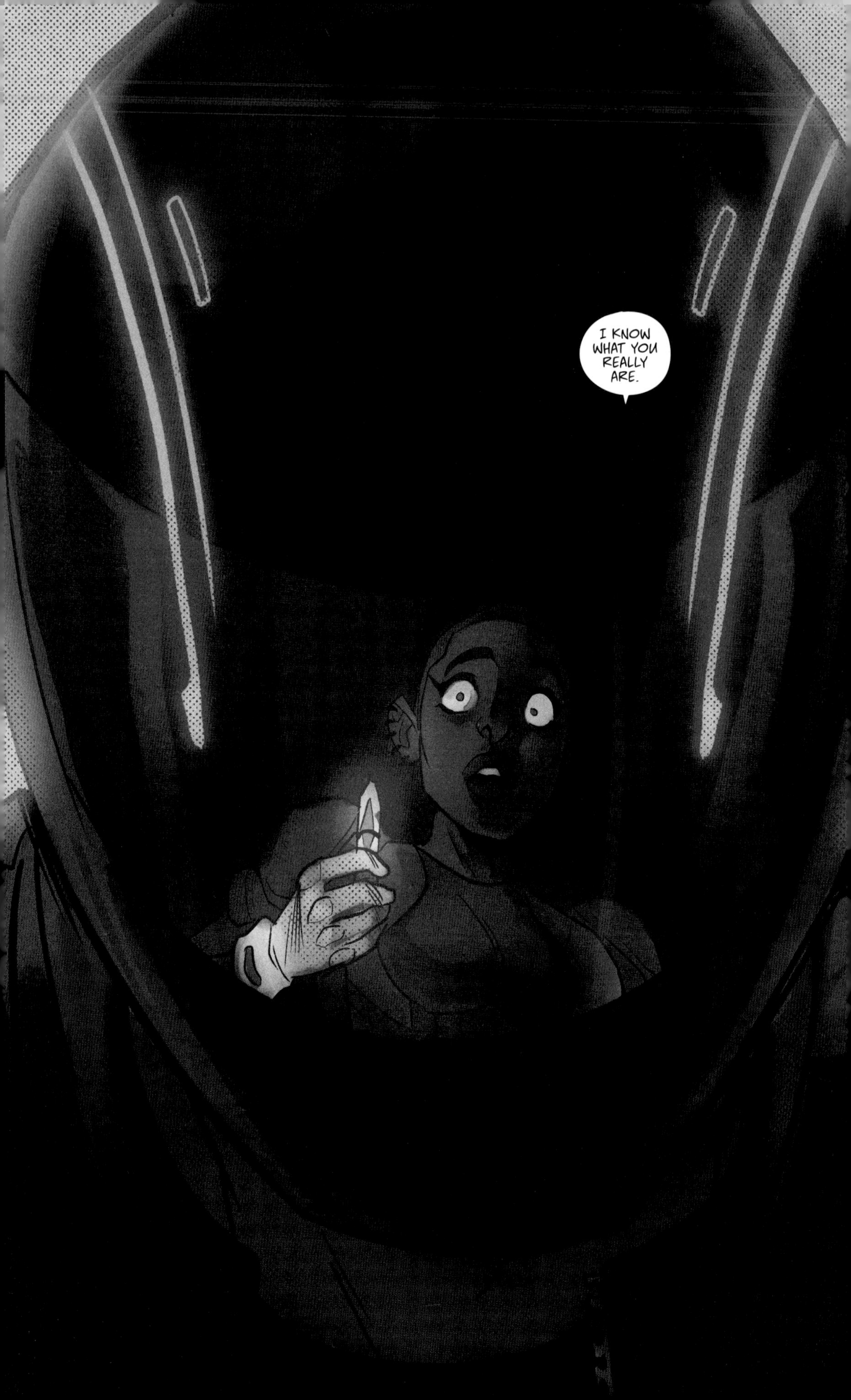
I KNOW WHAT YOU REALLY ARE.

WGP WARNING: SAY NO TO ILLEGAL ACCELERANTS!

MAD Agency—
TESTING IN PROGRESS

MACHINE ANTI DOPING

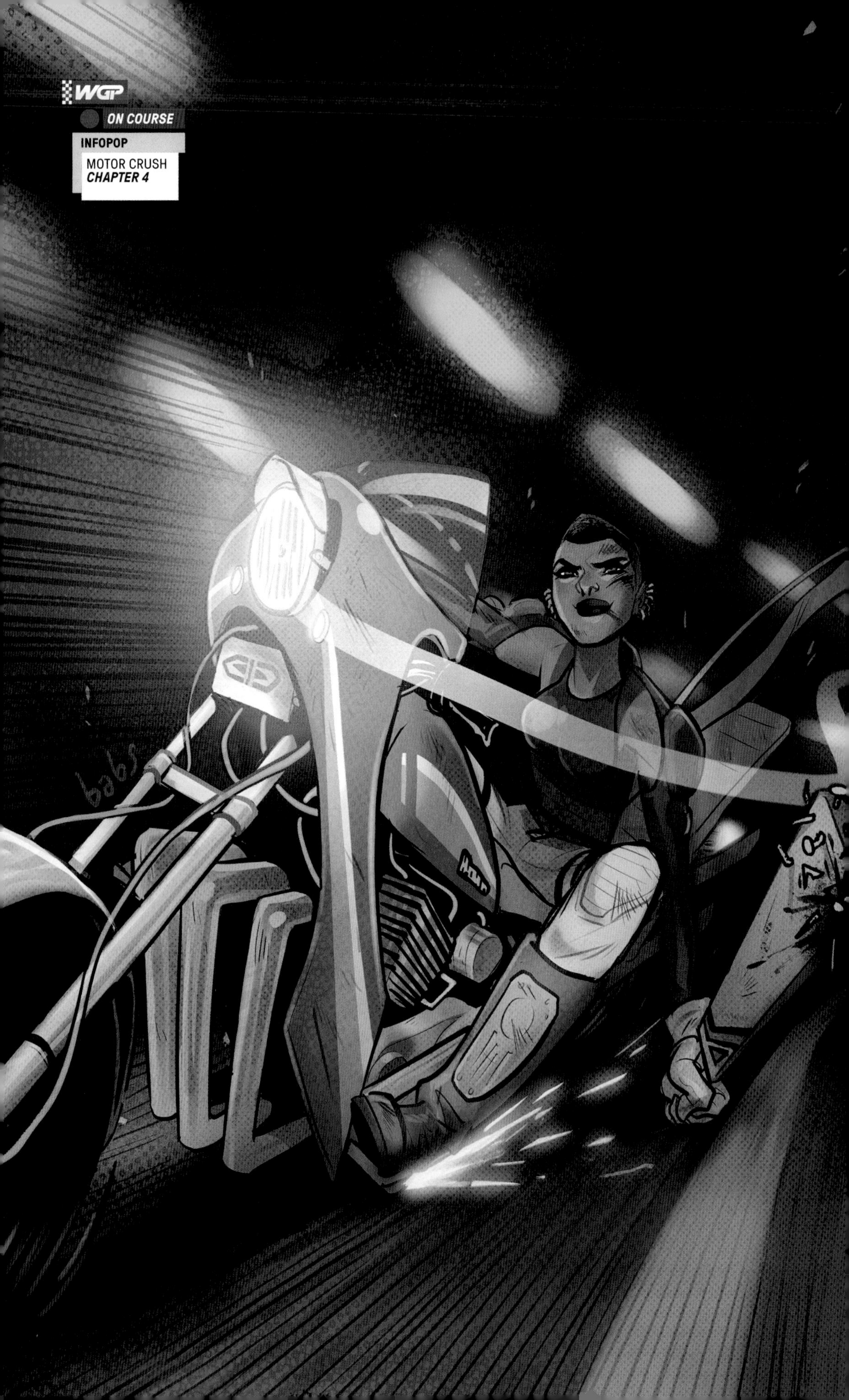
WGP
ON COURSE
INFOPOP
MOTOR CRUSH
CHAPTER 4
babs

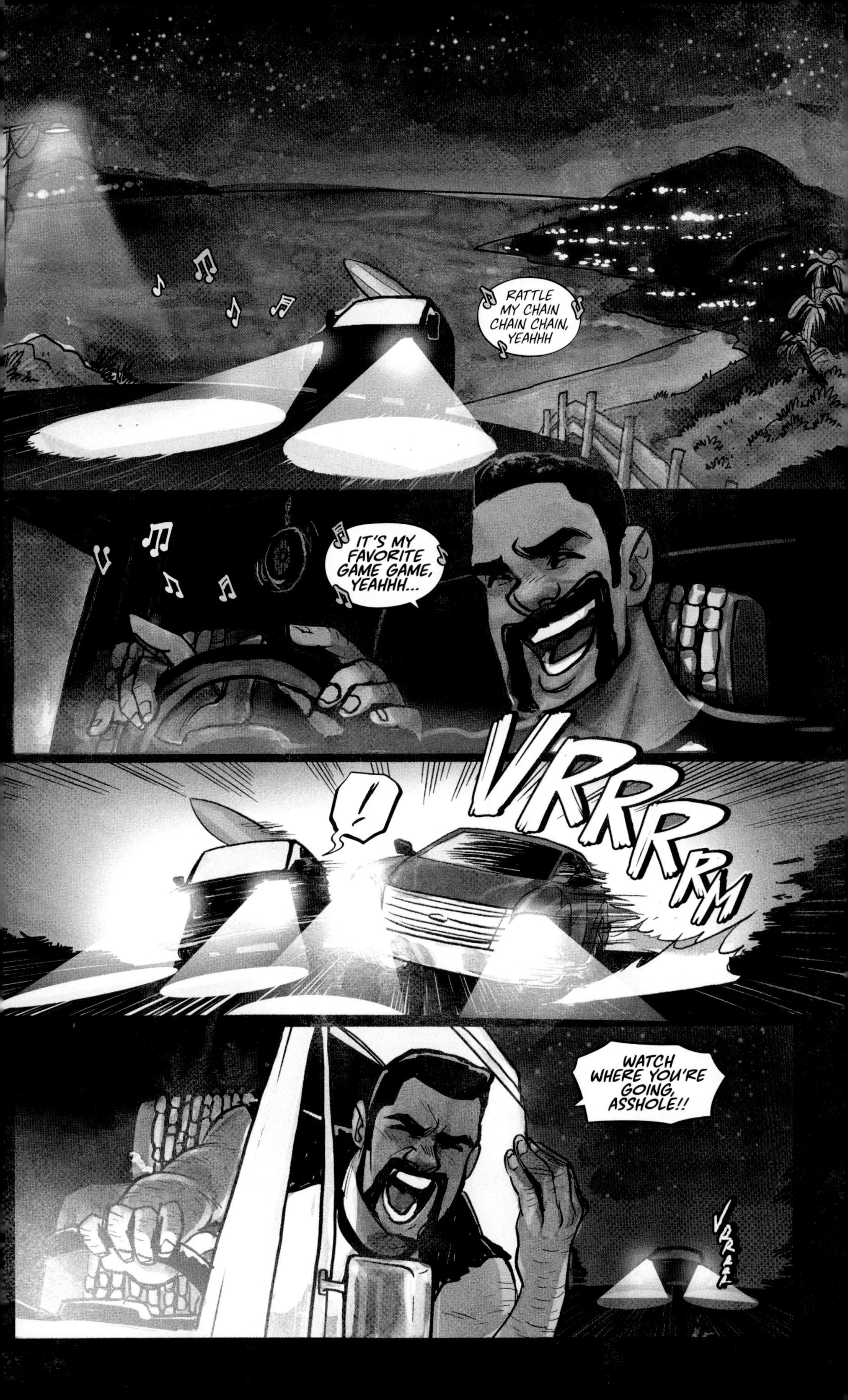
RATTLE MY CHAIN CHAIN CHAIN, YEAHHH
IT'S MY FAVORITE GAME GAME, YEAHHH...
!
VRRRRRM
WATCH WHERE YOU'RE GOING, ASSHOLE!!

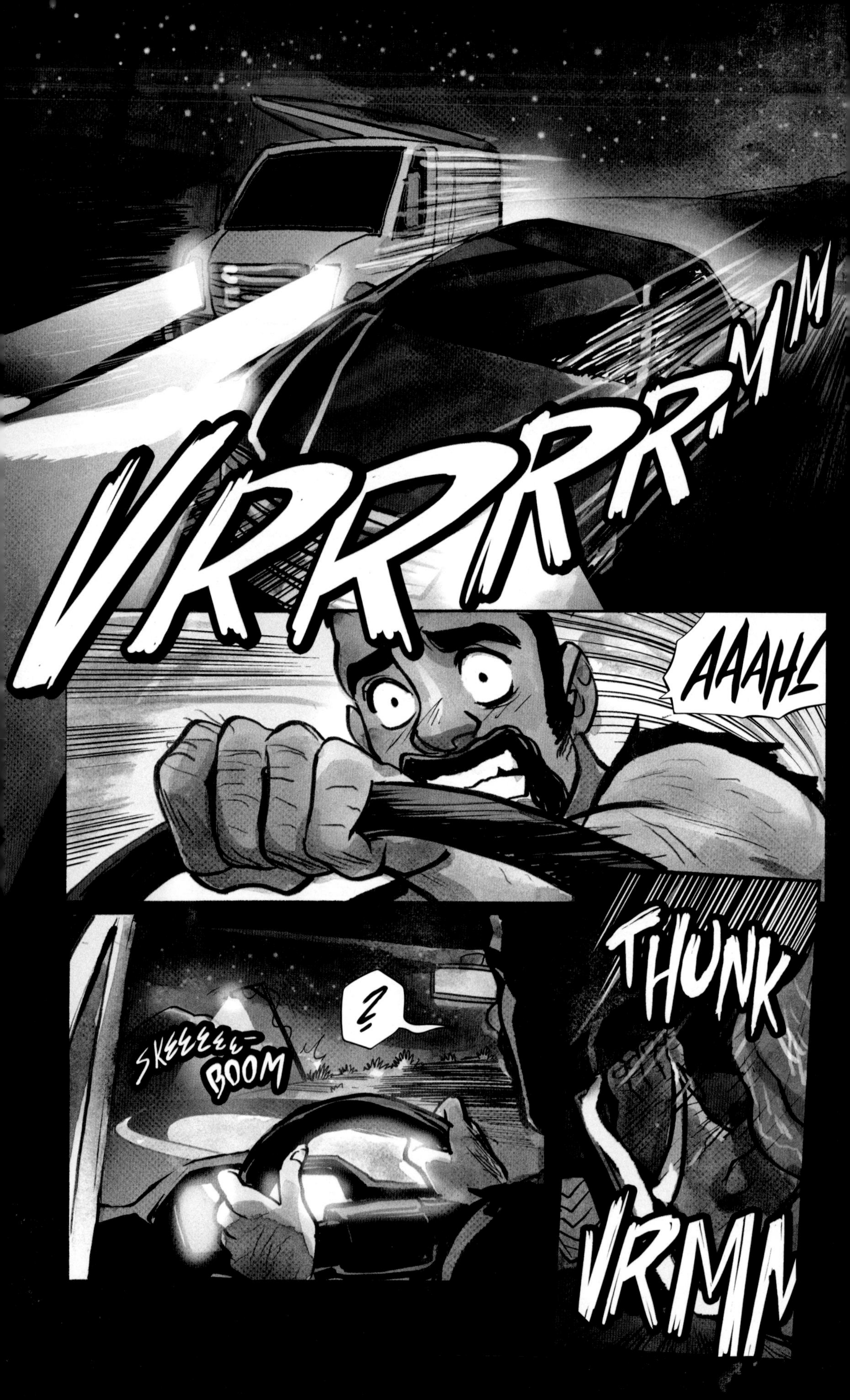
VRRRRRMM
AAAH!
THUNK
?
SKEEEEE-BOOM
VRMM

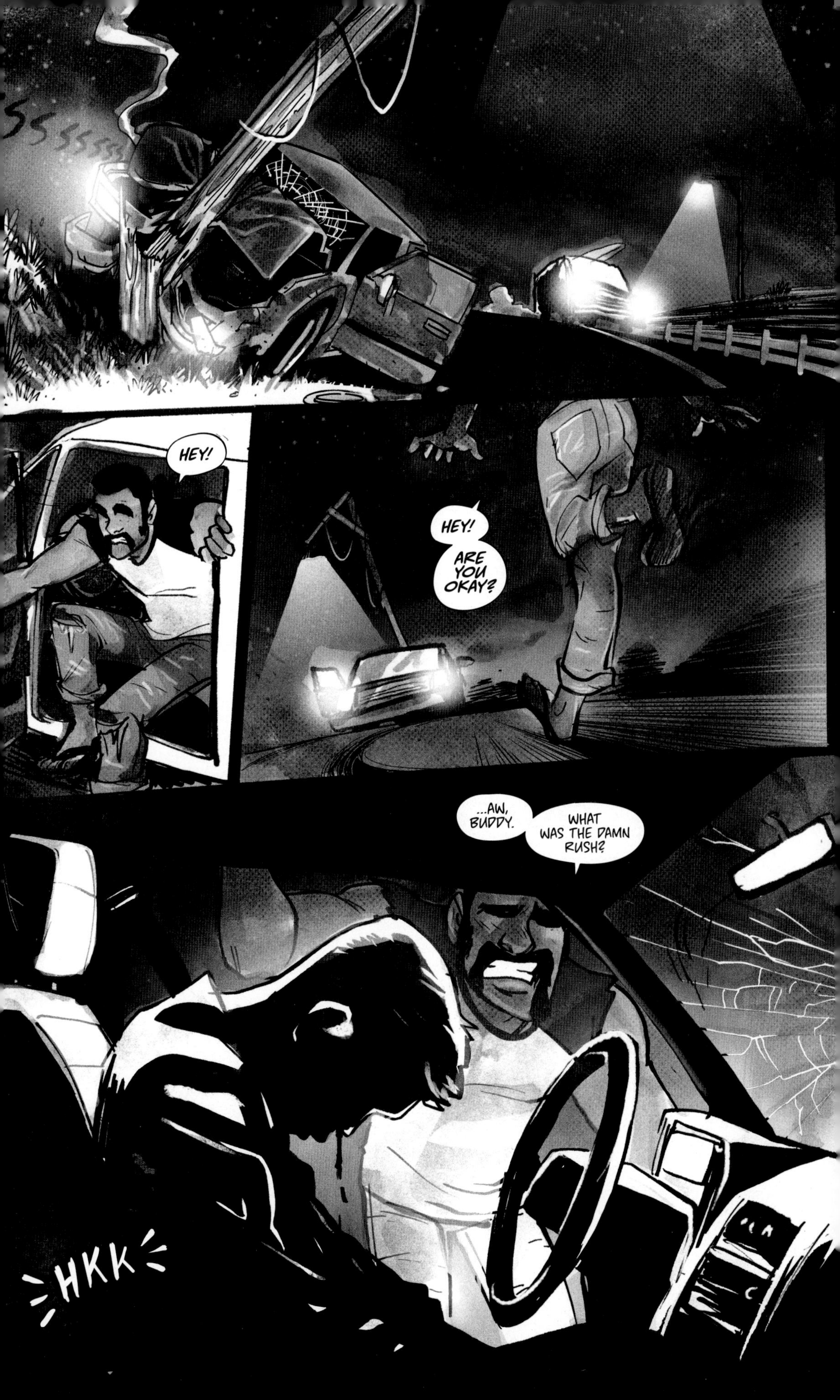
SSSSSSS
HEY!
HEY!
ARE YOU OKAY?
...AW, BUDDY.
WHAT WAS THE DAMN RUSH?
HKK

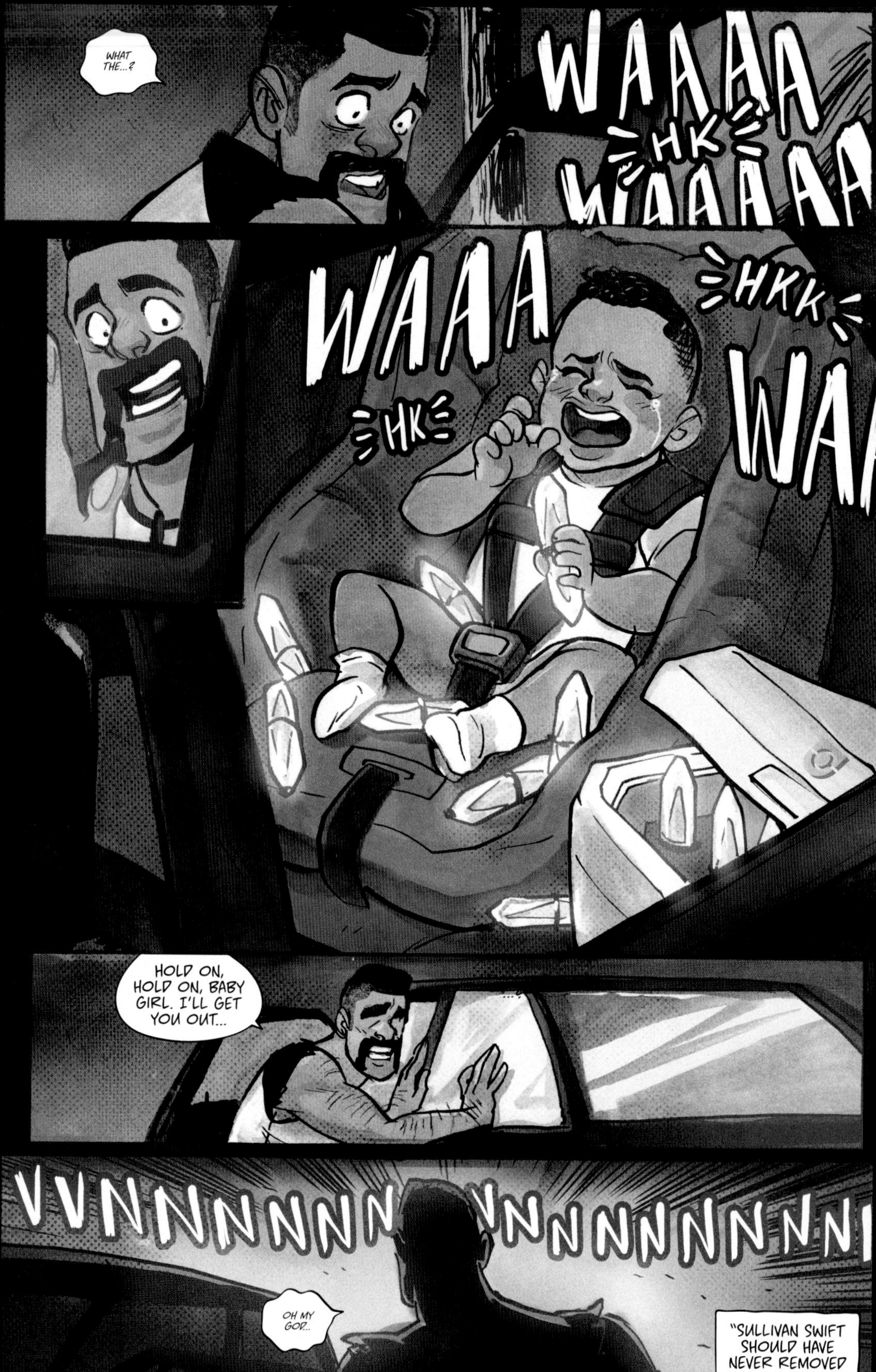
WHAT THE...?
WAAAA
HK
WAAAAAA
WAAA
HKK
HK
WAA
HOLD ON, HOLD ON, BABY GIRL. I'LL GET YOU OUT...
VVNNNNNNNNNNNNNNNN
OH MY GOD..
"SULLIVAN SWIFT SHOULD HAVE NEVER REMOVED THE CHILD FROM THAT CAR..."

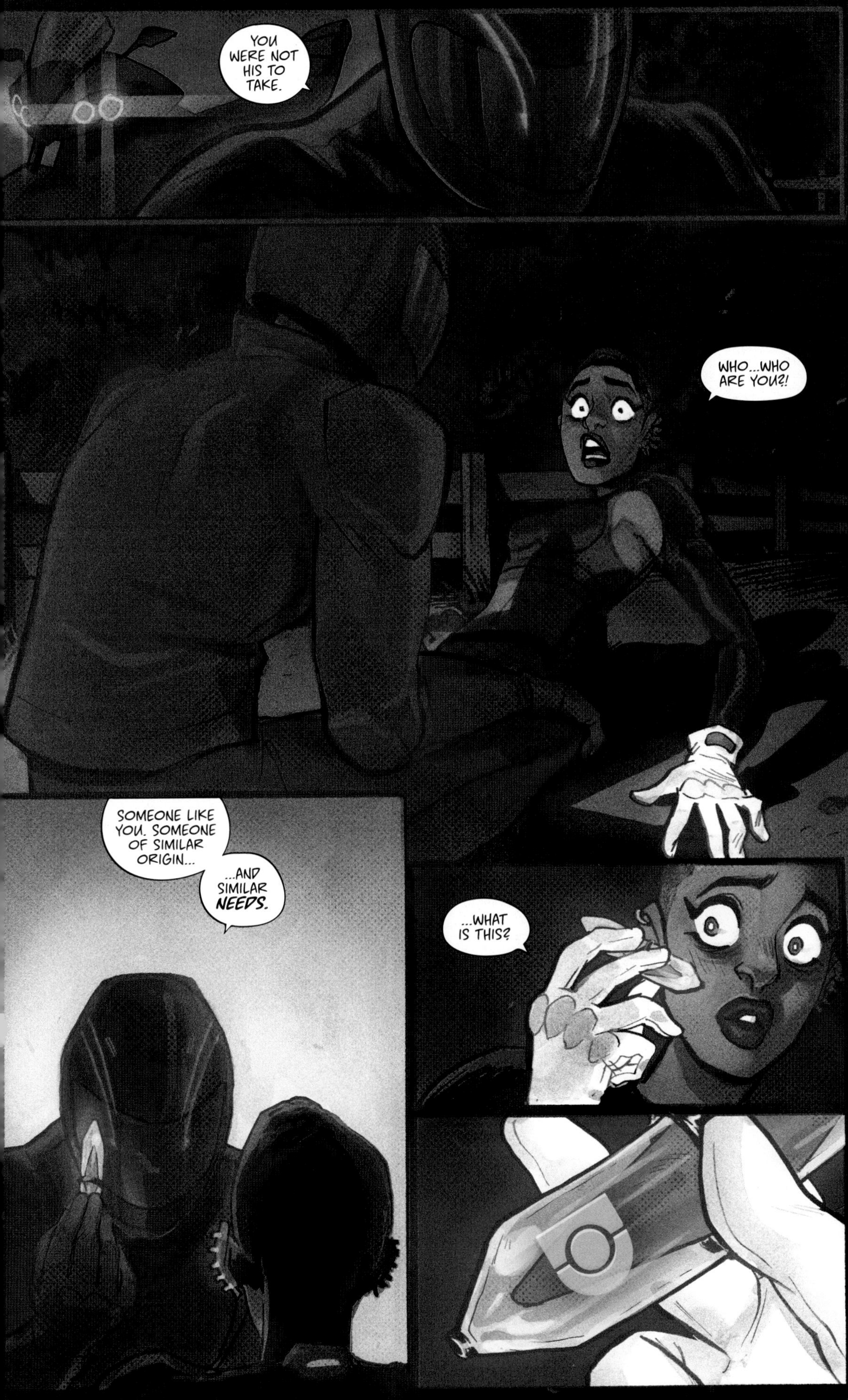
YOU WERE NOT HIS TO TAKE.
WHO...WHO ARE YOU?!
SOMEONE LIKE YOU. SOMEONE OF SIMILAR ORIGIN...
...AND SIMILAR NEEDS.
...WHAT IS THIS?

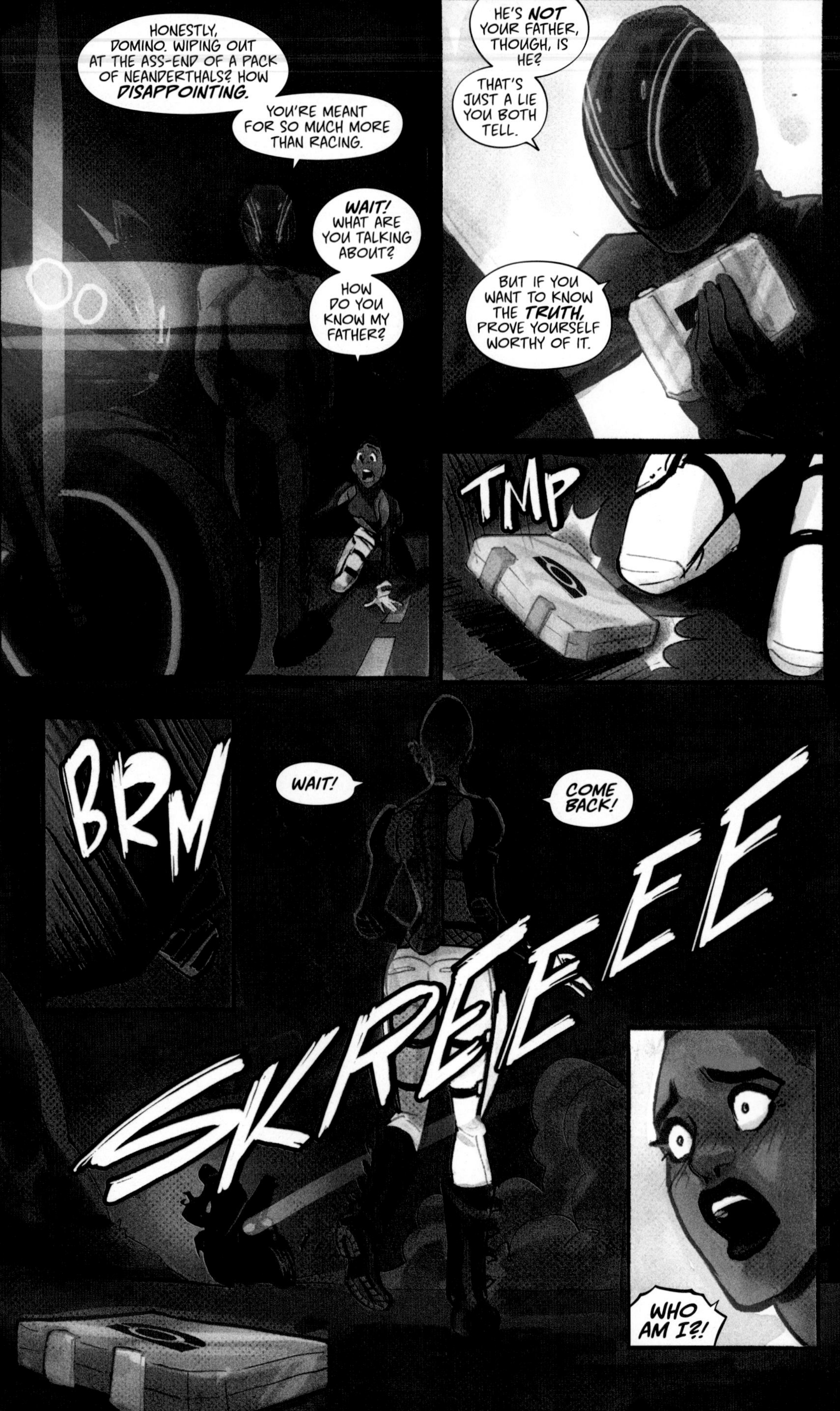
HONESTLY, DOMINO. WIPING OUT AT THE ASS-END OF A PACK OF NEANDERTHALS? HOW **DISAPPOINTING.**
YOU'RE MEANT FOR SO MUCH MORE THAN RACING.
WAIT! WHAT ARE YOU TALKING ABOUT?
HOW DO YOU KNOW MY FATHER?
HE'S **NOT** YOUR FATHER, THOUGH, IS HE?
THAT'S JUST A LIE YOU BOTH TELL.
BUT IF YOU WANT TO KNOW THE **TRUTH,** PROVE YOURSELF WORTHY OF IT.
TMP
BRM
WAIT!
COME BACK!
SKREEEEE
WHO AM I?!

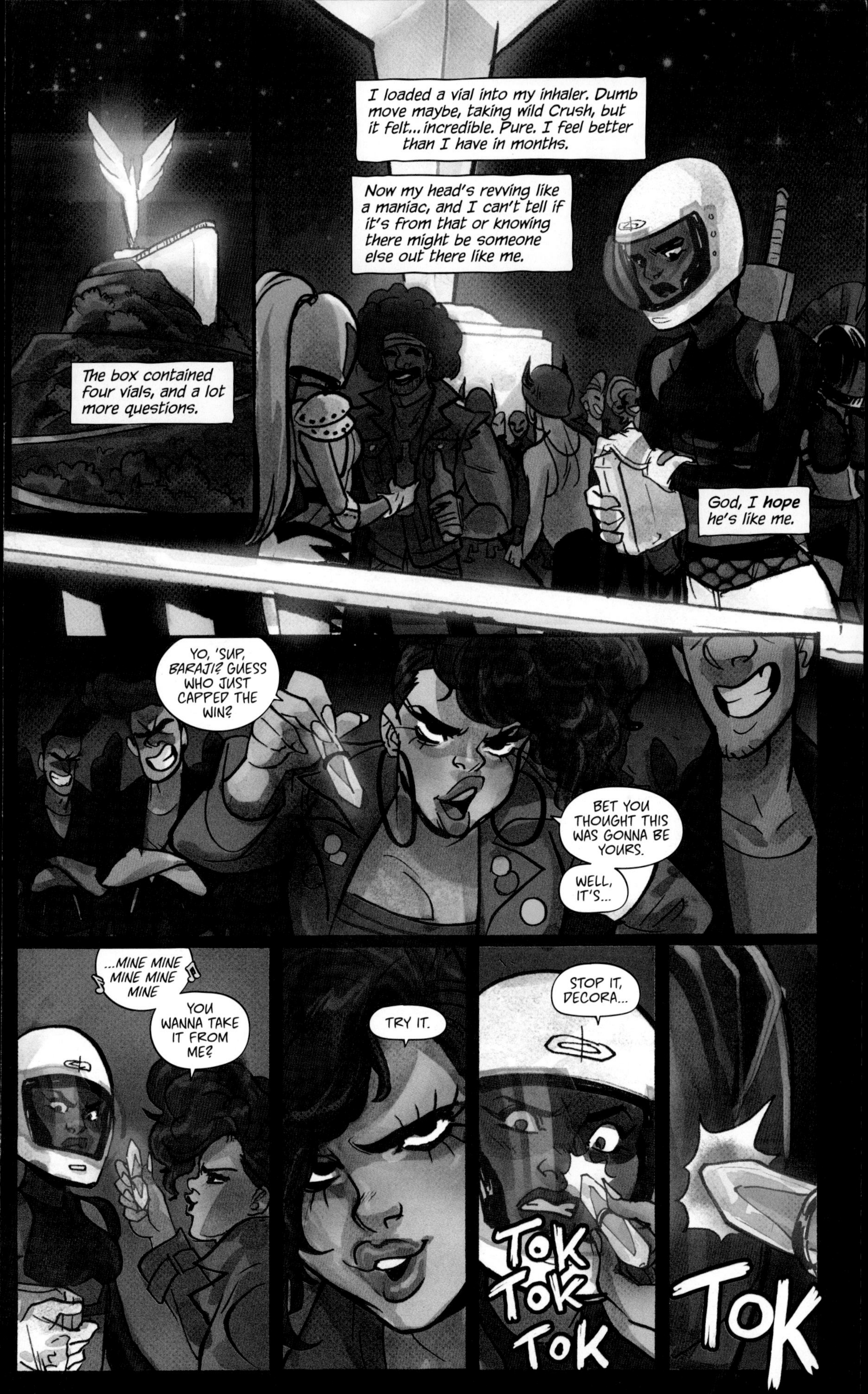
I loaded a vial into my inhaler. Dumb move maybe, taking wild Crush, but it felt... incredible. Pure. I feel better than I have in months.
Now my head's revving like a maniac, and I can't tell if it's from that or knowing there might be someone else out there like me.
The box contained four vials, and a lot more questions.
God, I **hope** he's like me.
YO, 'SUP, BARAJI? GUESS WHO JUST CAPPED THE WIN?
BET YOU THOUGHT THIS WAS GONNA BE YOURS.
WELL, IT'S...
...MINE MINE MINE MINE MINE
YOU WANNA TAKE IT FROM ME?
TRY IT.
STOP IT, DECORA...
TOK TOK TOK
TOK

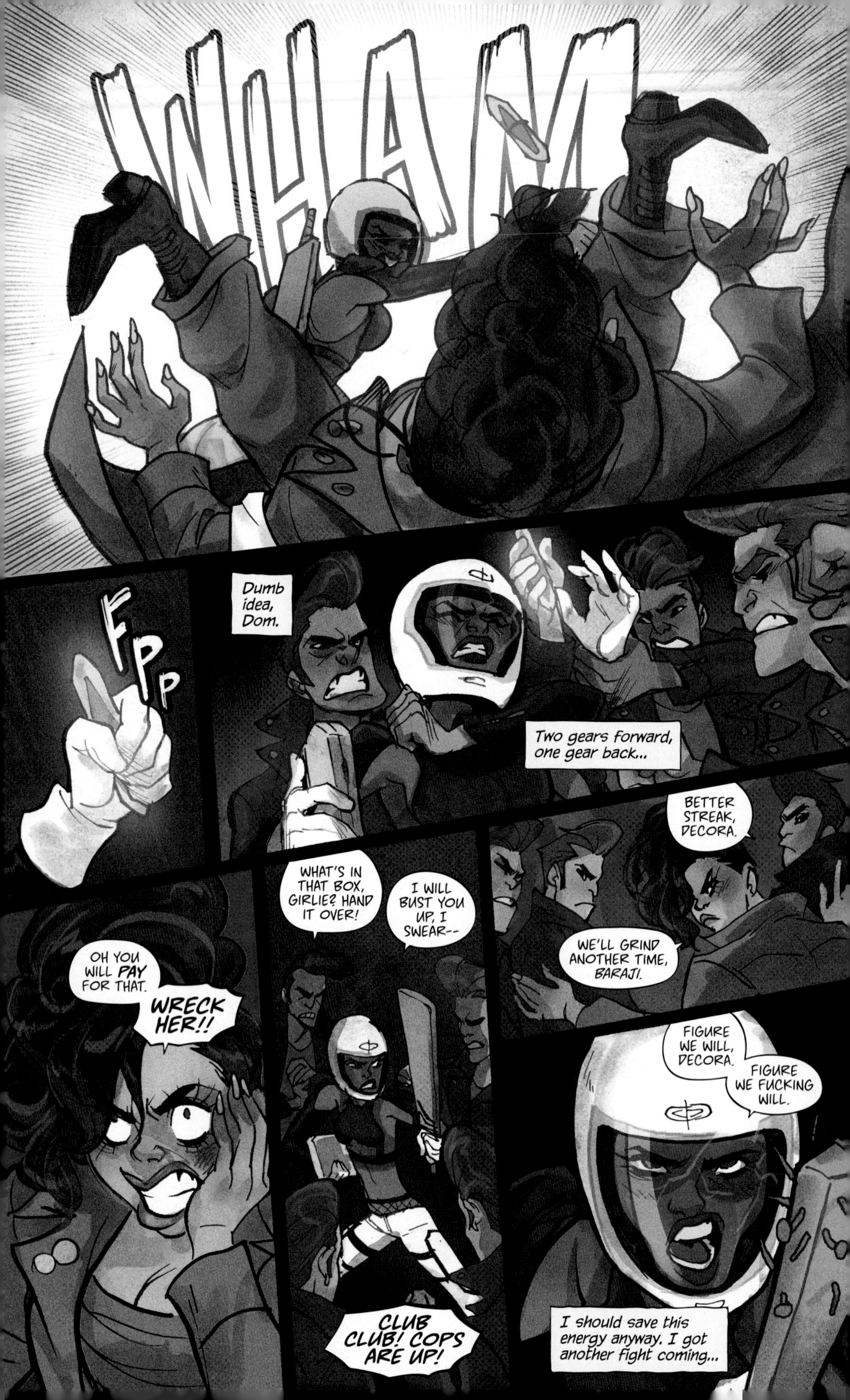
WHAM
FPP
Dumb idea, Dom.
Two gears forward, one gear back...
BETTER STREAK, DECORA.
WE'LL GRIND ANOTHER TIME, BARAJI.
OH YOU WILL PAY FOR THAT.
WRECK HER!!
WHAT'S IN THAT BOX, GIRLIE? HAND IT OVER!
I WILL BUST YOU UP, I SWEAR--
CLUB CLUB! COPS ARE UP!
FIGURE WE WILL, DECORA.
FIGURE WE FUCKING WILL.
I should save this energy anyway. I got another fight coming...

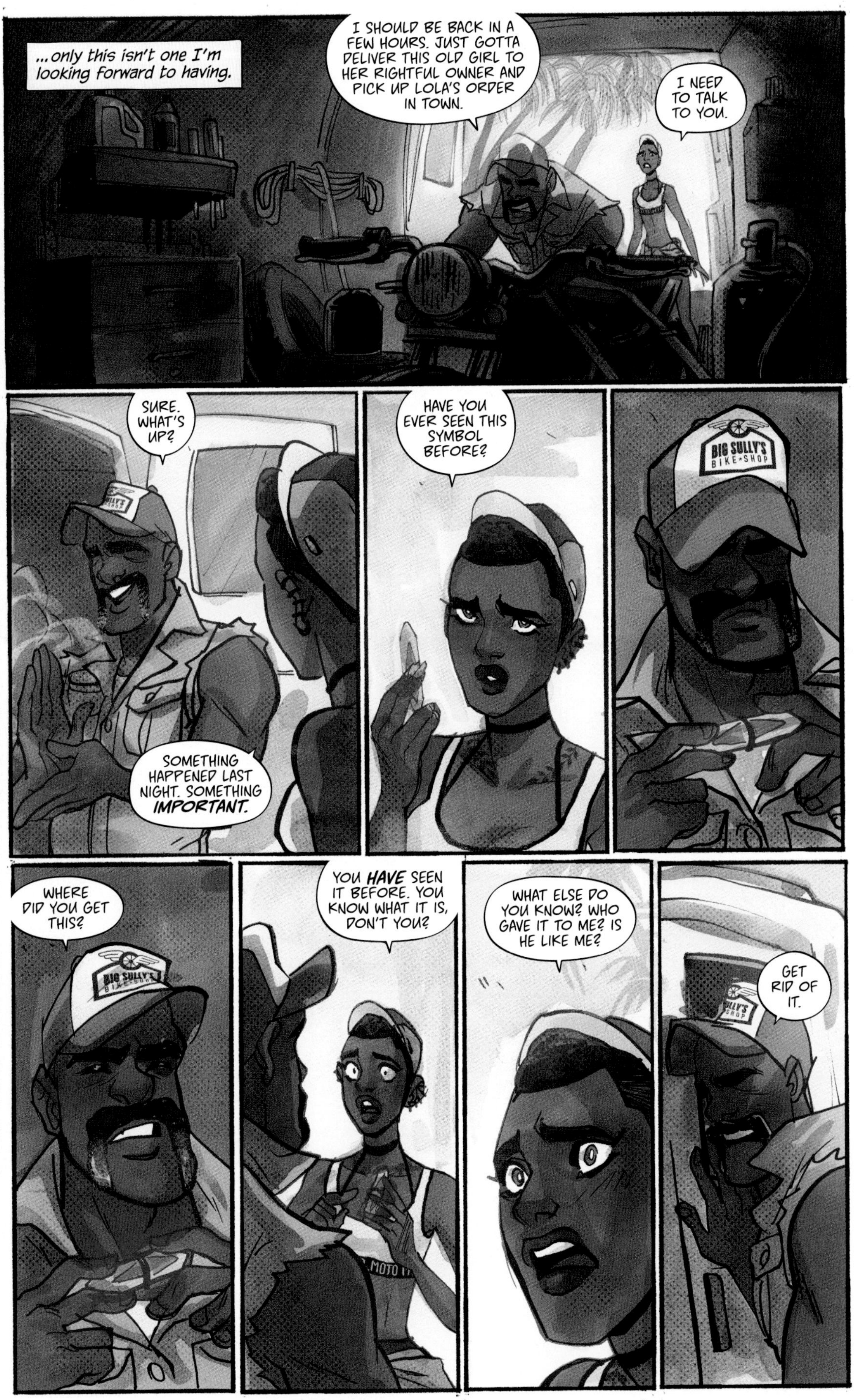
...only this isn't one I'm looking forward to having.
I SHOULD BE BACK IN A FEW HOURS. JUST GOTTA DELIVER THIS OLD GIRL TO HER RIGHTFUL OWNER AND PICK UP LOLA'S ORDER IN TOWN.
I NEED TO TALK TO YOU.
SURE. WHAT'S UP?
SOMETHING HAPPENED LAST NIGHT. SOMETHING IMPORTANT.
HAVE YOU EVER SEEN THIS SYMBOL BEFORE?
BIG SULLY'S BIKE SHOP
WHERE DID YOU GET THIS?
YOU HAVE SEEN IT BEFORE. YOU KNOW WHAT IT IS, DON'T YOU?
WHAT ELSE DO YOU KNOW? WHO GAVE IT TO ME? IS HE LIKE ME?
GET RID OF IT.

WHAT? *NO!* THIS IS A CLUE TO WHO I REALLY AM!

HE SAID I'M SUPPOSED TO *DO* SOMETHING, I'M SUPPOSED TO BE *MORE*--

DAD? DAD!

NOW YOU LISTEN TO ME. FORGET THIS.

I HAVE NEVER BEEN MORE SERIOUS. *DROP IT.*

DAD, PLEASE! THIS IS DRIVING ME CRAZY, DON'T YOU GET THAT?

THIS IS TOO *DANGEROUS,* DOM. DO YOU GET *THAT?*

THIS ISN'T THE WGP, IT'S NOT THE CANNONBALL. THIS IS LIFE AND DEATH. YOURS AND MINE AND--

I'M YOUR FATHER AND I'M TELLING YOU TO DROP IT.

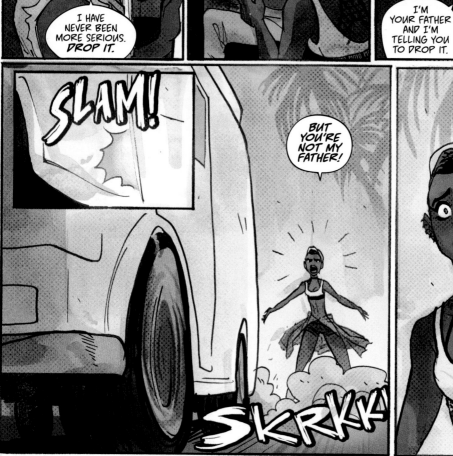

SLAM!

BUT YOU'RE NOT MY FATHER!

SKRKK!

And I've never felt less like his daughter.

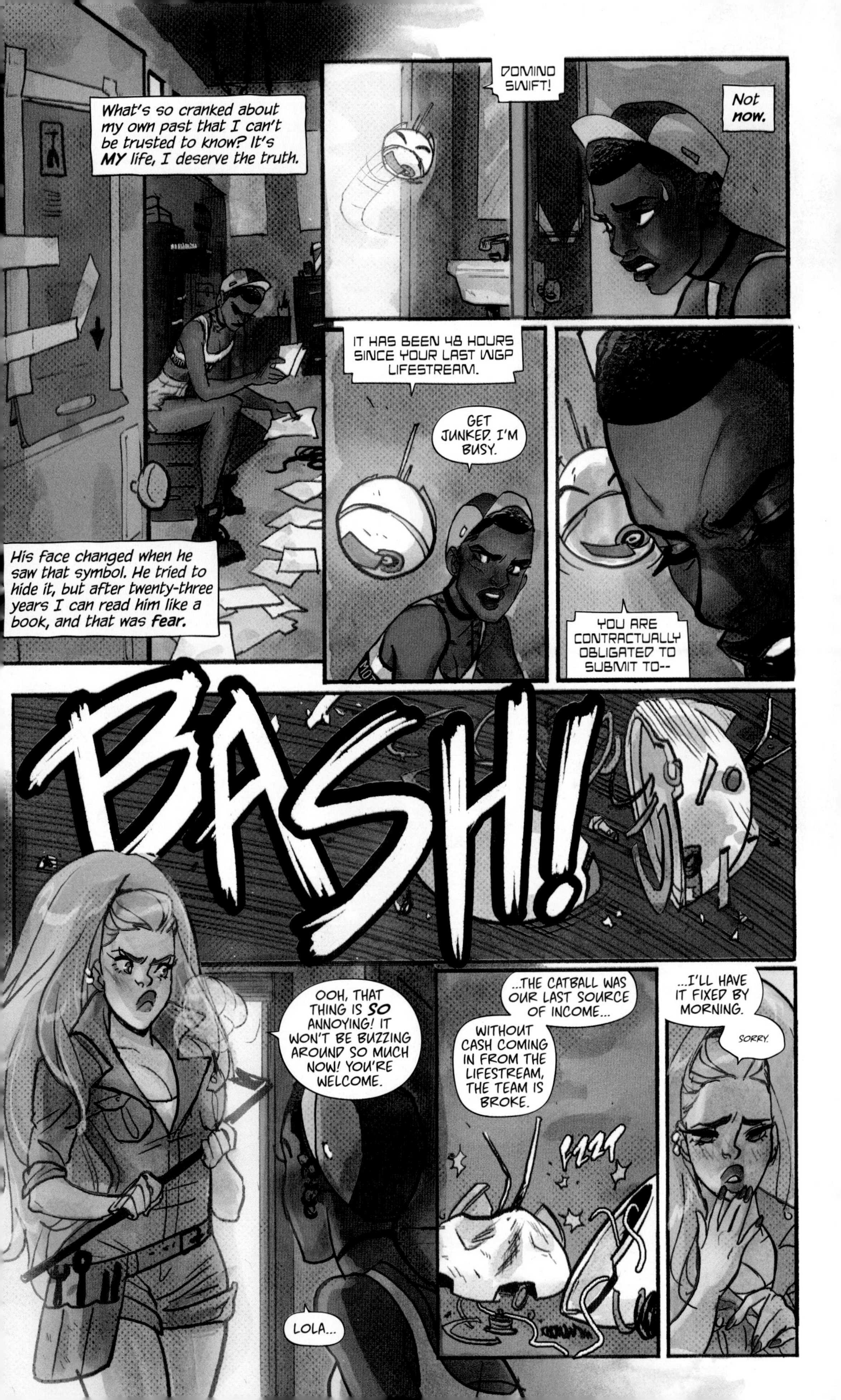

What's so cranked about my own past that I can't be trusted to know? It's MY life, I deserve the truth.
His face changed when he saw that symbol. He tried to hide it, but after twenty-three years I can read him like a book, and that was fear.
DOMINO SWIFT!
Not now.
IT HAS BEEN 48 HOURS SINCE YOUR LAST WGP LIFESTREAM.
GET JUNKED. I'M BUSY.
YOU ARE CONTRACTUALLY OBLIGATED TO SUBMIT TO--
BASH!
OOH, THAT THING IS SO ANNOYING! IT WON'T BE BUZZING AROUND SO MUCH NOW! YOU'RE WELCOME.
LOLA...
...THE CATBALL WAS OUR LAST SOURCE OF INCOME...
WITHOUT CASH COMING IN FROM THE LIFESTREAM, THE TEAM IS BROKE.
...I'LL HAVE IT FIXED BY MORNING.
SORRY.

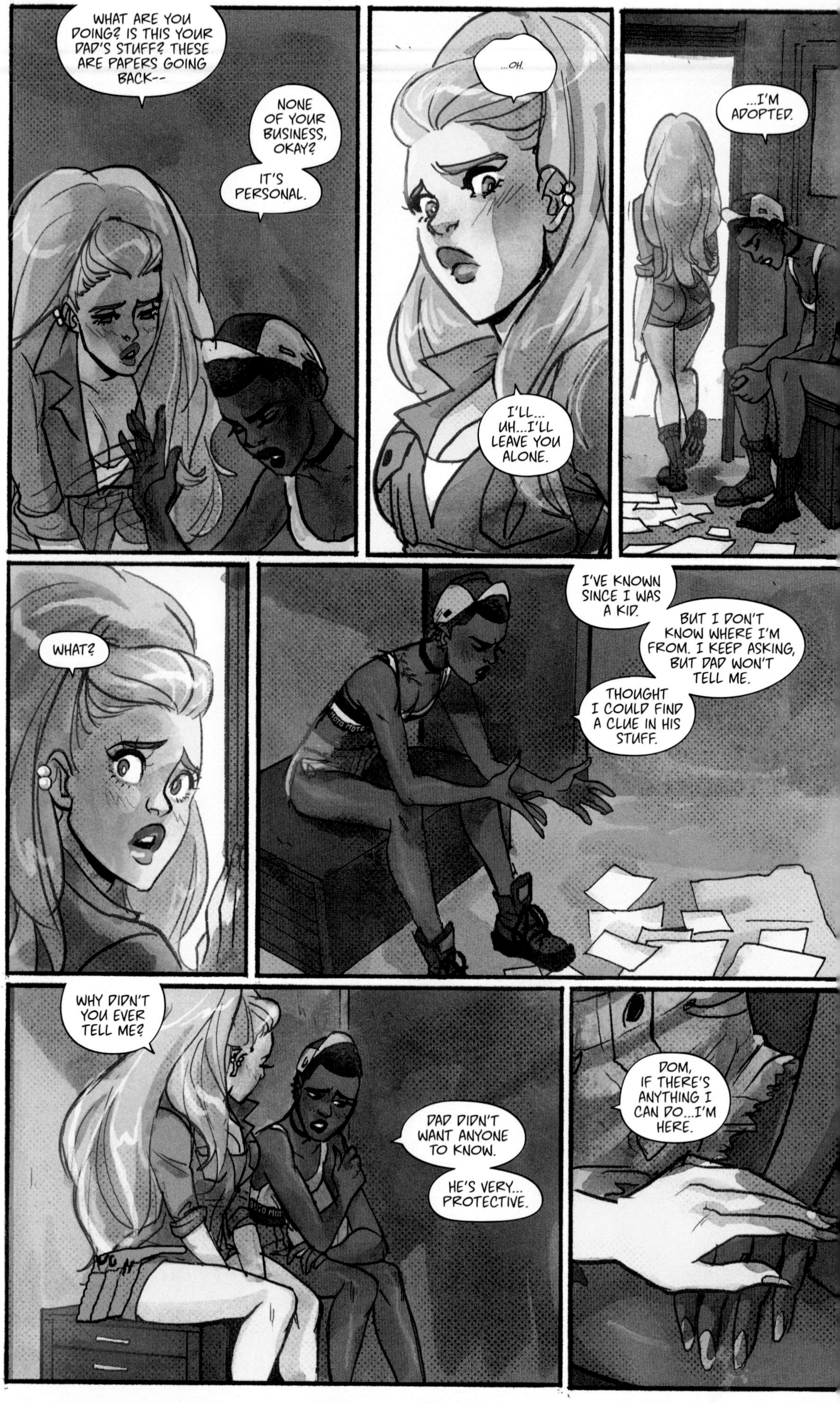
WHAT ARE YOU DOING? IS THIS YOUR DAD'S STUFF? THESE ARE PAPERS GOING BACK--
NONE OF YOUR BUSINESS, OKAY?
IT'S PERSONAL.
...OH.
I'LL... UH...I'LL LEAVE YOU ALONE.
...I'M ADOPTED.
WHAT?
I'VE KNOWN SINCE I WAS A KID.
BUT I DON'T KNOW WHERE I'M FROM. I KEEP ASKING, BUT DAD WON'T TELL ME.
THOUGHT I COULD FIND A CLUE IN HIS STUFF.
WHY DIDN'T YOU EVER TELL ME?
DAD DIDN'T WANT ANYONE TO KNOW.
HE'S VERY... PROTECTIVE.
DOM, IF THERE'S ANYTHING I CAN DO...I'M HERE.

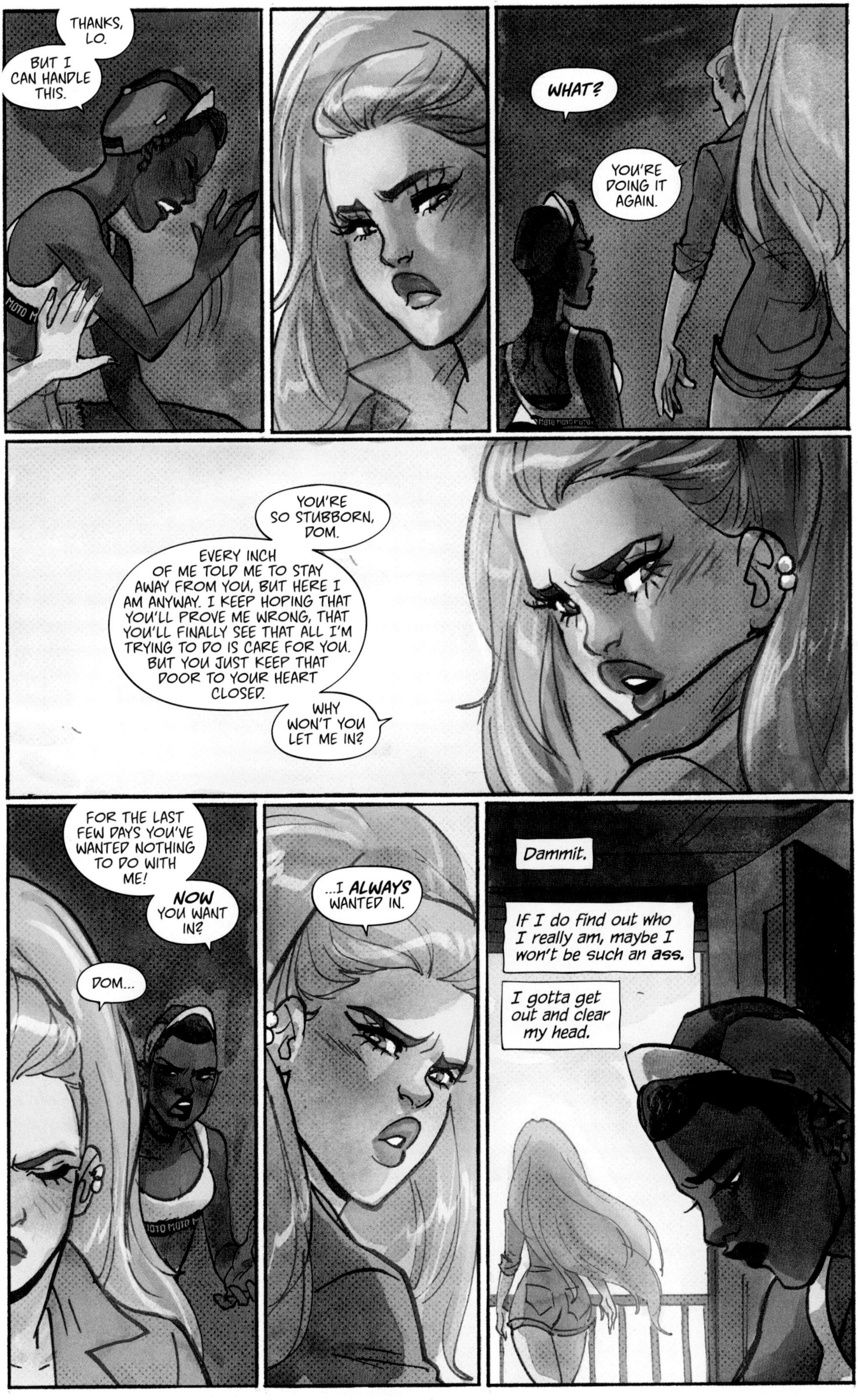
THANKS, LO.
BUT I CAN HANDLE THIS.
WHAT?
YOU'RE DOING IT AGAIN.
YOU'RE SO STUBBORN, DOM.
EVERY INCH OF ME TOLD ME TO STAY AWAY FROM YOU, BUT HERE I AM ANYWAY. I KEEP HOPING THAT YOU'LL PROVE ME WRONG, THAT YOU'LL FINALLY SEE THAT ALL I'M TRYING TO DO IS CARE FOR YOU. BUT YOU JUST KEEP THAT DOOR TO YOUR HEART CLOSED.
WHY WON'T YOU LET ME IN?
FOR THE LAST FEW DAYS YOU'VE WANTED NOTHING TO DO WITH ME!
NOW YOU WANT IN?
DOM...
...I ALWAYS WANTED IN.
Dammit.
If I do find out who I really am, maybe I won't be such an ass.
I gotta get out and clear my head.

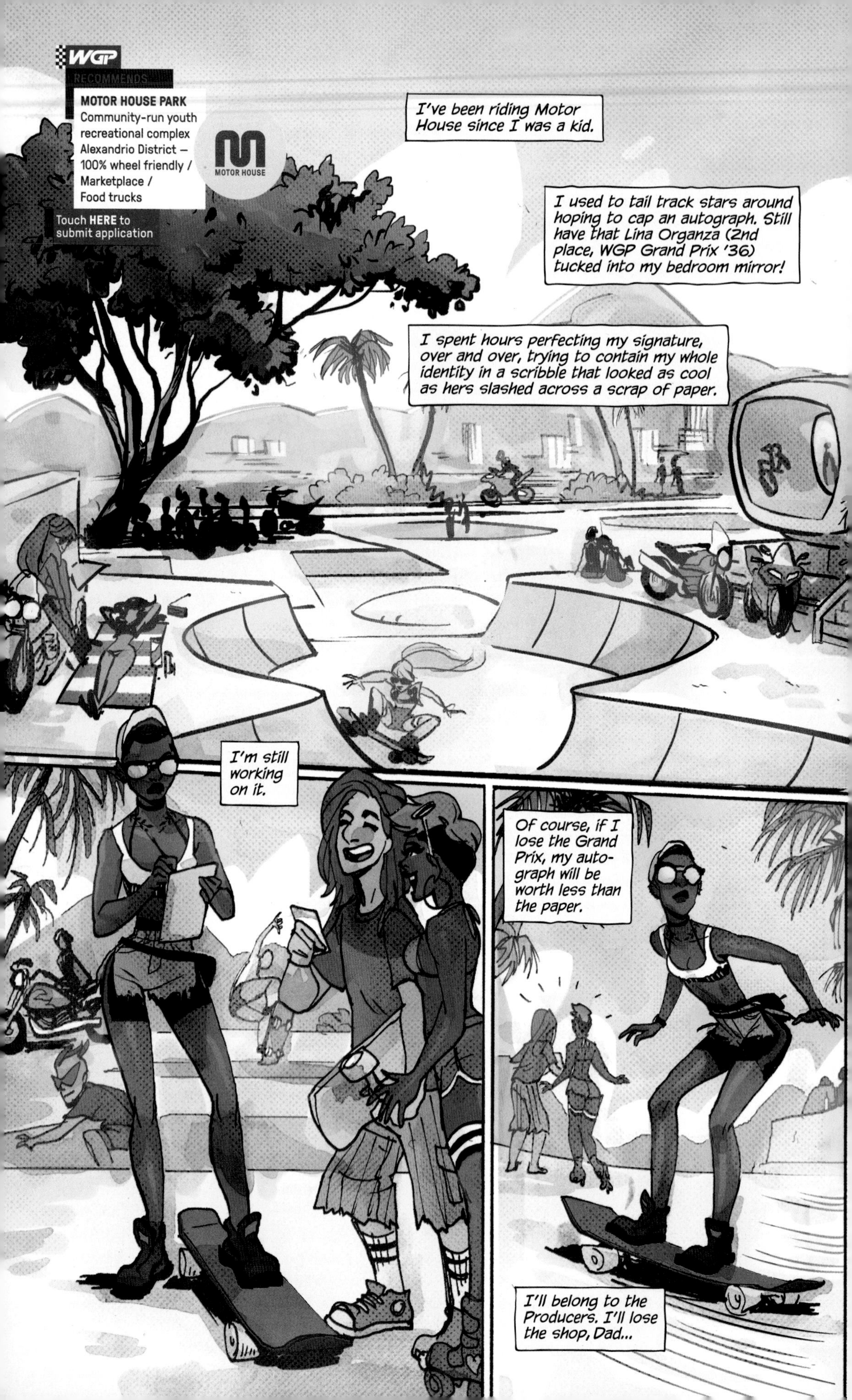
WGP
RECOMMENDS
MOTOR HOUSE PARK
Community-run youth recreational complex
Alexandrio District — 100% wheel friendly / Marketplace / Food trucks
MOTOR HOUSE
Touch HERE to submit application
I've been riding Motor House since I was a kid.
I used to tail track stars around hoping to cap an autograph. Still have that Lina Organza (2nd place, WGP Grand Prix '36) tucked into my bedroom mirror!
I spent hours perfecting my signature, over and over, trying to contain my whole identity in a scribble that looked as cool as hers slashed across a scrap of paper.
I'm still working on it.
Of course, if I lose the Grand Prix, my autograph will be worth less than the paper.
I'll belong to the Producers. I'll lose the shop, Dad...

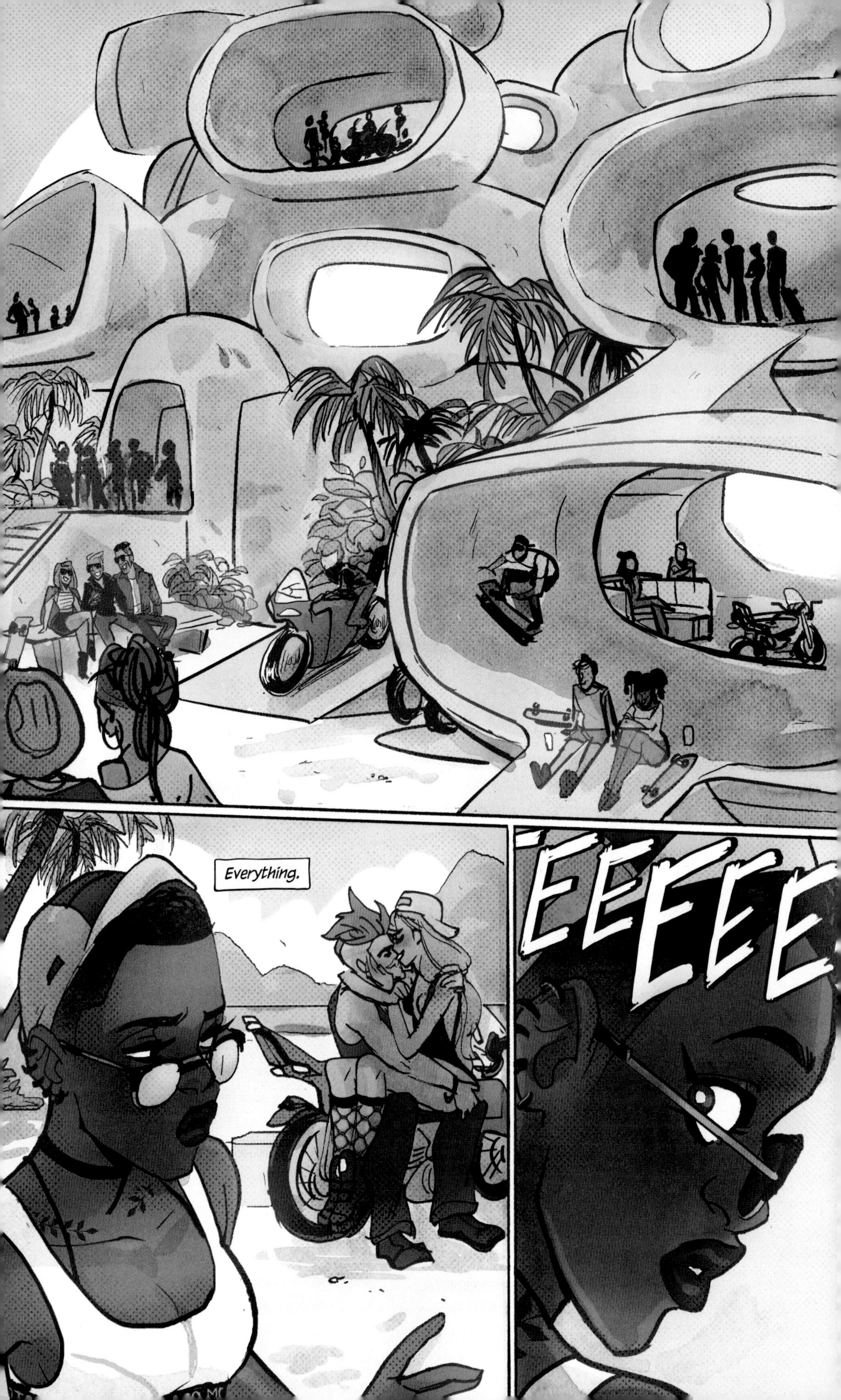
Everything.
EEEEEE

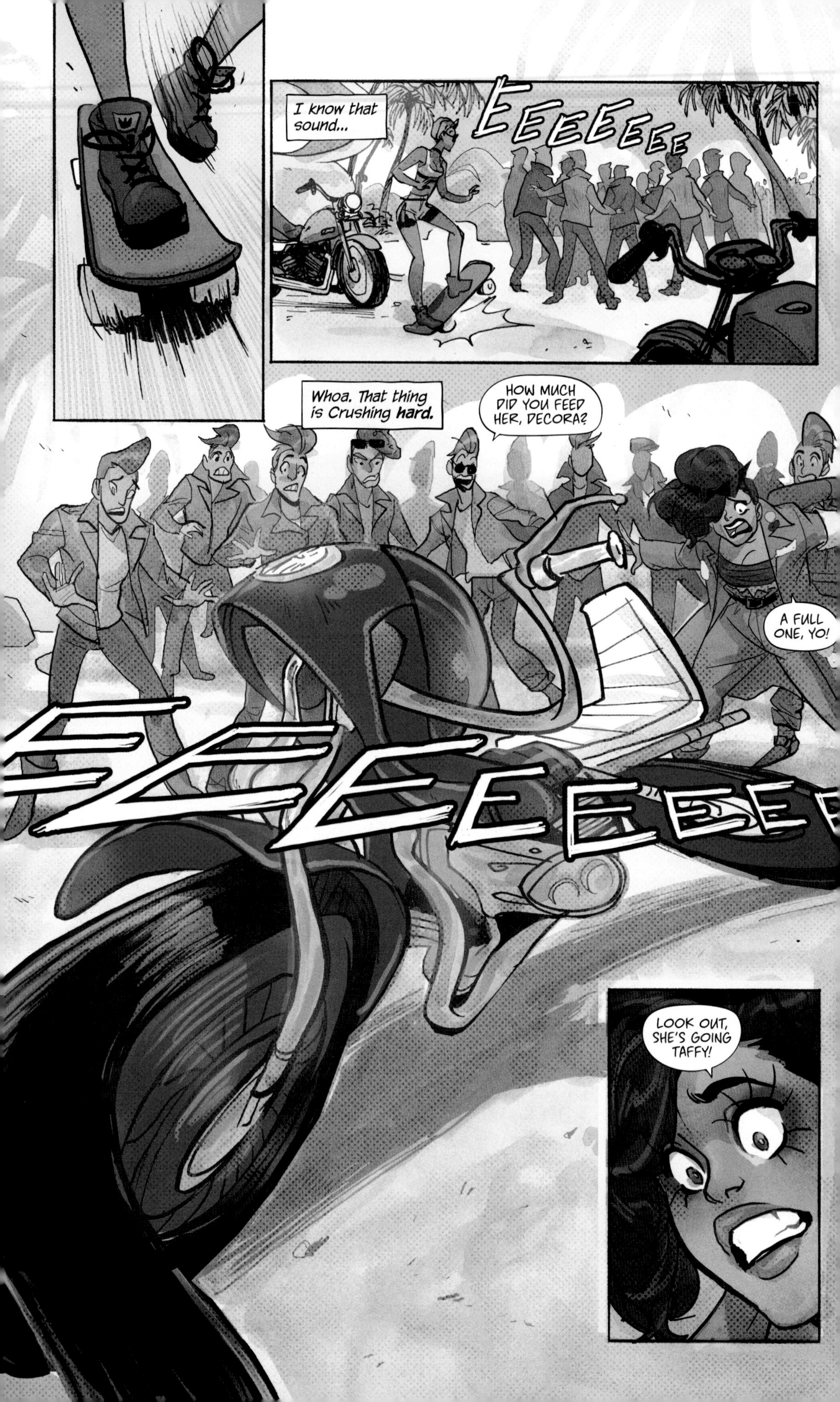
I know that sound...
EEEEEEEE
Whoa. That thing is Crushing **hard.**
HOW MUCH DID YOU FEED HER, DECORA?
A FULL ONE, YO!
EEEEEEEE
LOOK OUT, SHE'S GOING TAFFY!

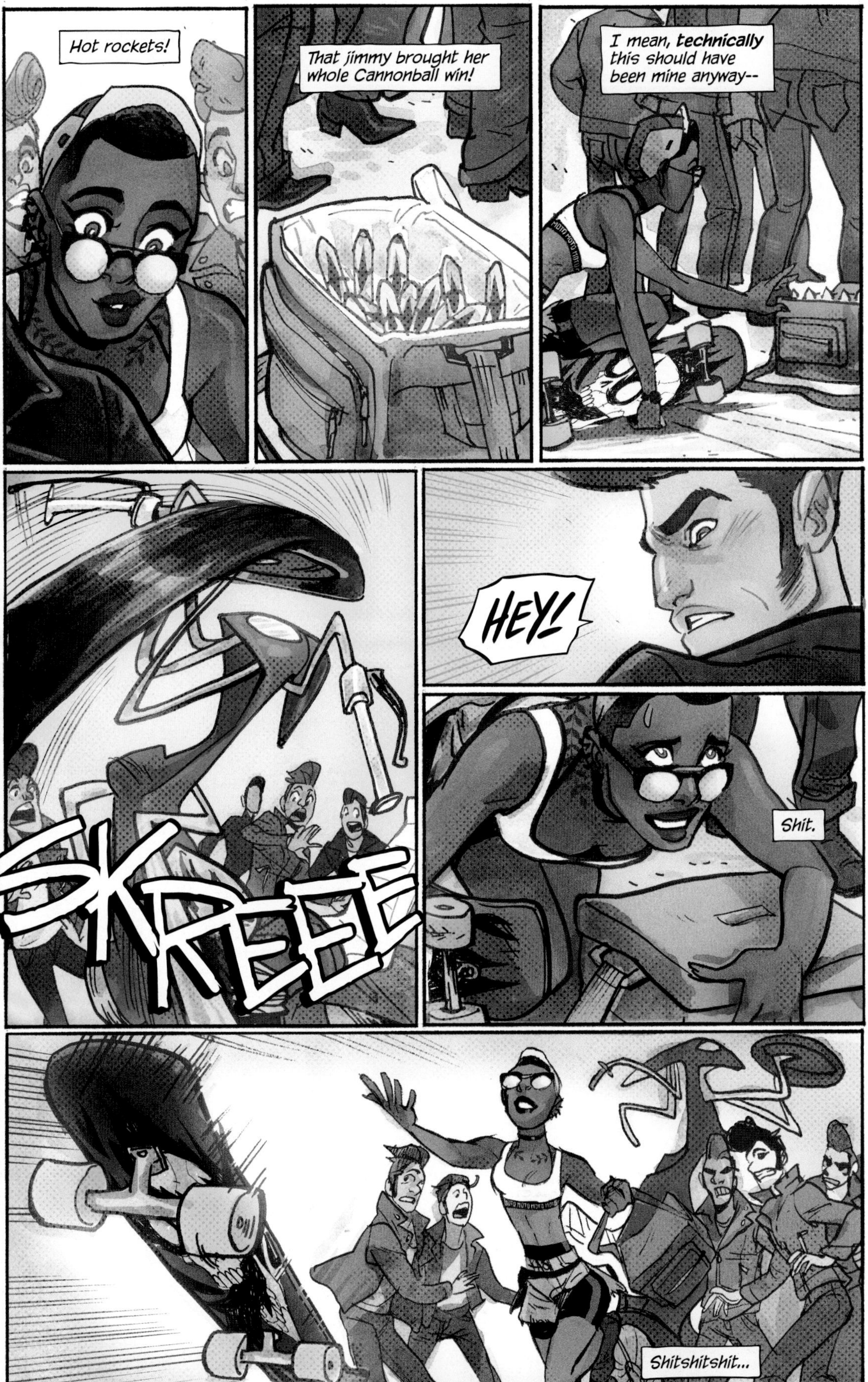
Hot rockets!
That jimmy brought her whole Cannonball win!
I mean, technically this should have been mine anyway--
SKREEEE
HEY!
Shit.
Shitshitshit...

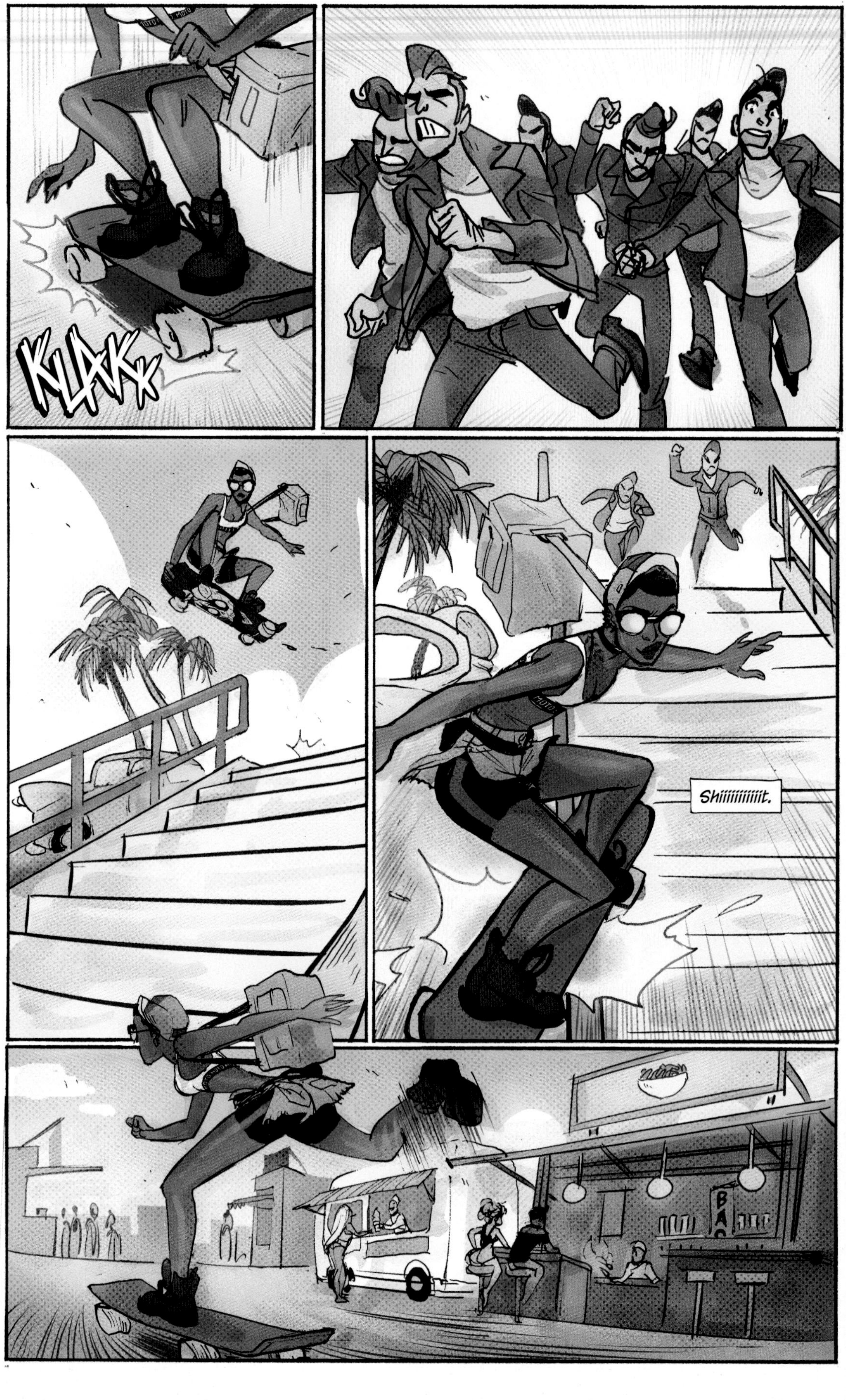
KLAKK
Shiiiiiiiiiiit.

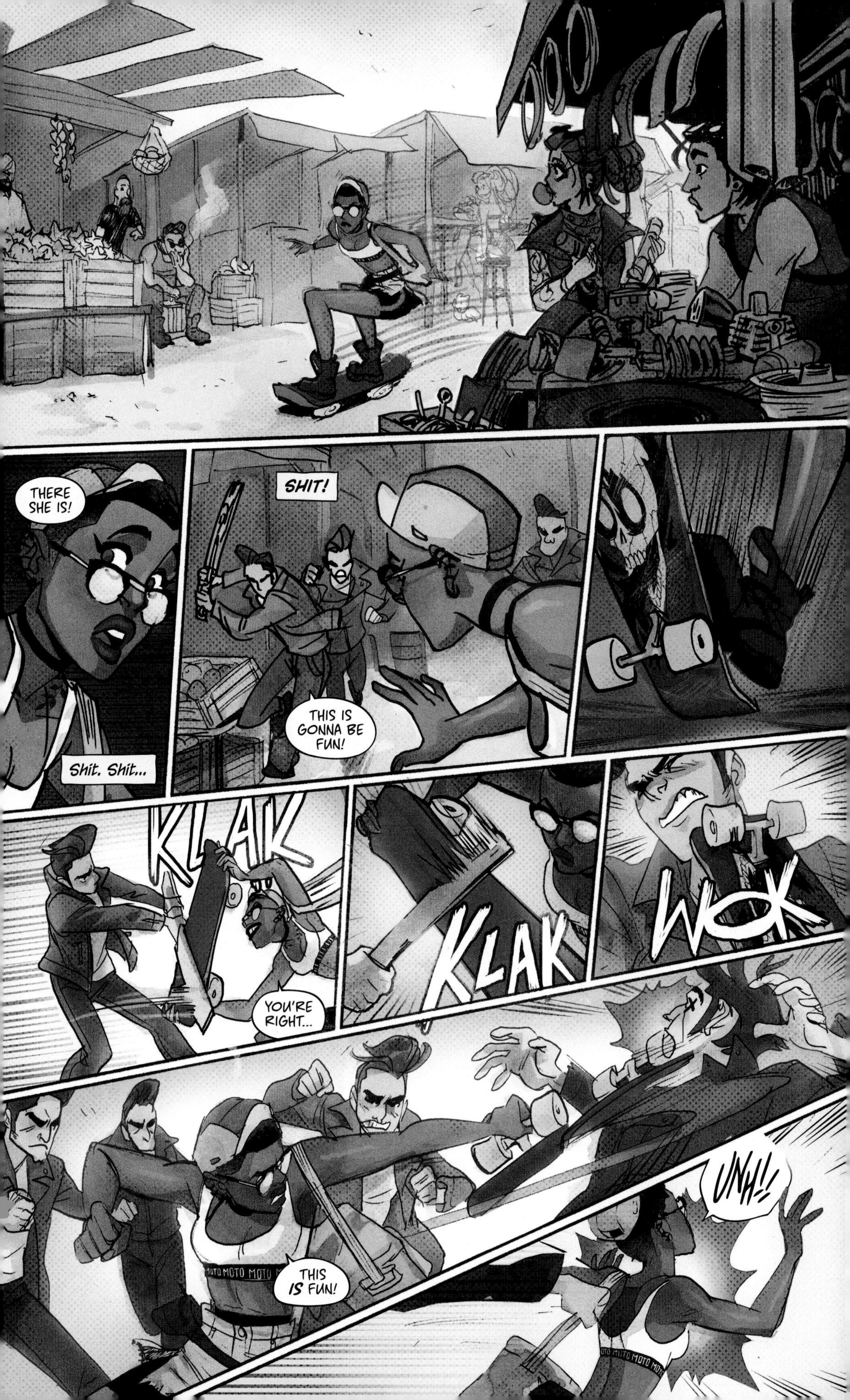
THERE SHE IS!
Shit. Shit...
SHIT!
THIS IS GONNA BE FUN!
KLAK
YOU'RE RIGHT...
KLAK
WOK
UNH!!
THIS *IS* FUN!
MOTO MOTO MOTO

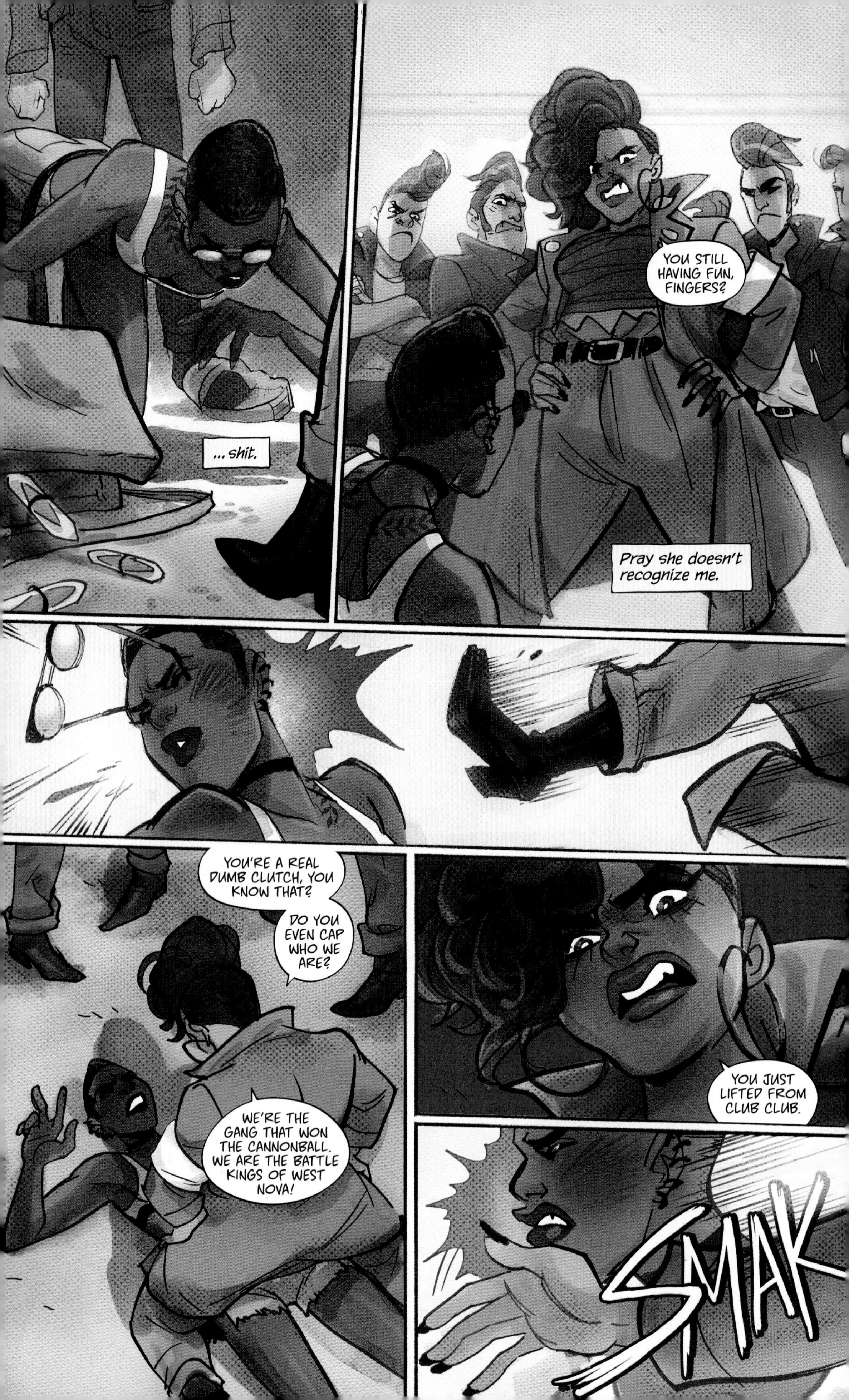

...shit.
YOU STILL HAVING FUN, FINGERS?
Pray she doesn't recognize me.
YOU'RE A REAL DUMB CLUTCH, YOU KNOW THAT?
DO YOU EVEN CAP WHO WE ARE?
WE'RE THE GANG THAT WON THE CANNONBALL. WE ARE THE BATTLE KINGS OF WEST NOVA!
YOU JUST LIFTED FROM CLUB CLUB.
SMAK

I thought he might have been trying to help me.

But he's just standing there, watching.

YOU'RE GONNA LEARN A LESSON, FINGERS...

He's here.

What is this, a *game?* You're just gonna fuck with my head and watch me squirm?

Well, *fuck you,* too! I'll--

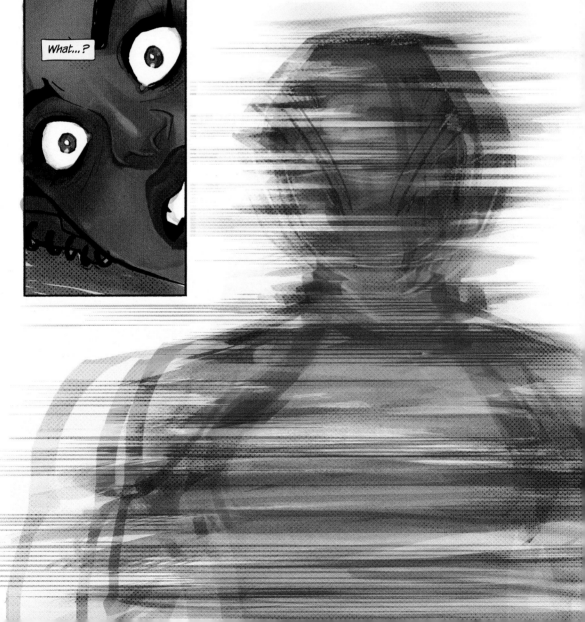

What...?

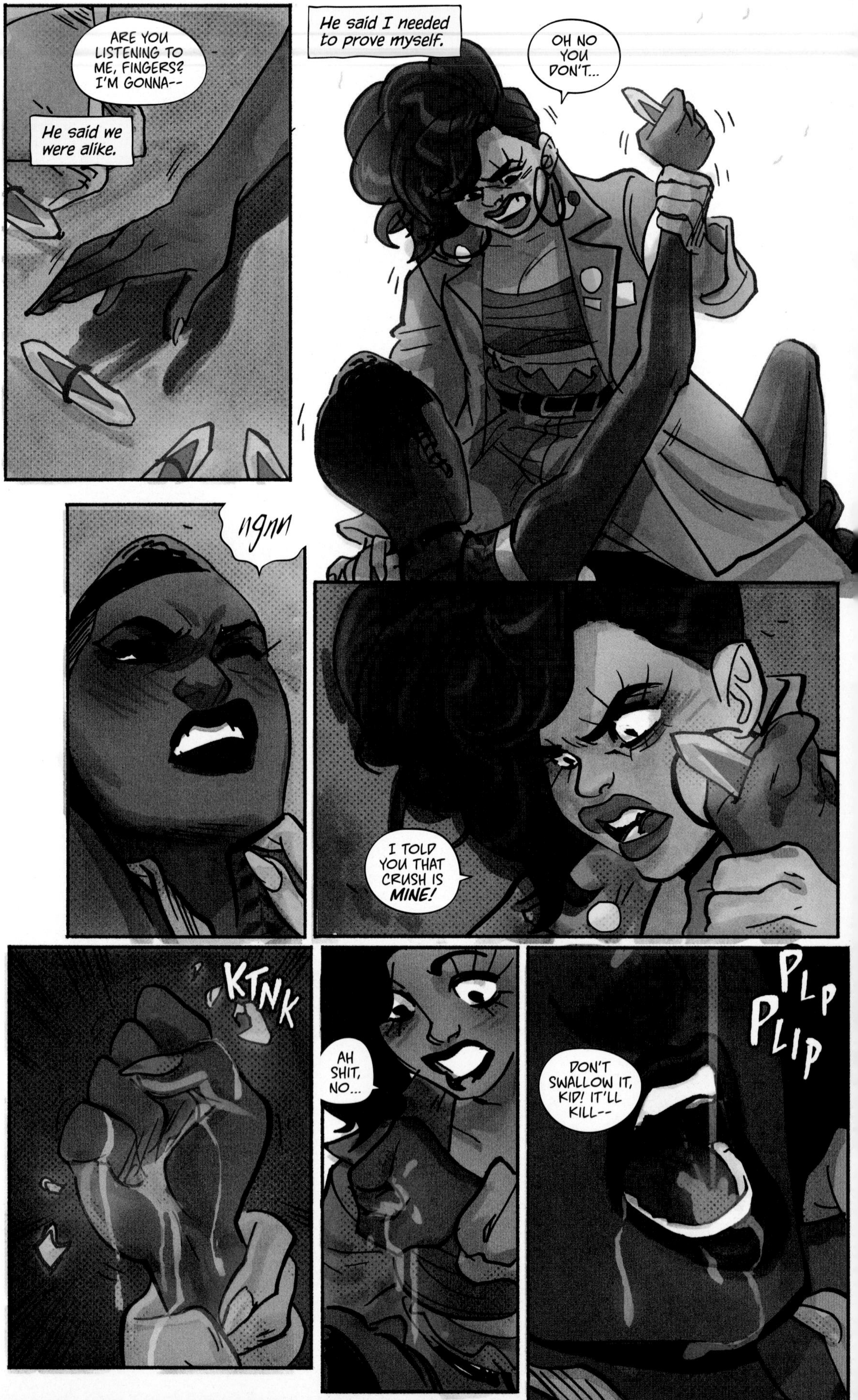
ARE YOU LISTENING TO ME, FINGERS? I'M GONNA--
He said we were alike.
He said I needed to prove myself.
OH NO YOU DON'T...
ngnn
I TOLD YOU THAT CRUSH IS MINE!
KTNK
AH SHIT, NO...
PLP PLIP
DON'T SWALLOW IT, KID! IT'LL KILL--

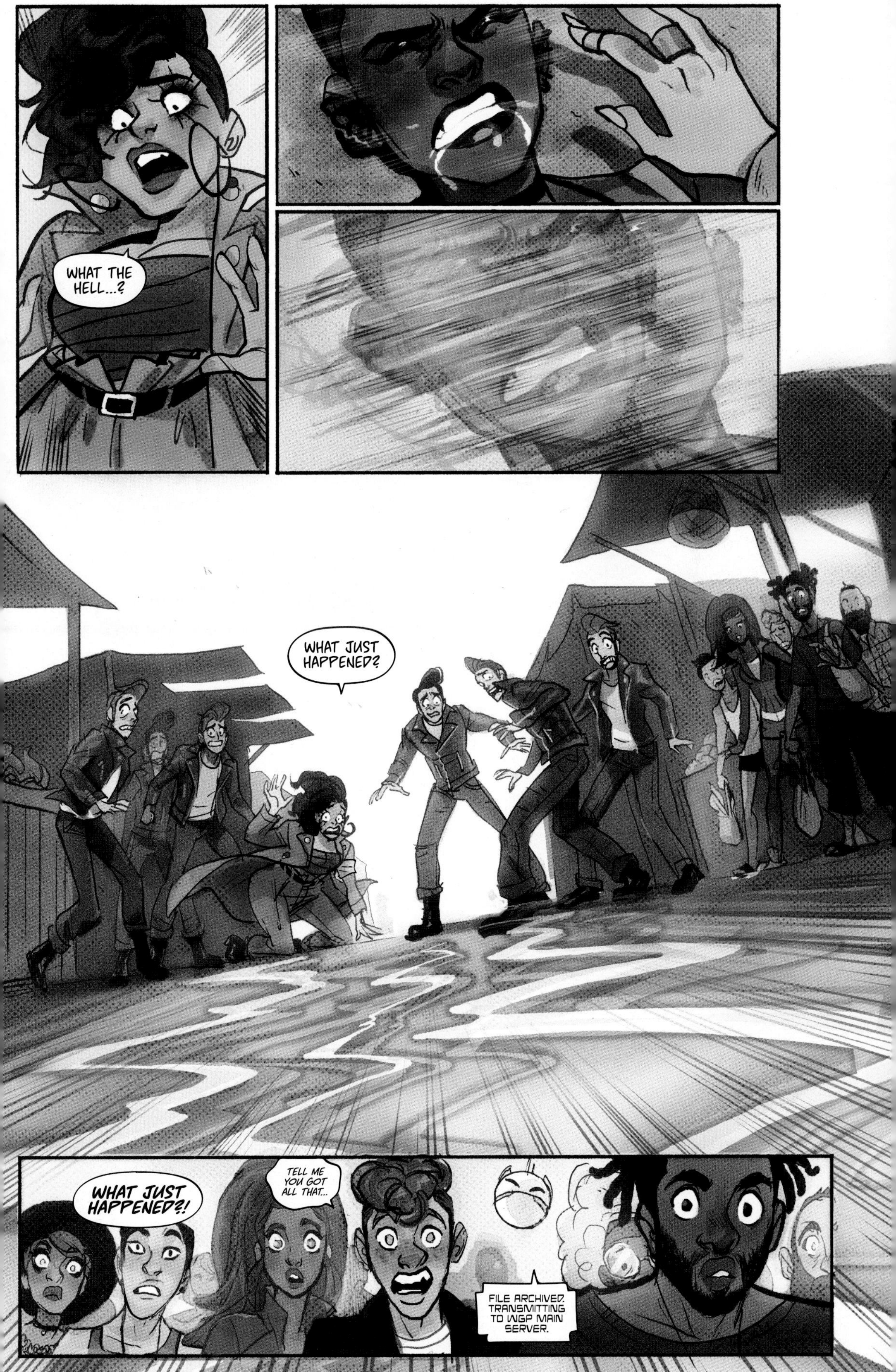
WHAT THE HELL...?
WHAT JUST HAPPENED?
WHAT JUST HAPPENED?!
TELL ME YOU GOT ALL THAT...
FILE ARCHIVED. TRANSMITTING TO WGP MAIN SERVER.

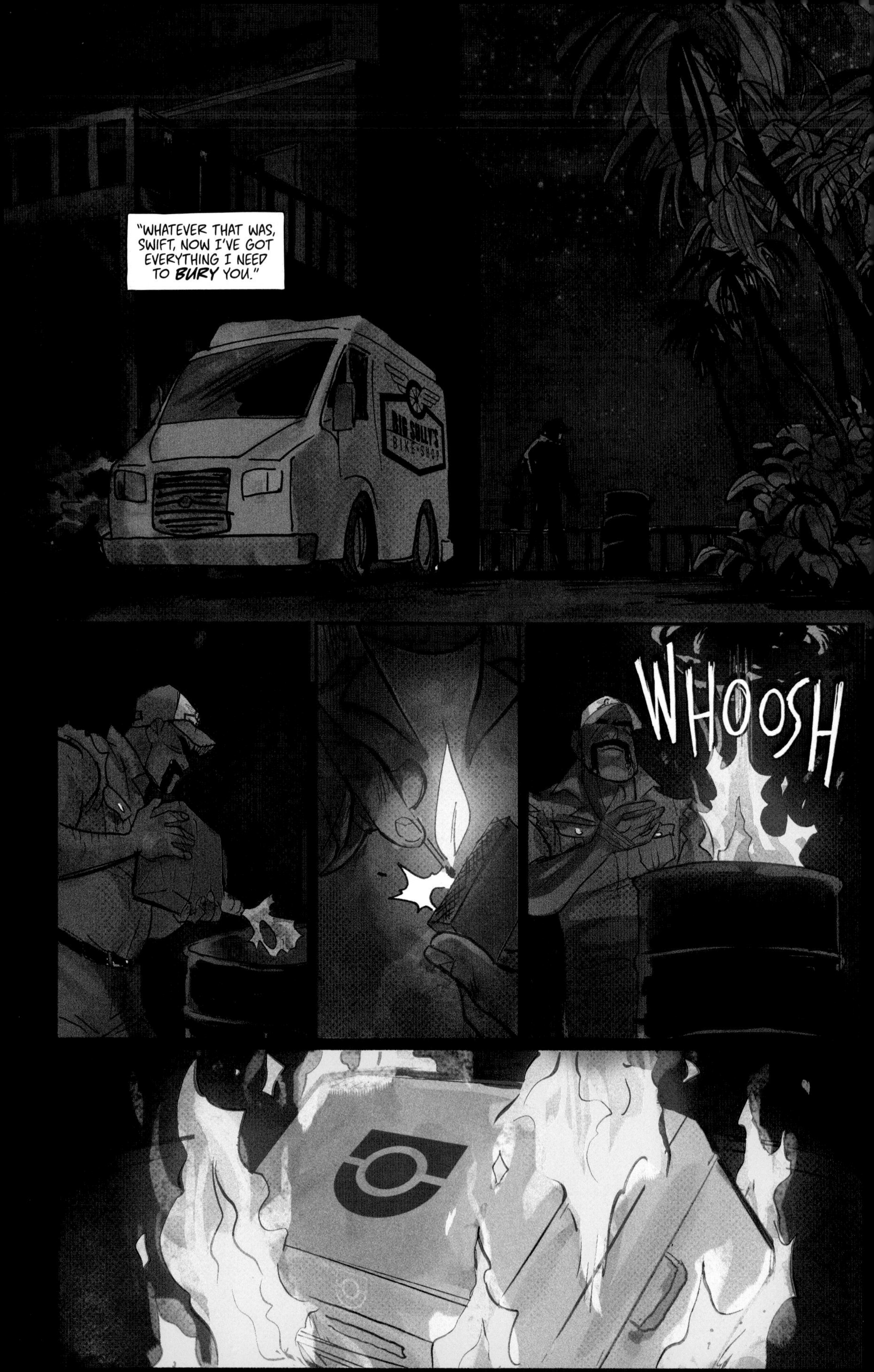
"WHATEVER THAT WAS, SWIFT, NOW I'VE GOT EVERYTHING I NEED TO BURY YOU."
BIG SULLY'S BIKE SHOP
WHOOSH

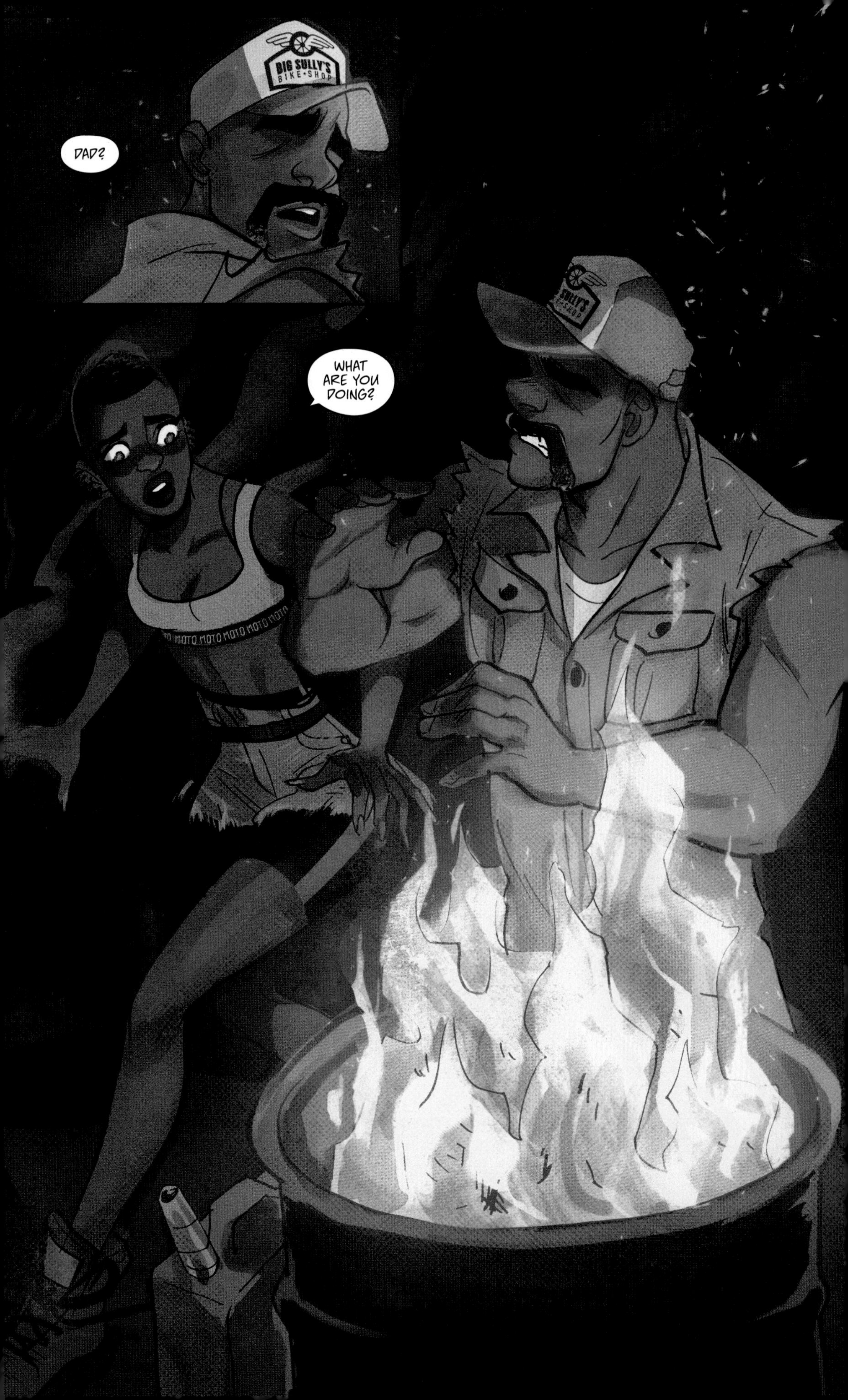
DAD?
WHAT ARE YOU DOING?

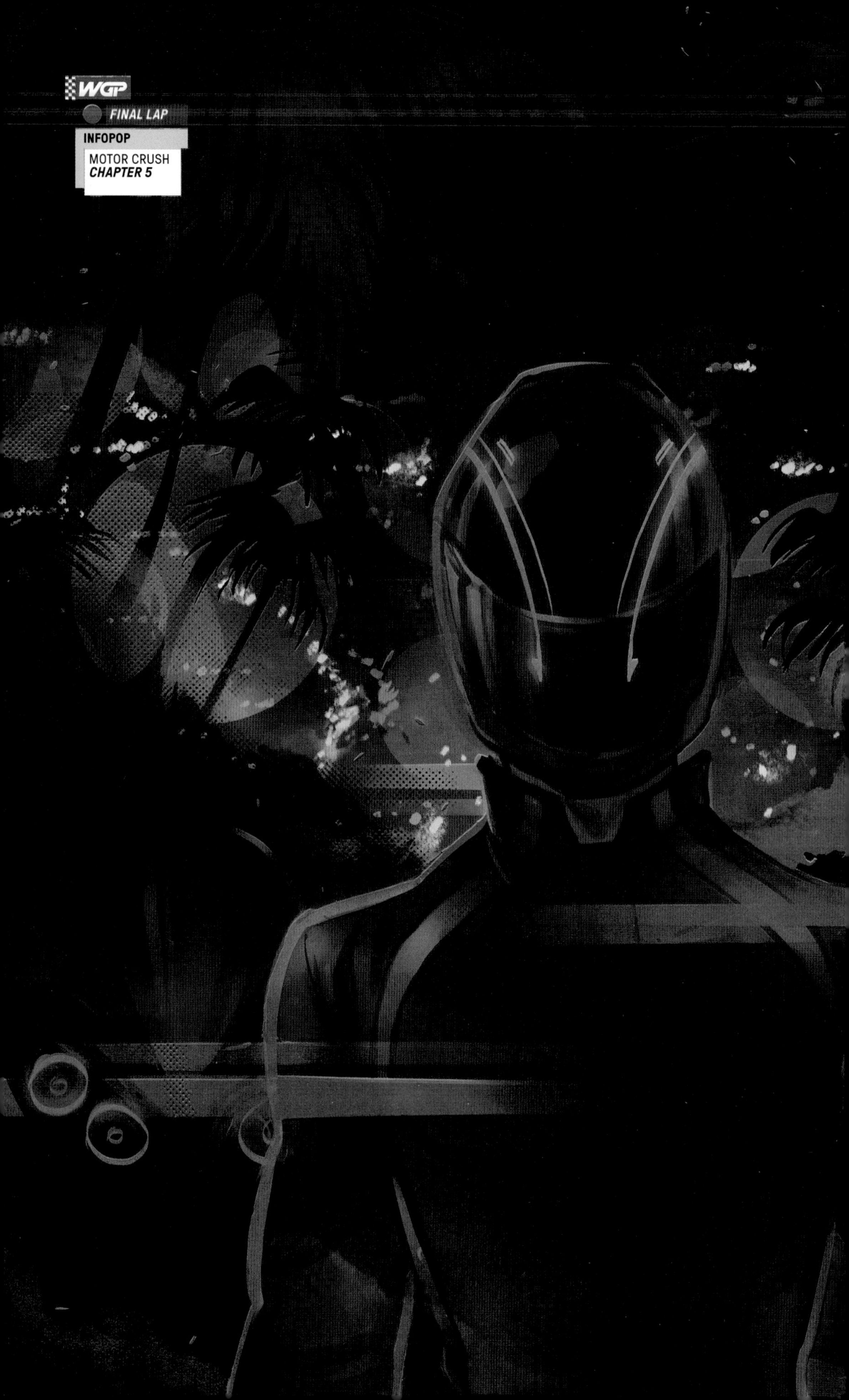
WGP
FINAL LAP
INFOPOP
MOTOR CRUSH
CHAPTER 5

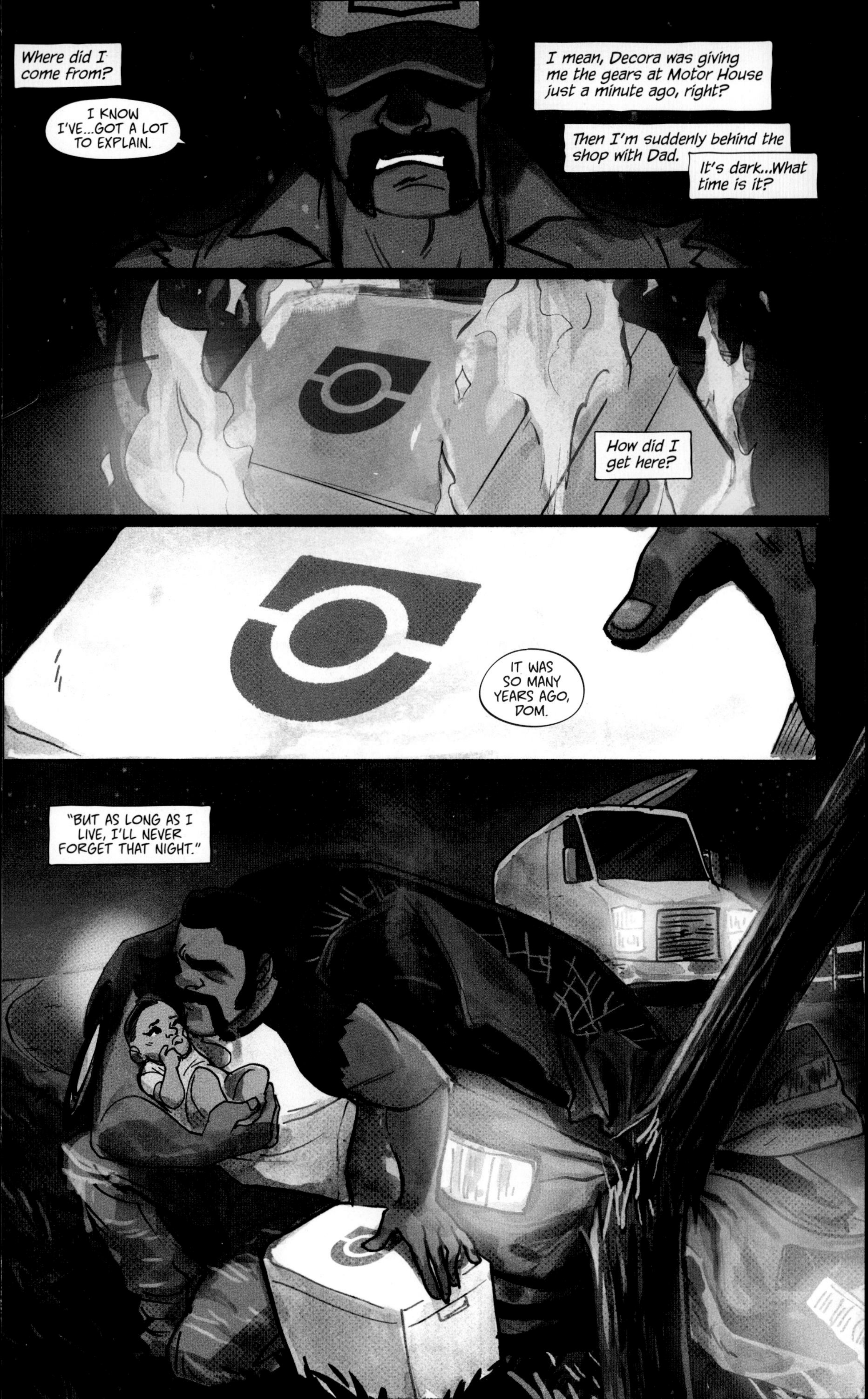
Where did I come from?
I KNOW I'VE...GOT A LOT TO EXPLAIN.
I mean, Decora was giving me the gears at Motor House just a minute ago, right?
Then I'm suddenly behind the shop with Dad.
It's dark...What time is it?
How did I get here?
IT WAS SO MANY YEARS AGO, DOM.
"BUT AS LONG AS I LIVE, I'LL NEVER FORGET THAT NIGHT."

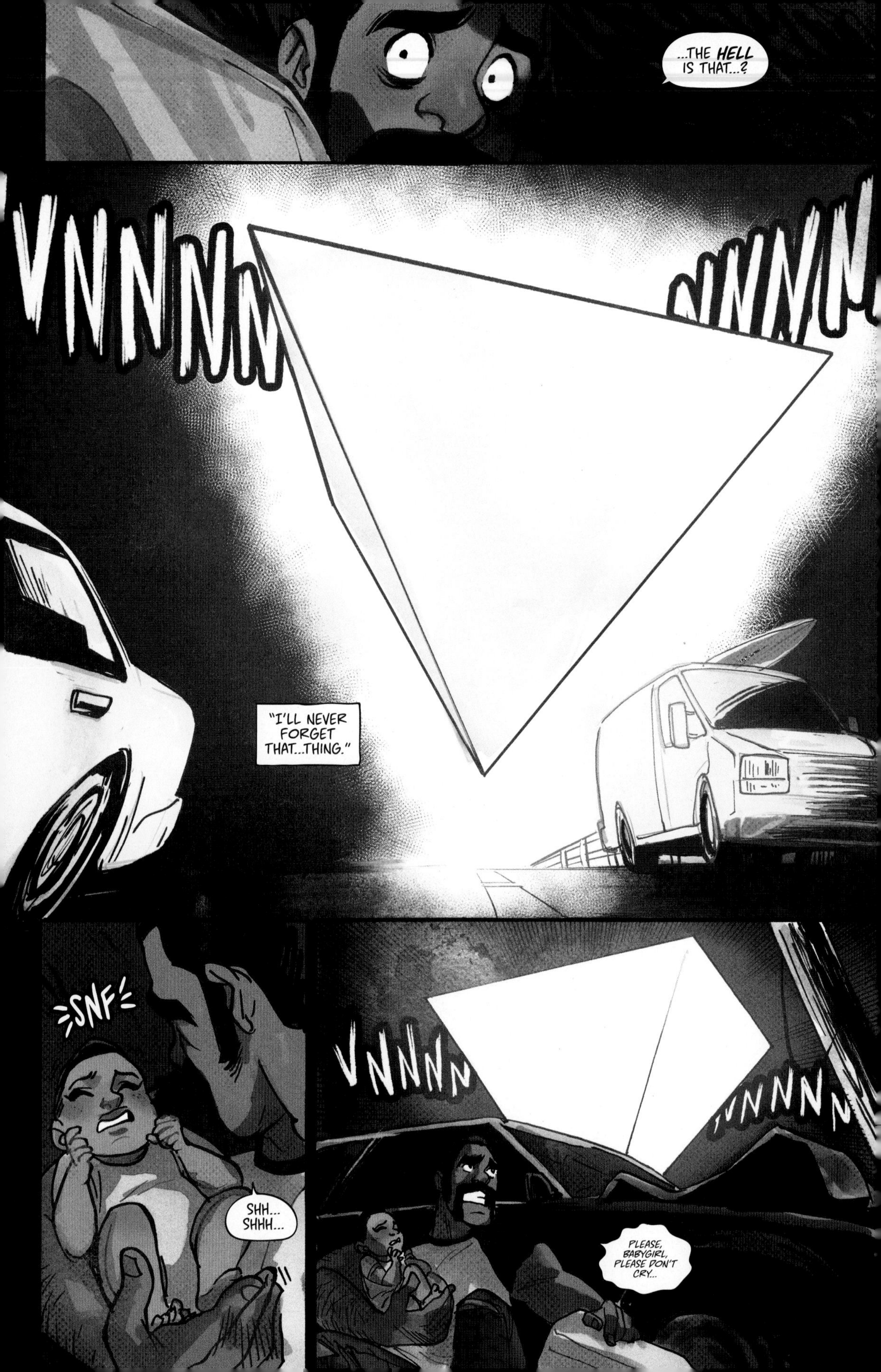

...THE HELL IS THAT...?
VNNNN
VNNNN
"I'LL NEVER FORGET THAT...THING."
SNF
SHH... SHHH...
VNNNN
VNNNN
PLEASE, BABYGIRL, PLEASE DON'T CRY...

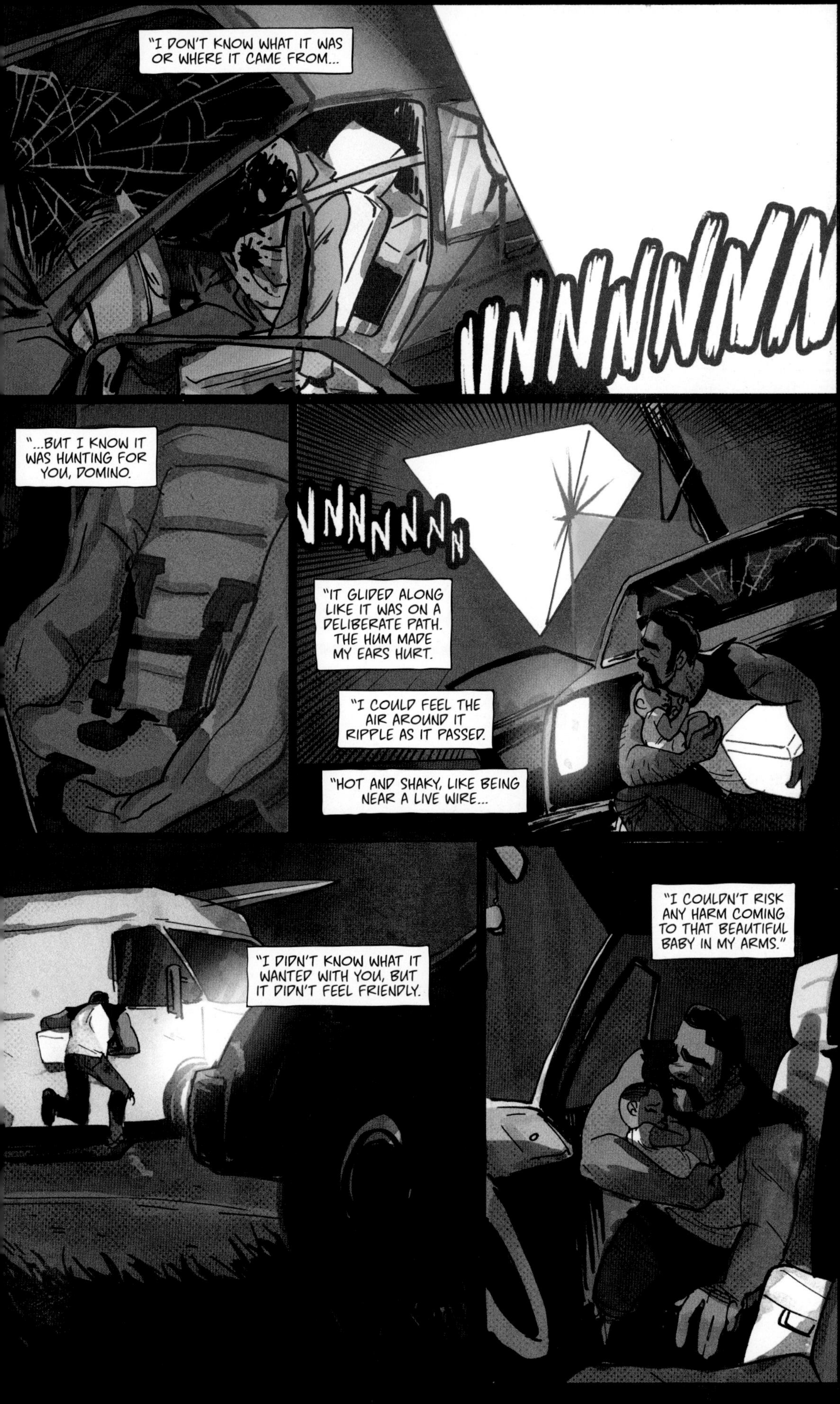
"I DON'T KNOW WHAT IT WAS OR WHERE IT CAME FROM...
NNNNNNNNM
"...BUT I KNOW IT WAS HUNTING FOR YOU, DOMINO.
NNNNNNNN
"IT GLIDED ALONG LIKE IT WAS ON A DELIBERATE PATH. THE HUM MADE MY EARS HURT.
"I COULD FEEL THE AIR AROUND IT RIPPLE AS IT PASSED.
"HOT AND SHAKY, LIKE BEING NEAR A LIVE WIRE...
"I DIDN'T KNOW WHAT IT WANTED WITH YOU, BUT IT DIDN'T FEEL FRIENDLY.
"I COULDN'T RISK ANY HARM COMING TO THAT BEAUTIFUL BABY IN MY ARMS."

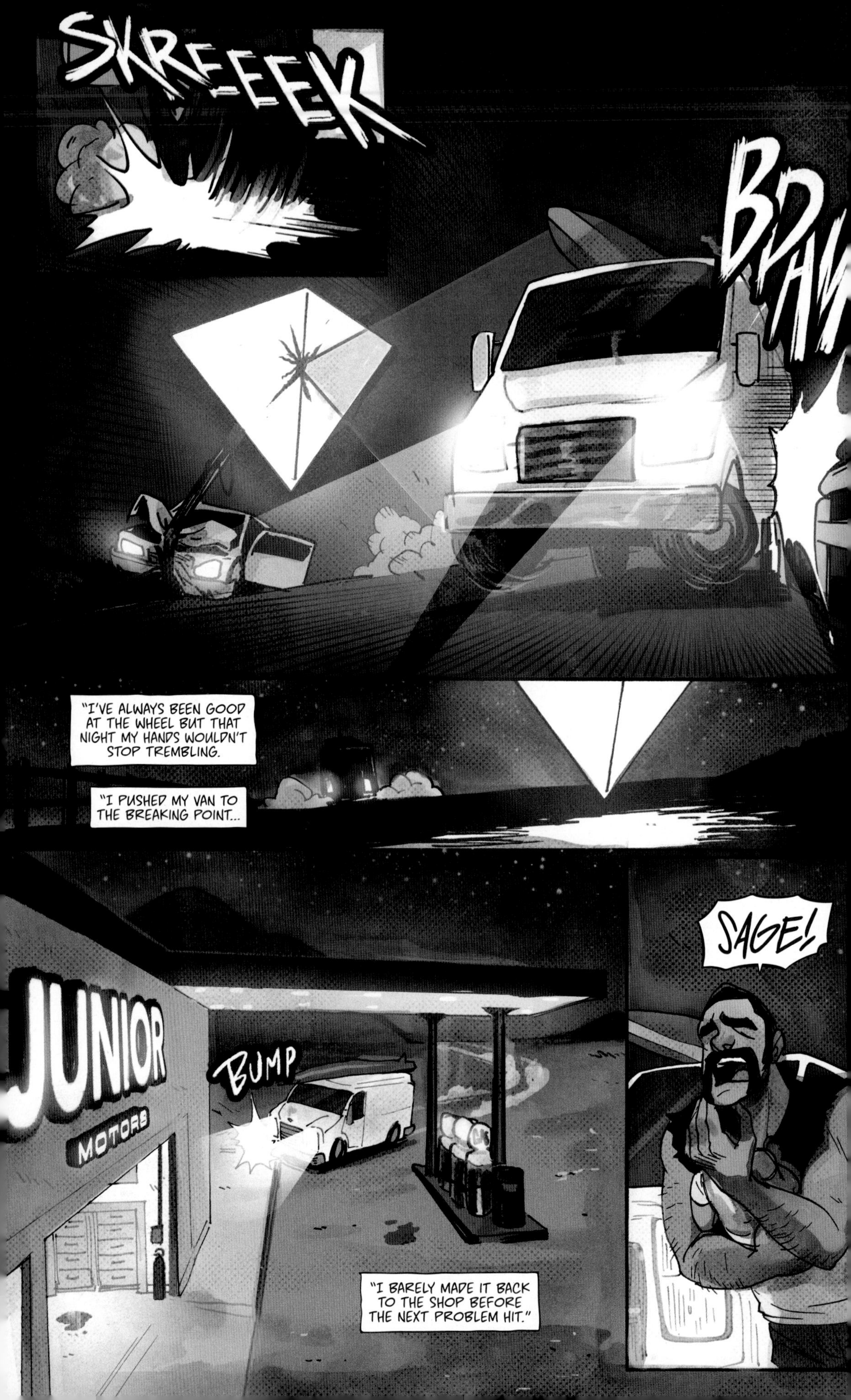
SKREEEEK
BRAM
"I'VE ALWAYS BEEN GOOD AT THE WHEEL BUT THAT NIGHT MY HANDS WOULDN'T STOP TREMBLING.
"I PUSHED MY VAN TO THE BREAKING POINT...
JUNIOR
MOTORS
BUMP
"I BARELY MADE IT BACK TO THE SHOP BEFORE THE NEXT PROBLEM HIT."
SAGE!

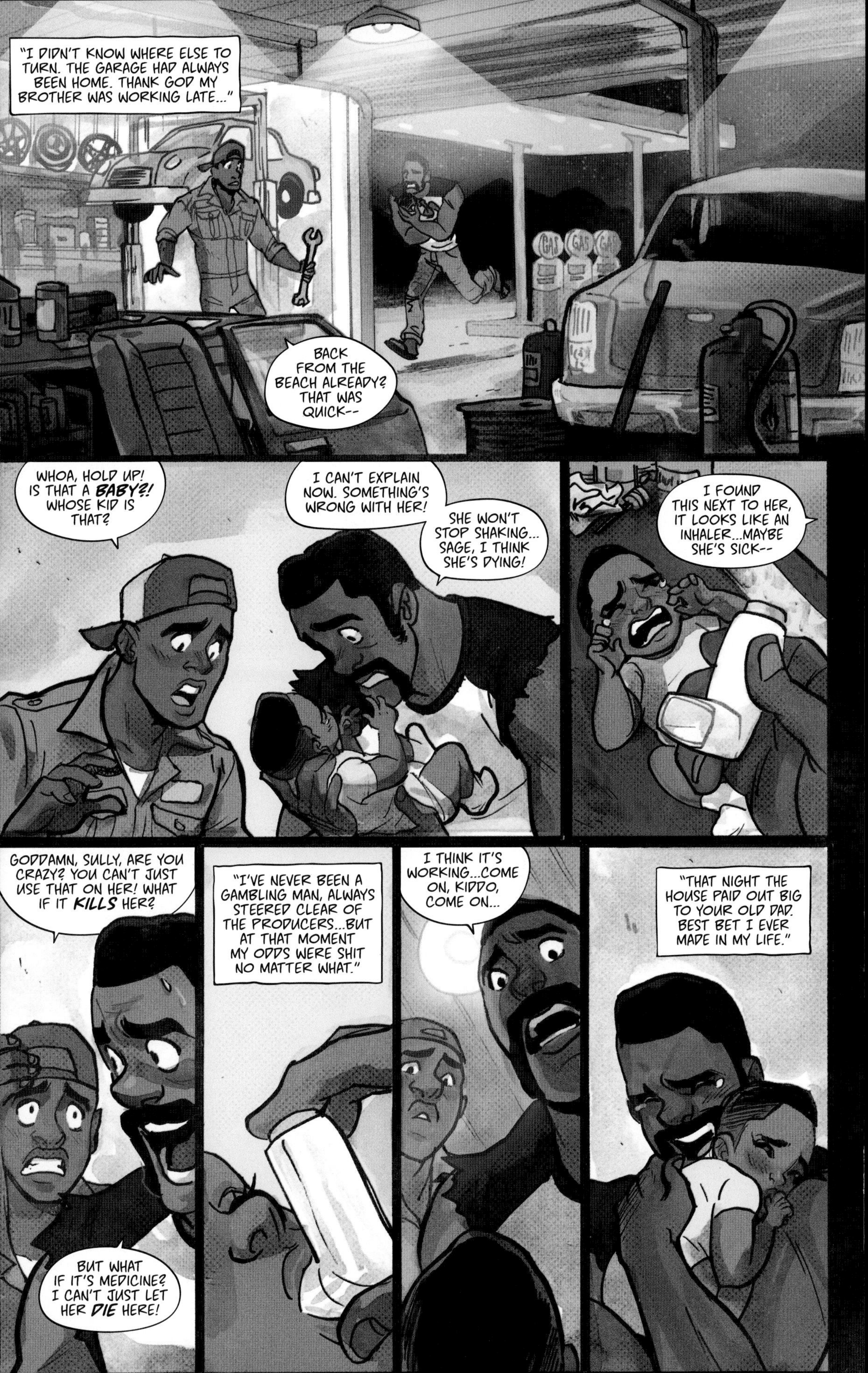
"I DIDN'T KNOW WHERE ELSE TO TURN. THE GARAGE HAD ALWAYS BEEN HOME. THANK GOD MY BROTHER WAS WORKING LATE..."
BACK FROM THE BEACH ALREADY? THAT WAS QUICK--
WHOA, HOLD UP! IS THAT A BABY?! WHOSE KID IS THAT?
I CAN'T EXPLAIN NOW. SOMETHING'S WRONG WITH HER!
SHE WON'T STOP SHAKING... SAGE, I THINK SHE'S DYING!
I FOUND THIS NEXT TO HER, IT LOOKS LIKE AN INHALER...MAYBE SHE'S SICK--
GODDAMN, SULLY, ARE YOU CRAZY? YOU CAN'T JUST USE THAT ON HER! WHAT IF IT KILLS HER?
BUT WHAT IF IT'S MEDICINE? I CAN'T JUST LET HER DIE HERE!
"I'VE NEVER BEEN A GAMBLING MAN, ALWAYS STEERED CLEAR OF THE PRODUCERS...BUT AT THAT MOMENT MY ODDS WERE SHIT NO MATTER WHAT."
I THINK IT'S WORKING...COME ON, KIDDO, COME ON...
"THAT NIGHT THE HOUSE PAID OUT BIG TO YOUR OLD DAD. BEST BET I EVER MADE IN MY LIFE."

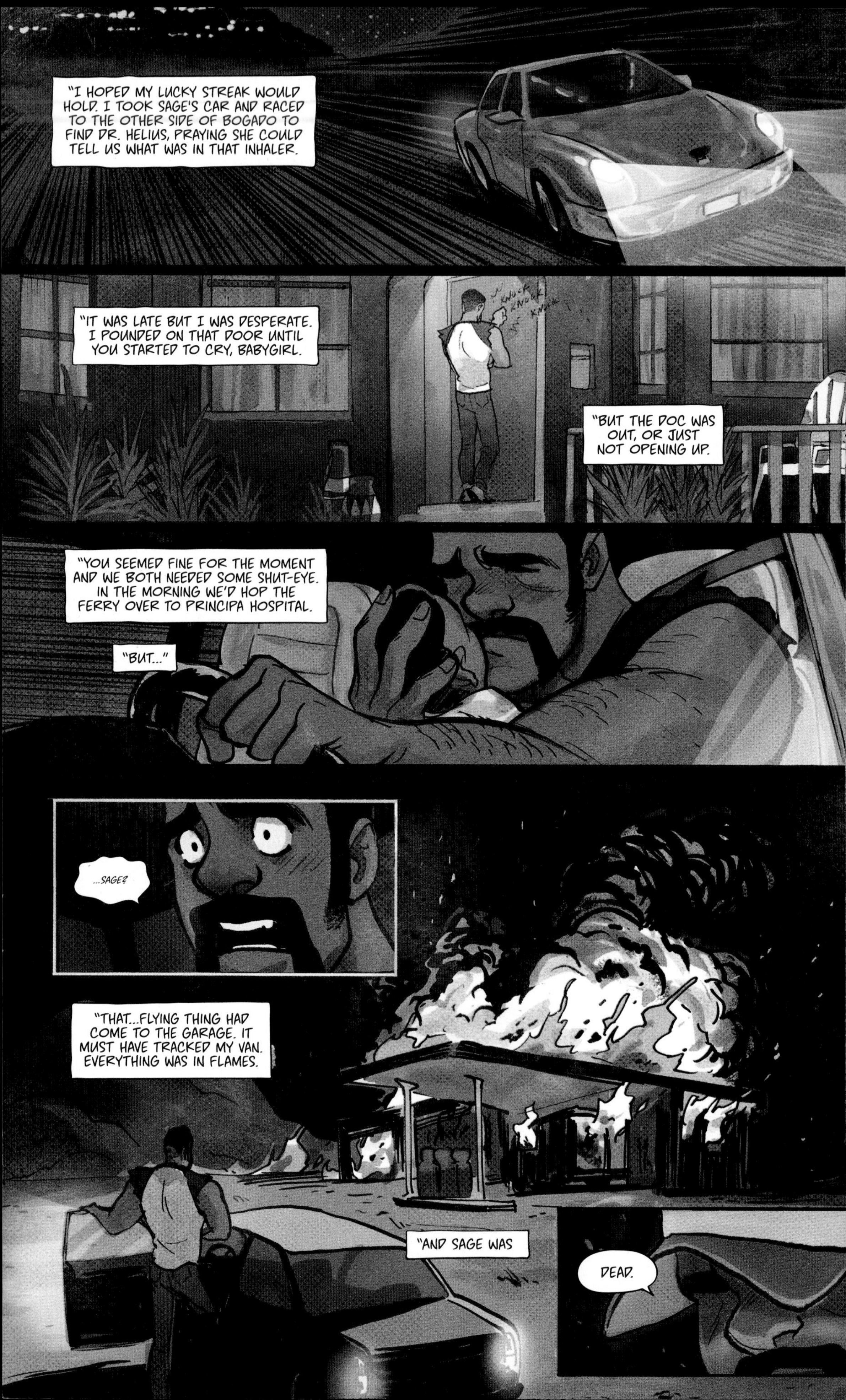
"I HOPED MY LUCKY STREAK WOULD HOLD. I TOOK SAGE'S CAR AND RACED TO THE OTHER SIDE OF BOGADO TO FIND DR. HELIUS, PRAYING SHE COULD TELL US WHAT WAS IN THAT INHALER.
"IT WAS LATE BUT I WAS DESPERATE. I POUNDED ON THAT DOOR UNTIL YOU STARTED TO CRY, BABYGIRL.
KNOCK KNOCK KNOCK
"BUT THE DOC WAS OUT, OR JUST NOT OPENING UP.
"YOU SEEMED FINE FOR THE MOMENT AND WE BOTH NEEDED SOME SHUT-EYE. IN THE MORNING WE'D HOP THE FERRY OVER TO PRINCIPA HOSPITAL.
"BUT..."
...SAGE?
"THAT...FLYING THING HAD COME TO THE GARAGE. IT MUST HAVE TRACKED MY VAN. EVERYTHING WAS IN FLAMES.
"AND SAGE WAS
DEAD.

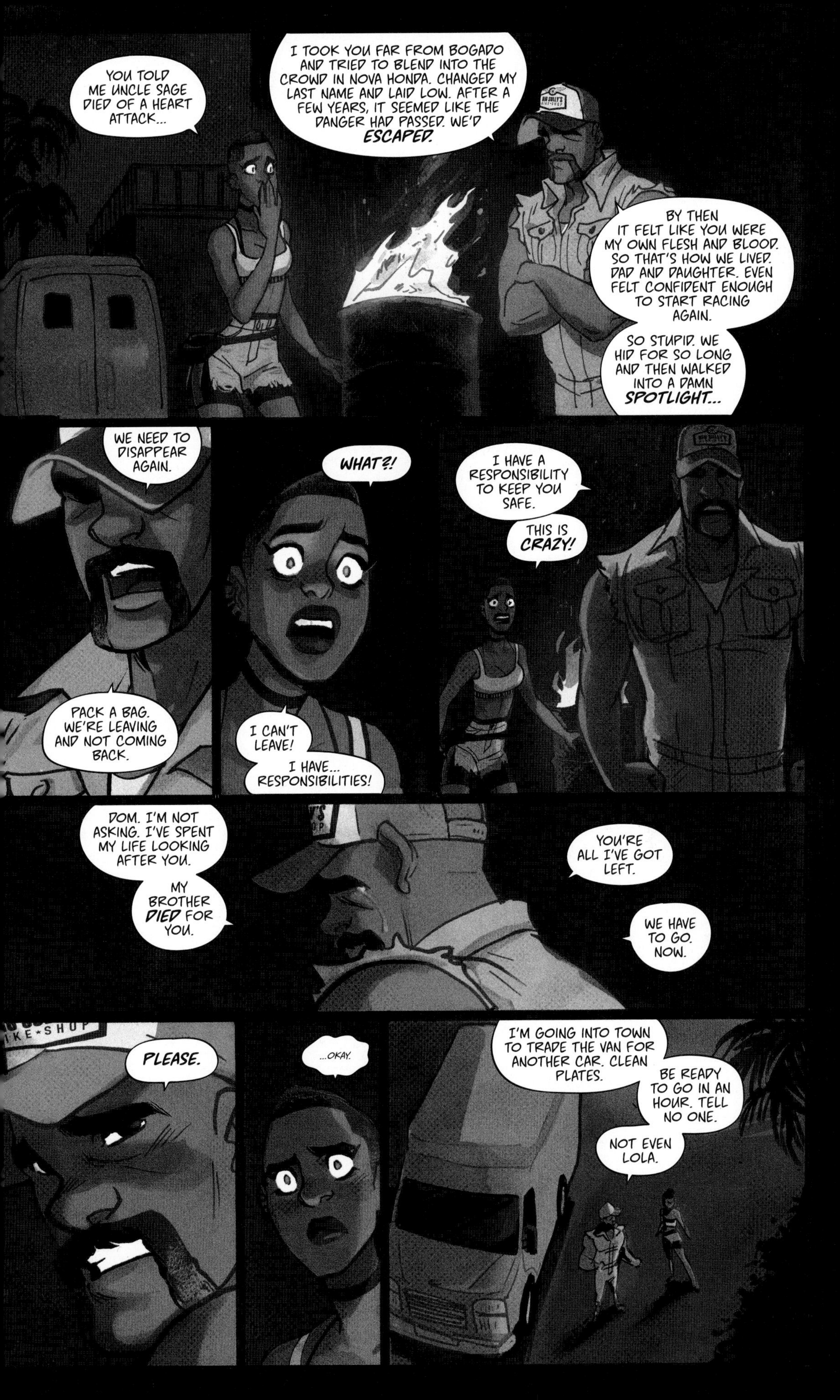
YOU TOLD ME UNCLE SAGE DIED OF A HEART ATTACK...
I TOOK YOU FAR FROM BOGADO AND TRIED TO BLEND INTO THE CROWD IN NOVA HONDA. CHANGED MY LAST NAME AND LAID LOW. AFTER A FEW YEARS, IT SEEMED LIKE THE DANGER HAD PASSED. WE'D ESCAPED.
BIG SULLY'S BIKE SHOP
BY THEN IT FELT LIKE YOU WERE MY OWN FLESH AND BLOOD. SO THAT'S HOW WE LIVED. DAD AND DAUGHTER. EVEN FELT CONFIDENT ENOUGH TO START RACING AGAIN.
SO STUPID. WE HID FOR SO LONG AND THEN WALKED INTO A DAMN SPOTLIGHT...
WE NEED TO DISAPPEAR AGAIN.
PACK A BAG. WE'RE LEAVING AND NOT COMING BACK.
WHAT?!
I CAN'T LEAVE!
I HAVE... RESPONSIBILITIES!
I HAVE A RESPONSIBILITY TO KEEP YOU SAFE.
THIS IS CRAZY!
DOM. I'M NOT ASKING. I'VE SPENT MY LIFE LOOKING AFTER YOU.
MY BROTHER DIED FOR YOU.
YOU'RE ALL I'VE GOT LEFT.
WE HAVE TO GO. NOW.
PLEASE.
...OKAY.
I'M GOING INTO TOWN TO TRADE THE VAN FOR ANOTHER CAR. CLEAN PLATES.
BE READY TO GO IN AN HOUR. TELL NO ONE.
NOT EVEN LOLA.

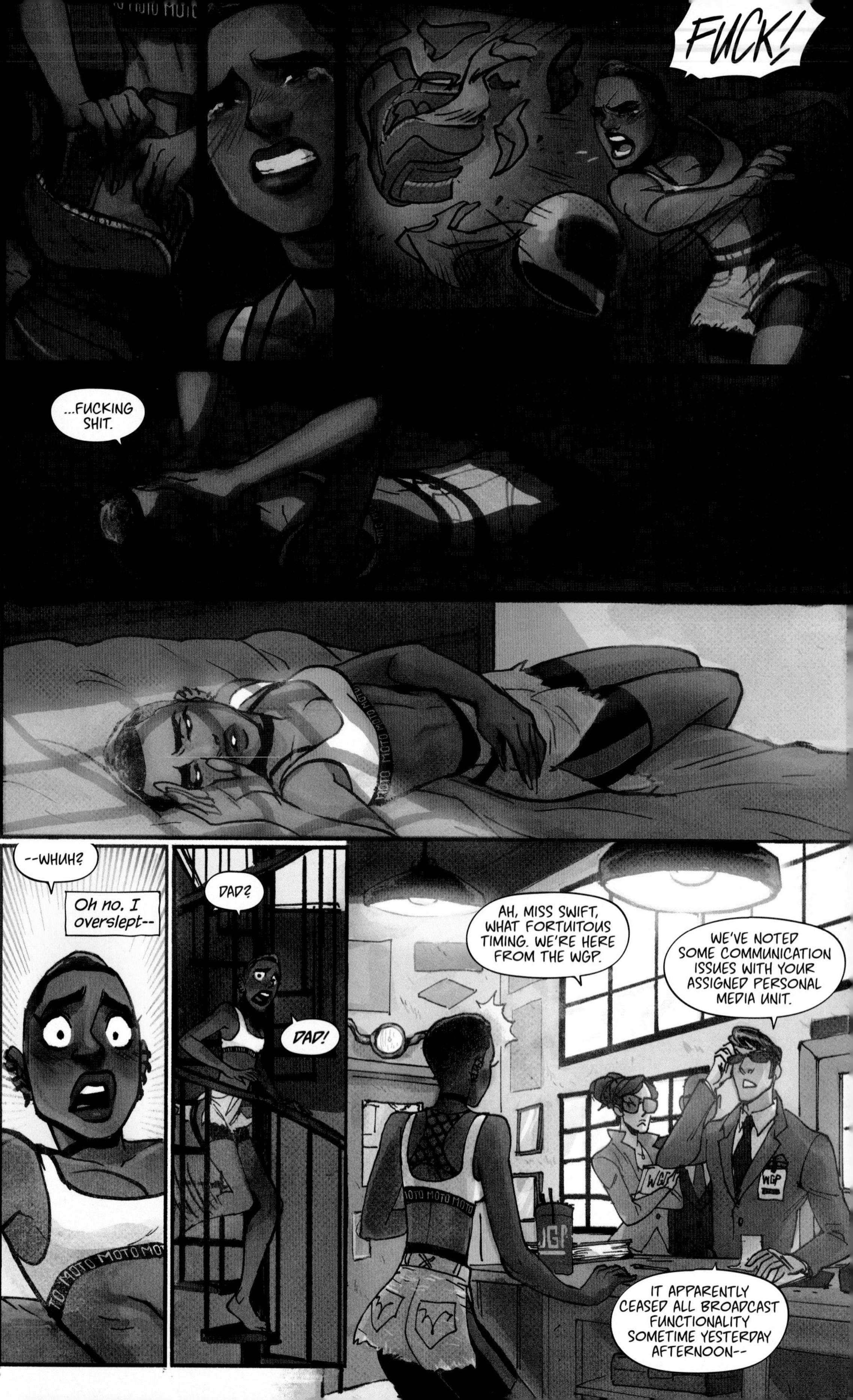
FUCK!
...FUCKING SHIT.
--WHUH?
Oh no. I overslept--
DAD?
DAD!
AH, MISS SWIFT, WHAT FORTUITOUS TIMING. WE'RE HERE FROM THE WGP.
WE'VE NOTED SOME COMMUNICATION ISSUES WITH YOUR ASSIGNED PERSONAL MEDIA UNIT.
IT APPARENTLY CEASED ALL BROADCAST FUNCTIONALITY SOMETIME YESTERDAY AFTERNOON--

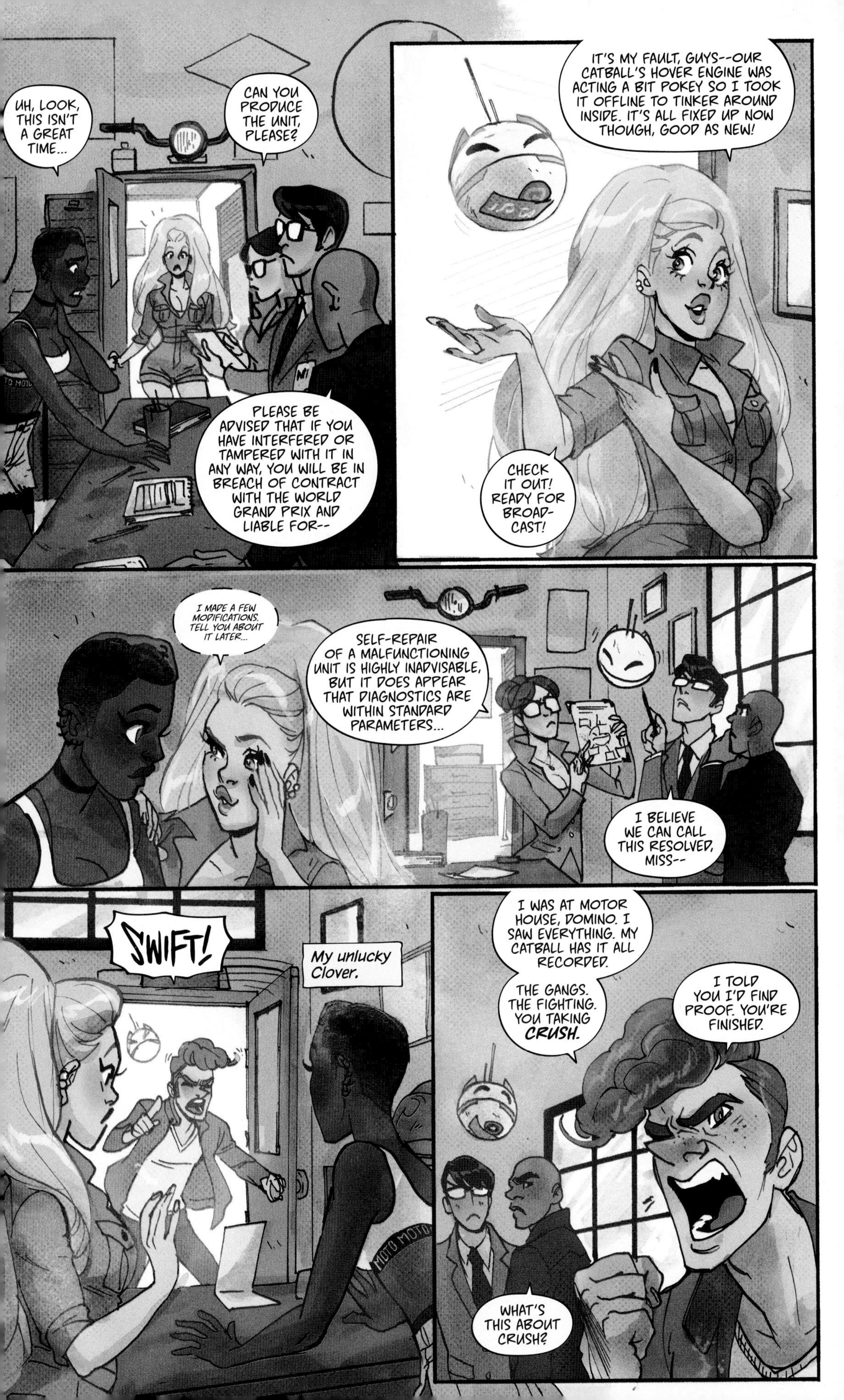
UH, LOOK, THIS ISN'T A GREAT TIME...
CAN YOU PRODUCE THE UNIT, PLEASE?
PLEASE BE ADVISED THAT IF YOU HAVE INTERFERED OR TAMPERED WITH IT IN ANY WAY, YOU WILL BE IN BREACH OF CONTRACT WITH THE WORLD GRAND PRIX AND LIABLE FOR--
IT'S MY FAULT, GUYS--OUR CATBALL'S HOVER ENGINE WAS ACTING A BIT POKEY SO I TOOK IT OFFLINE TO TINKER AROUND INSIDE. IT'S ALL FIXED UP NOW THOUGH, GOOD AS NEW!
CHECK IT OUT! READY FOR BROAD-CAST!
I MADE A FEW MODIFICATIONS. TELL YOU ABOUT IT LATER...
SELF-REPAIR OF A MALFUNCTIONING UNIT IS HIGHLY INADVISABLE, BUT IT DOES APPEAR THAT DIAGNOSTICS ARE WITHIN STANDARD PARAMETERS...
I BELIEVE WE CAN CALL THIS RESOLVED, MISS--
SWIFT!
My unlucky Clover.
I WAS AT MOTOR HOUSE, DOMINO. I SAW EVERYTHING. MY CATBALL HAS IT ALL RECORDED.
THE GANGS. THE FIGHTING. YOU TAKING CRUSH.
I TOLD YOU I'D FIND PROOF. YOU'RE FINISHED.
WHAT'S THIS ABOUT CRUSH?

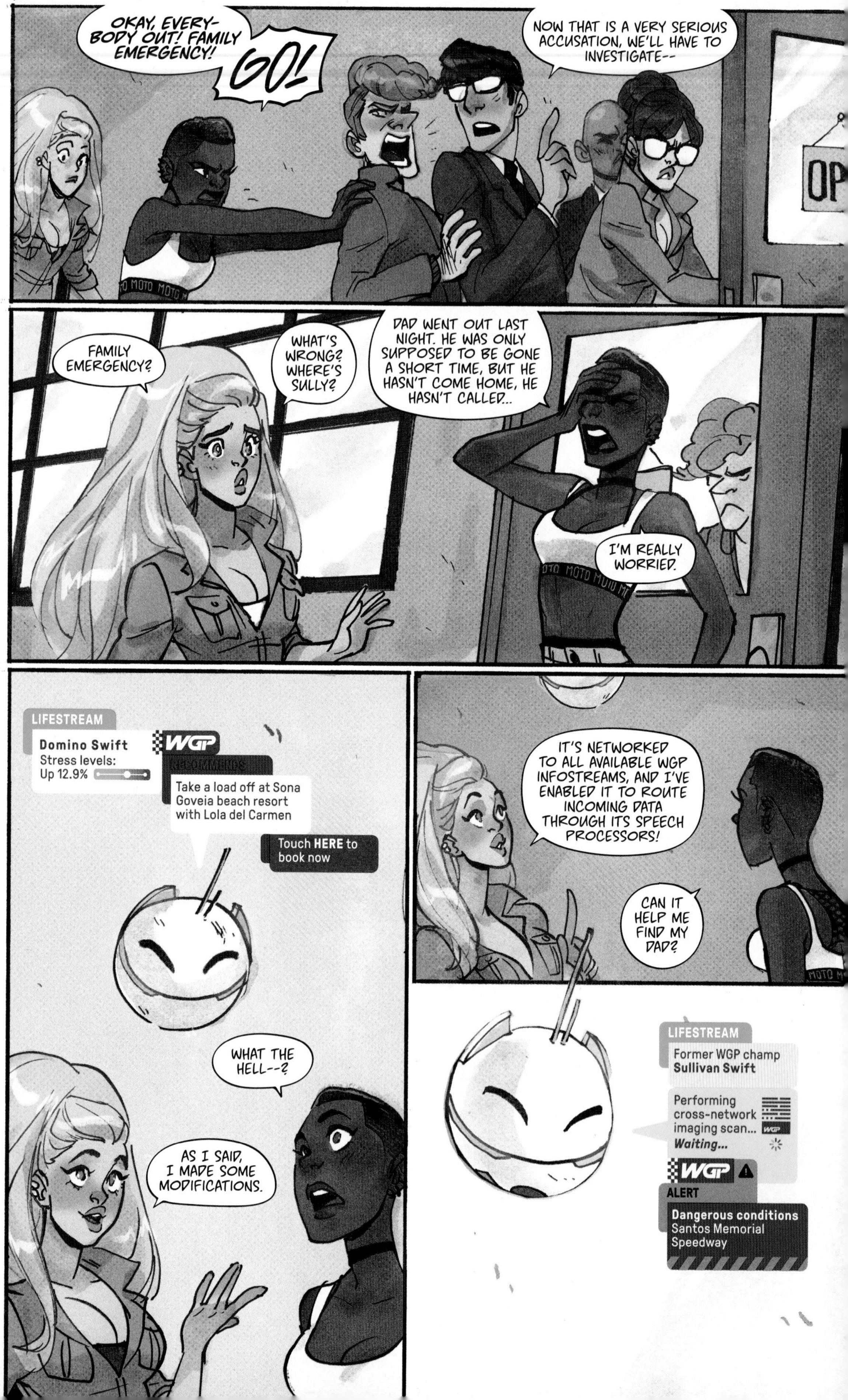

OKAY, EVERY-BODY OUT! FAMILY EMERGENCY!
GO!
NOW THAT IS A VERY SERIOUS ACCUSATION, WE'LL HAVE TO INVESTIGATE--
OP
FAMILY EMERGENCY?
WHAT'S WRONG? WHERE'S SULLY?
DAD WENT OUT LAST NIGHT. HE WAS ONLY SUPPOSED TO BE GONE A SHORT TIME, BUT HE HASN'T COME HOME, HE HASN'T CALLED...
I'M REALLY WORRIED.
LIFESTREAM
Domino Swift
Stress levels:
Up 12.9%
WGP
RECOMMENDS
Take a load off at Sona Goveia beach resort with Lola del Carmen
Touch HERE to book now
WHAT THE HELL--?
AS I SAID, I MADE SOME MODIFICATIONS.
IT'S NETWORKED TO ALL AVAILABLE WGP INFOSTREAMS, AND I'VE ENABLED IT TO ROUTE INCOMING DATA THROUGH ITS SPEECH PROCESSORS!
CAN IT HELP ME FIND MY DAD?
LIFESTREAM
Former WGP champ
Sullivan Swift
Performing cross-network imaging scan...
Waiting...
WGP
ALERT
Dangerous conditions
Santos Memorial Speedway

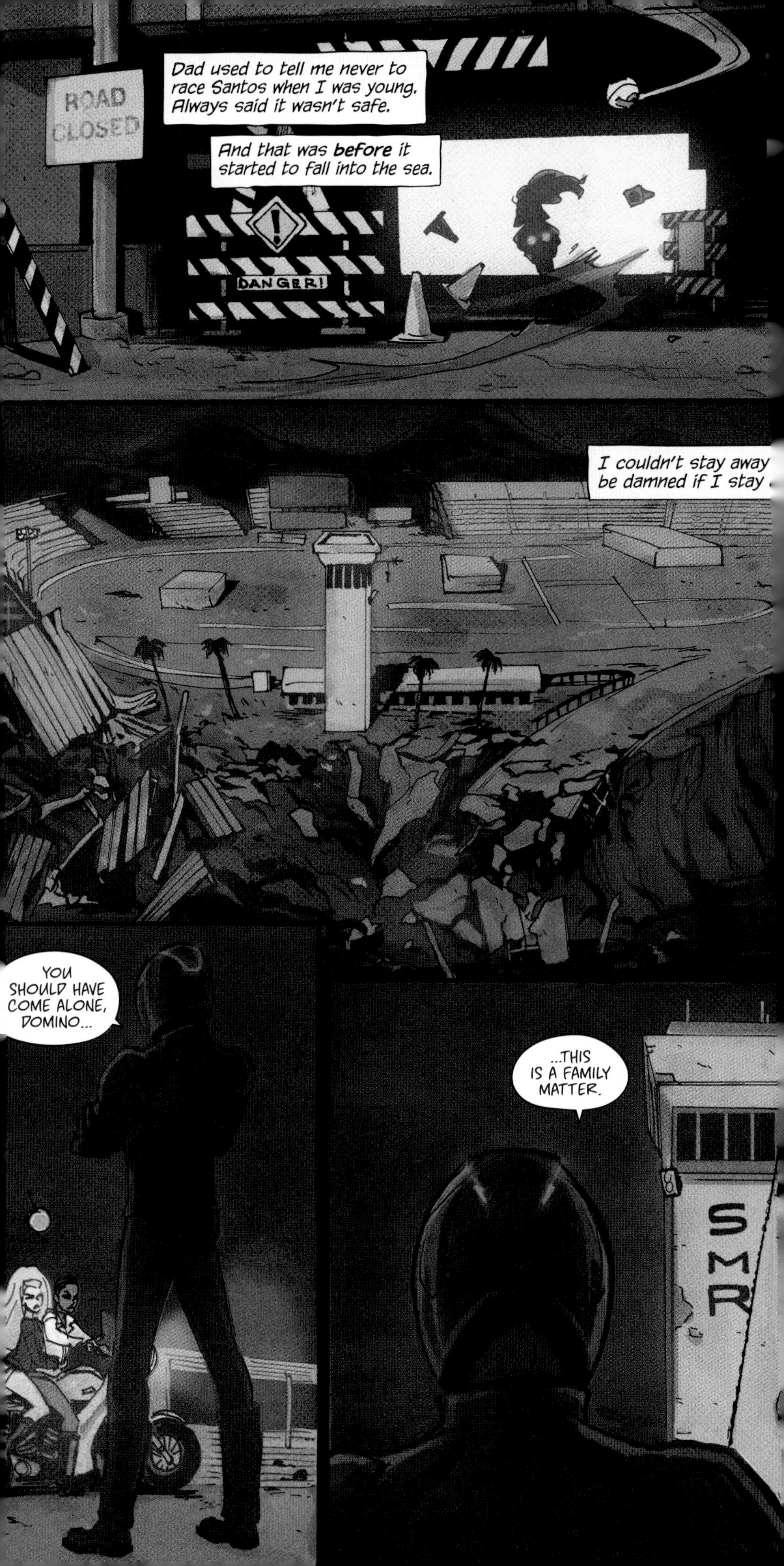
ROAD CLOSED
Dad used to tell me never to race Santos when I was young. Always said it wasn't safe.
And that was **before** it started to fall into the sea.
DANGER!
I couldn't stay away
be damned if I stay
YOU SHOULD HAVE COME ALONE, DOMINO...
...THIS IS A FAMILY MATTER.
SMR

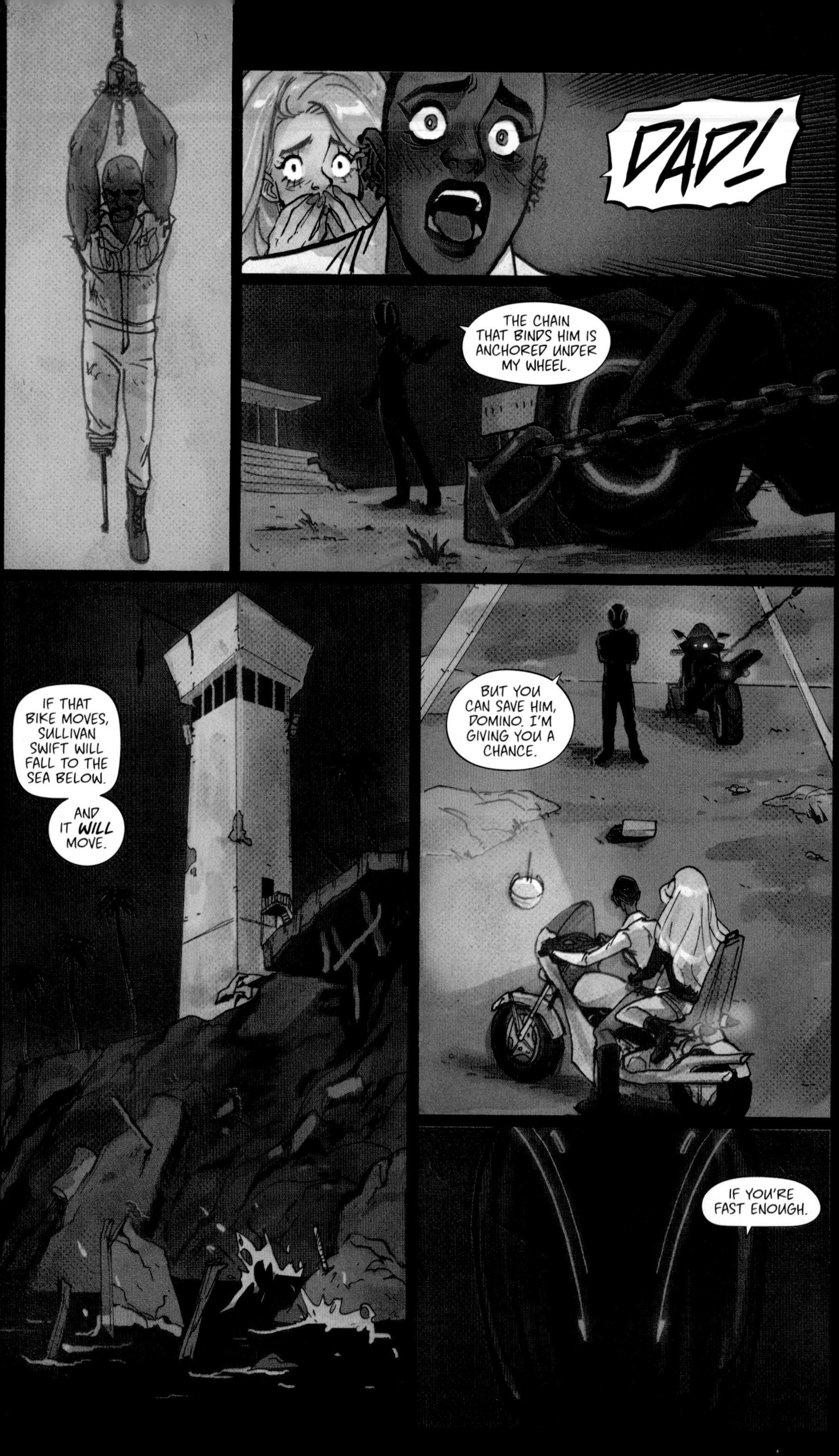
DAD!
THE CHAIN THAT BINDS HIM IS ANCHORED UNDER MY WHEEL.
IF THAT BIKE MOVES, SULLIVAN SWIFT WILL FALL TO THE SEA BELOW.
AND IT WILL MOVE.
BUT YOU CAN SAVE HIM, DOMINO. I'M GIVING YOU A CHANCE.
IF YOU'RE FAST ENOUGH.

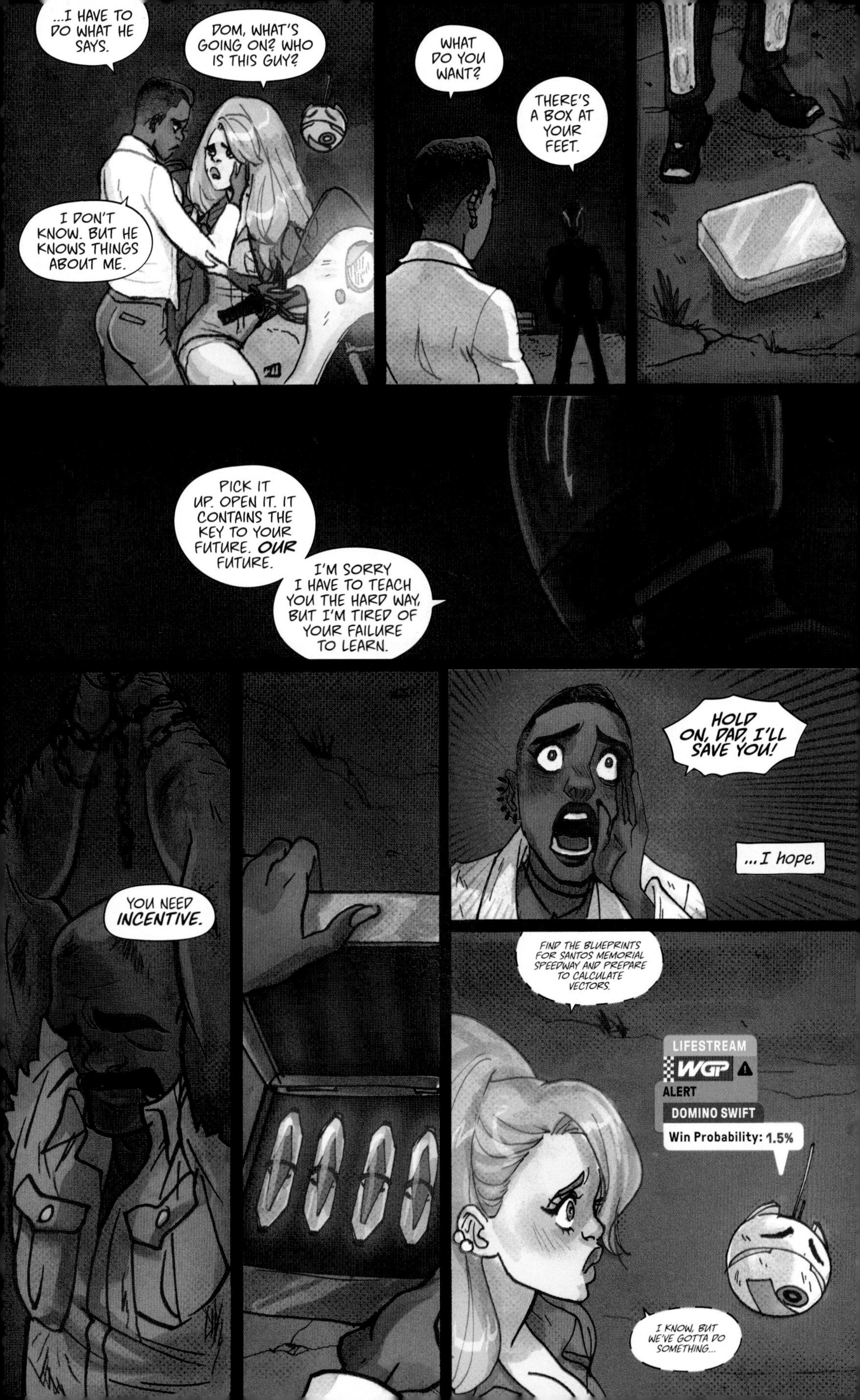
...I HAVE TO DO WHAT HE SAYS.
DOM, WHAT'S GOING ON? WHO IS THIS GUY?
I DON'T KNOW. BUT HE KNOWS THINGS ABOUT ME.
WHAT DO YOU WANT?
THERE'S A BOX AT YOUR FEET.
PICK IT UP. OPEN IT. IT CONTAINS THE KEY TO YOUR FUTURE. ***OUR*** FUTURE.
I'M SORRY I HAVE TO TEACH YOU THE HARD WAY, BUT I'M TIRED OF YOUR FAILURE TO LEARN.
YOU NEED **INCENTIVE.**
HOLD ON, DAD, I'LL SAVE YOU!
...I hope.
FIND THE BLUEPRINTS FOR SANTOS MEMORIAL SPEEDWAY AND PREPARE TO CALCULATE VECTORS.
LIFESTREAM
WGP
ALERT
DOMINO SWIFT
Win Probability: 1.5%
I KNOW, BUT WE'VE GOTTA DO SOMETHING...

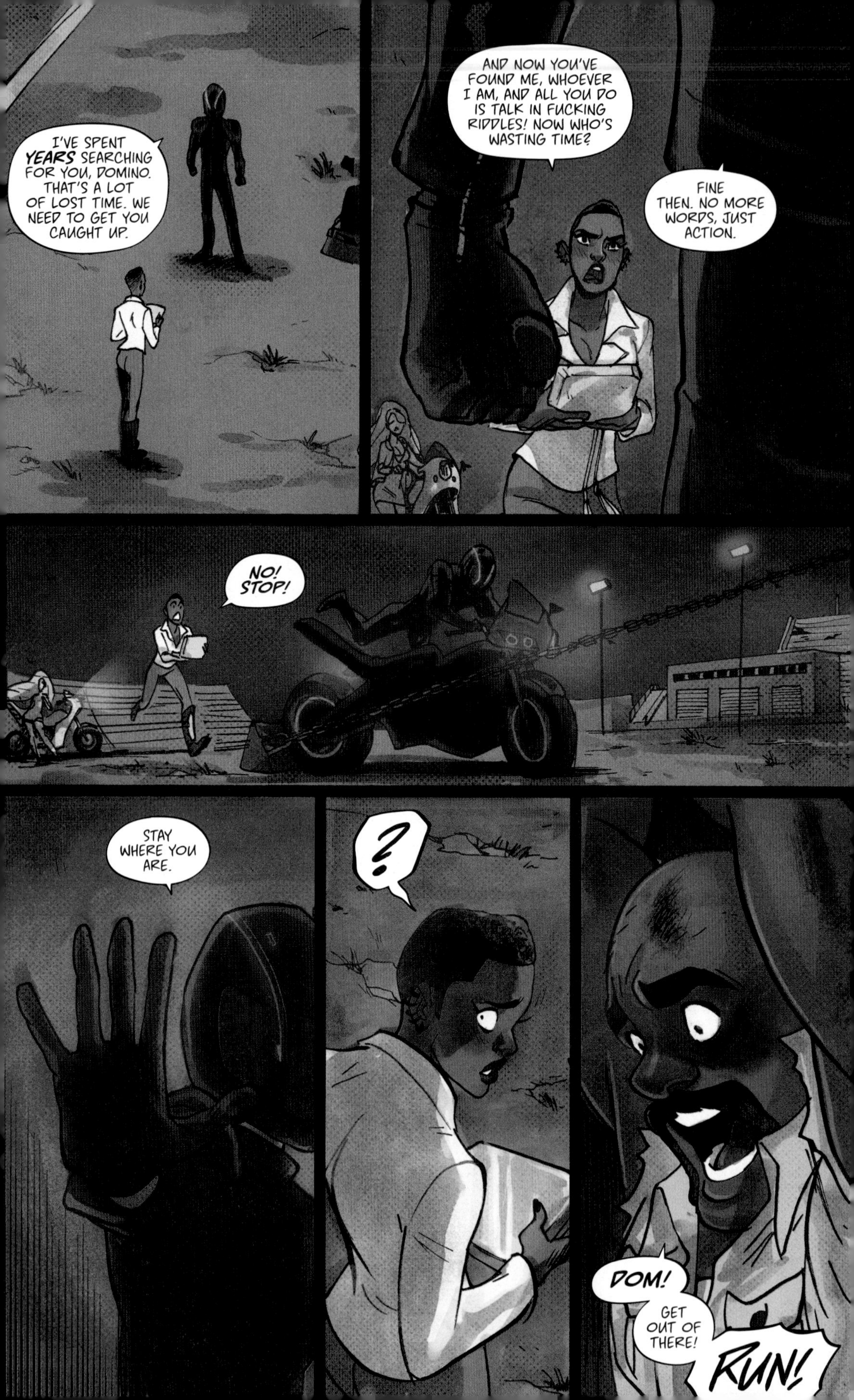
I'VE SPENT YEARS SEARCHING FOR YOU, DOMINO. THAT'S A LOT OF LOST TIME. WE NEED TO GET YOU CAUGHT UP.
AND NOW YOU'VE FOUND ME, WHOEVER I AM, AND ALL YOU DO IS TALK IN FUCKING RIDDLES! NOW WHO'S WASTING TIME?
FINE THEN. NO MORE WORDS, JUST ACTION.
NO! STOP!
STAY WHERE YOU ARE.
?
DOM!
GET OUT OF THERE!
RUN!

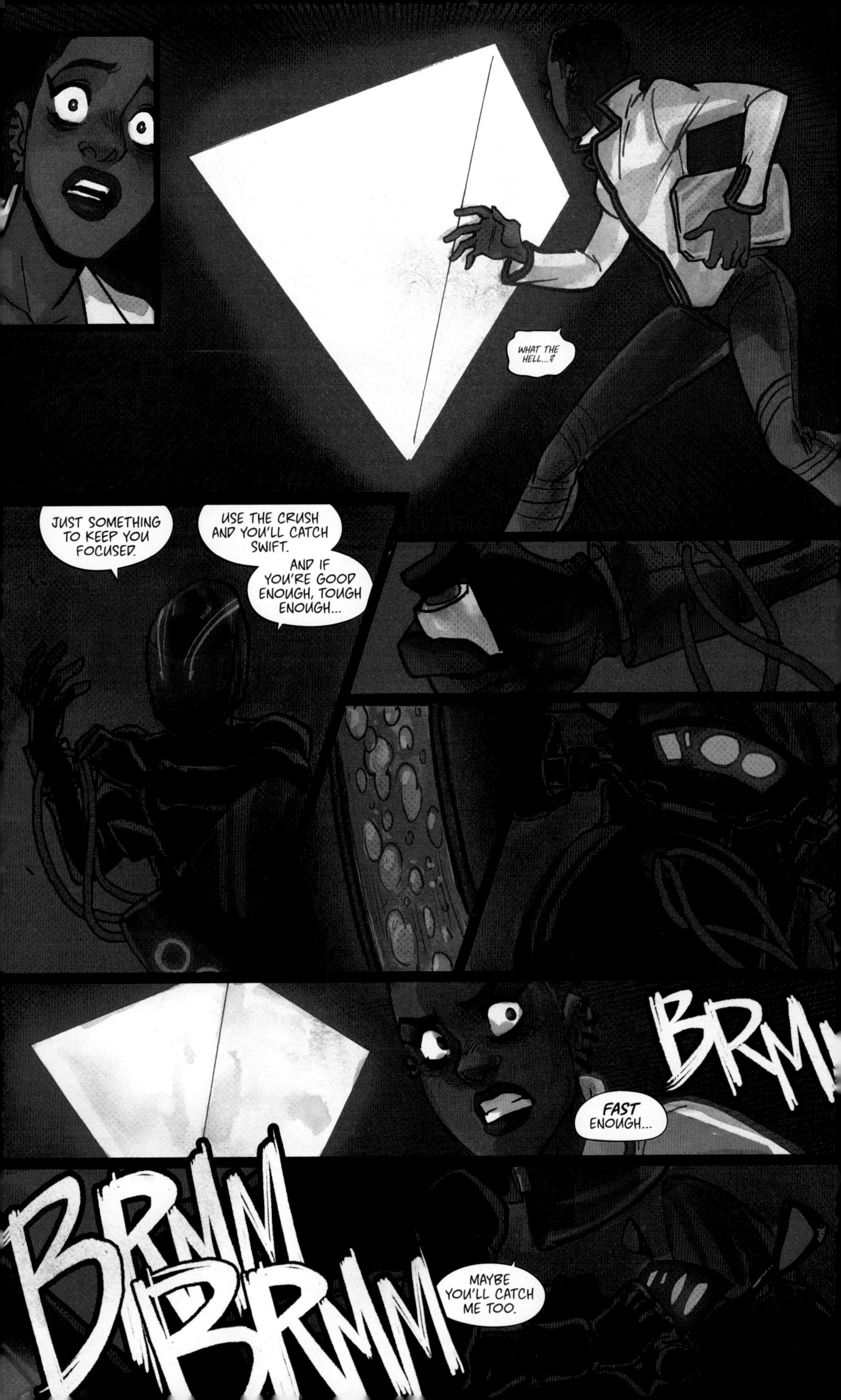
WHAT THE HELL...?
JUST SOMETHING TO KEEP YOU FOCUSED.
USE THE CRUSH AND YOU'LL CATCH SWIFT.
AND IF YOU'RE GOOD ENOUGH, TOUGH ENOUGH...
BRM
FAST ENOUGH...
BRMM
BRMM
MAYBE YOU'LL CATCH ME TOO.

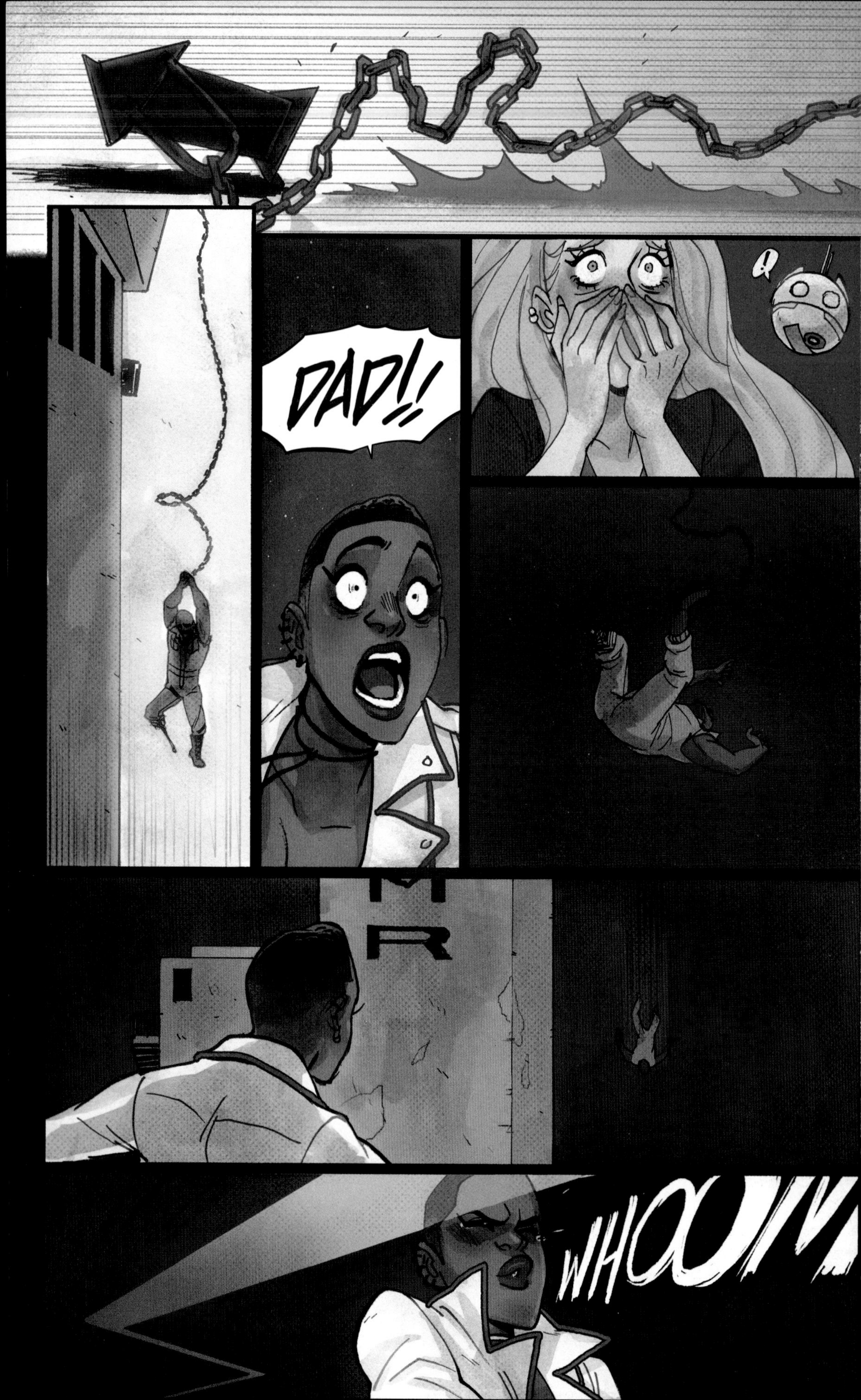

DAD!!
WHOOM

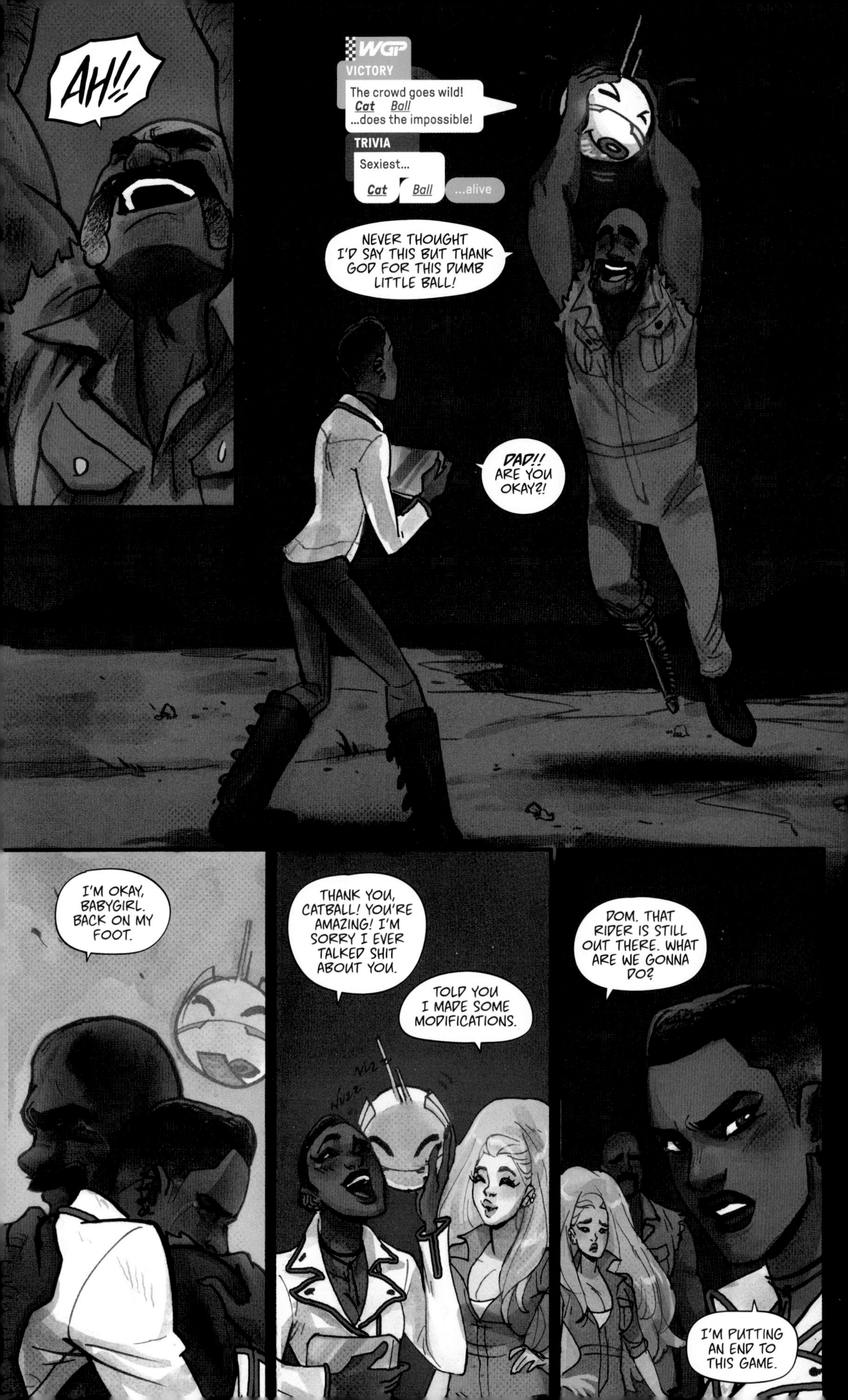
AH!!
WGP
VICTORY
The crowd goes wild!
Cat Ball
...does the impossible!
TRIVIA
Sexiest...
Cat Ball ...alive
NEVER THOUGHT I'D SAY THIS BUT THANK GOD FOR THIS DUMB LITTLE BALL!
DAD!! ARE YOU OKAY?!
I'M OKAY, BABYGIRL. BACK ON MY FOOT.
THANK YOU, CATBALL! YOU'RE AMAZING! I'M SORRY I EVER TALKED SHIT ABOUT YOU.
TOLD YOU I MADE SOME MODIFICATIONS.
DOM. THAT RIDER IS STILL OUT THERE. WHAT ARE WE GONNA DO?
I'M PUTTING AN END TO THIS GAME.

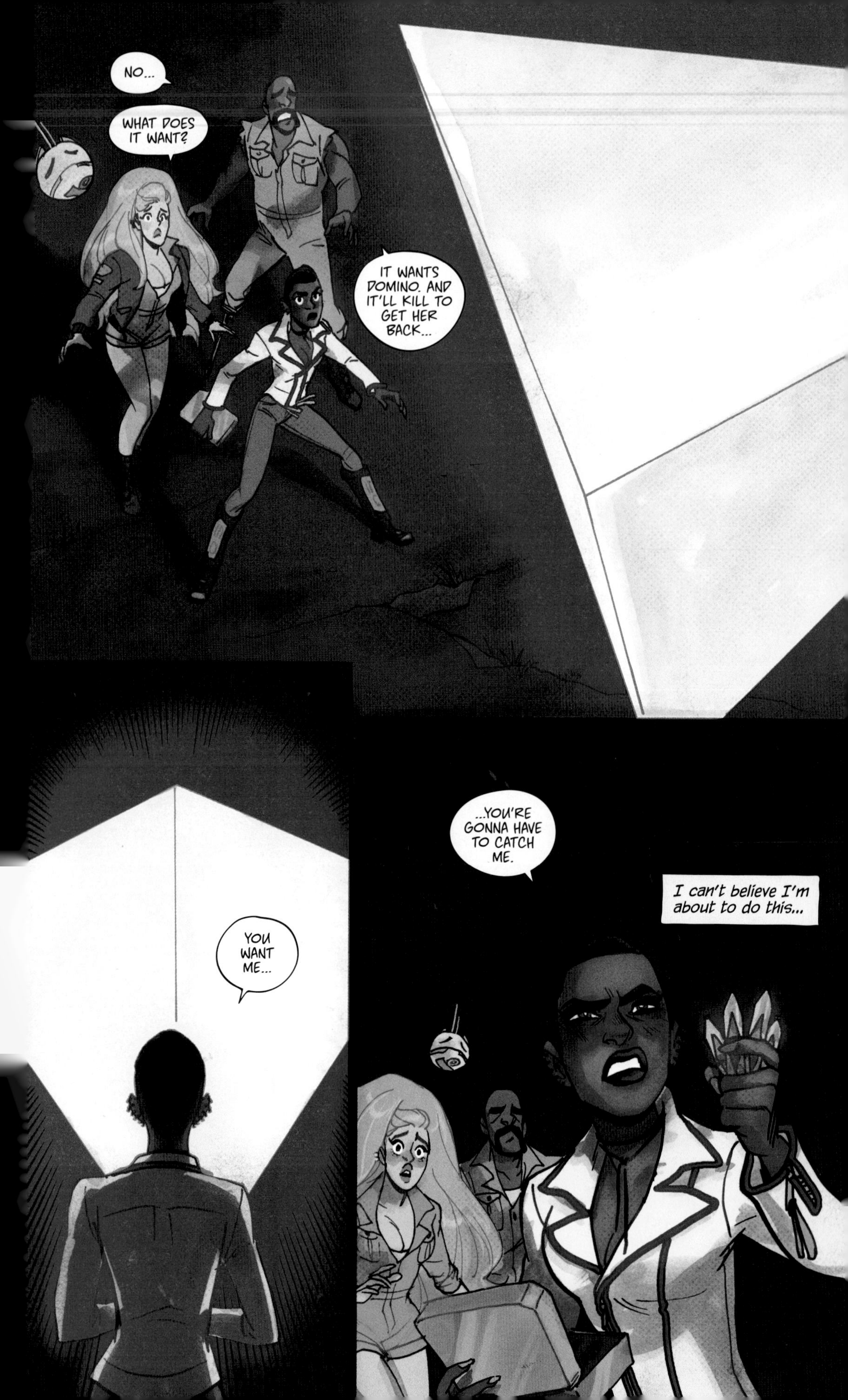
NO...
WHAT DOES IT WANT?
IT WANTS DOMINO. AND IT'LL KILL TO GET HER BACK...
YOU WANT ME...
...YOU'RE GONNA HAVE TO CATCH ME.
I can't believe I'm about to do this...

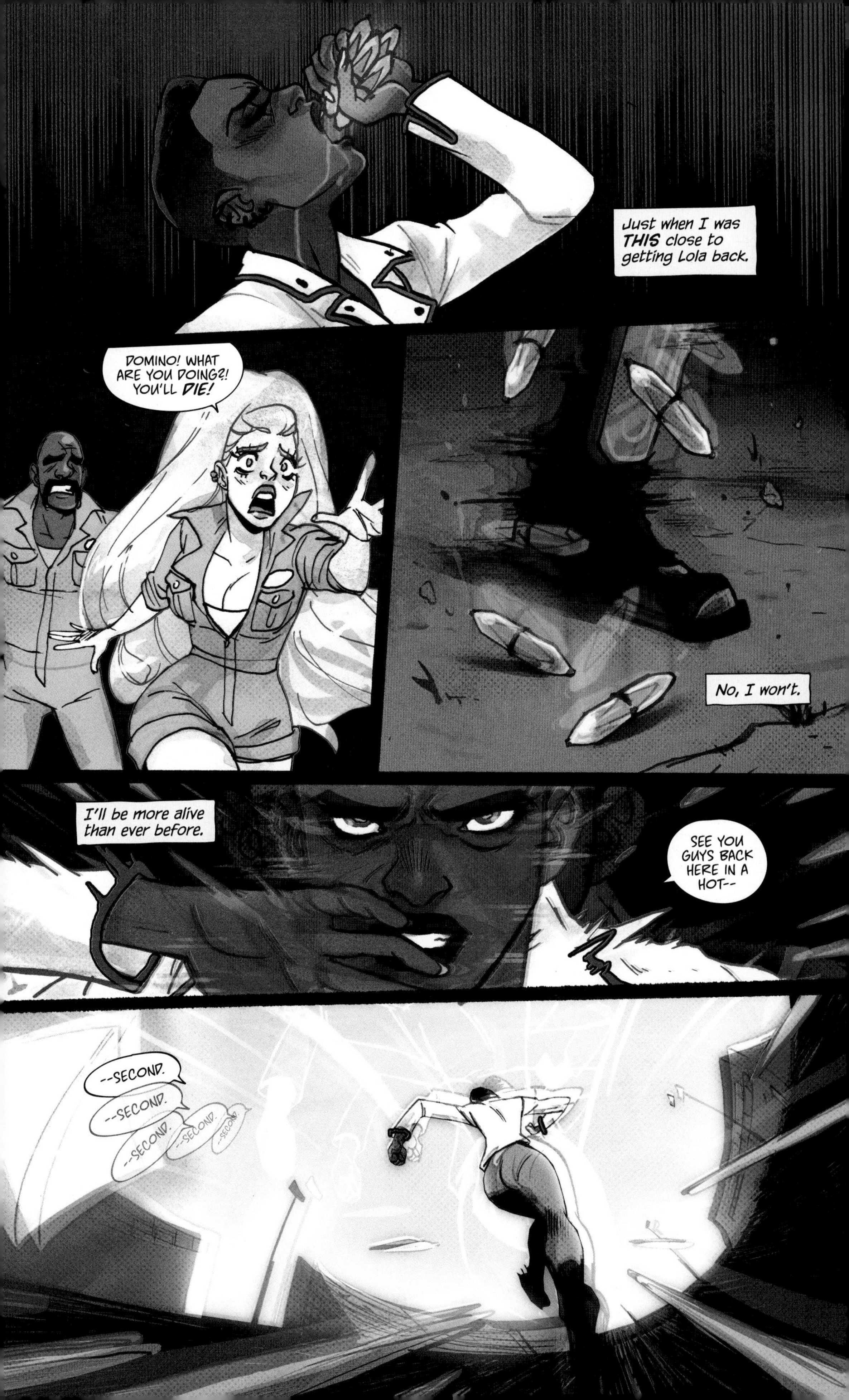
Just when I was THIS close to getting Lola back.
DOMINO! WHAT ARE YOU DOING?! YOU'LL DIE!
No, I won't.
I'll be more alive than ever before.
SEE YOU GUYS BACK HERE IN A HOT--
--SECOND.
--SECOND.
--SECOND.
--SECOND.
--SECOND.

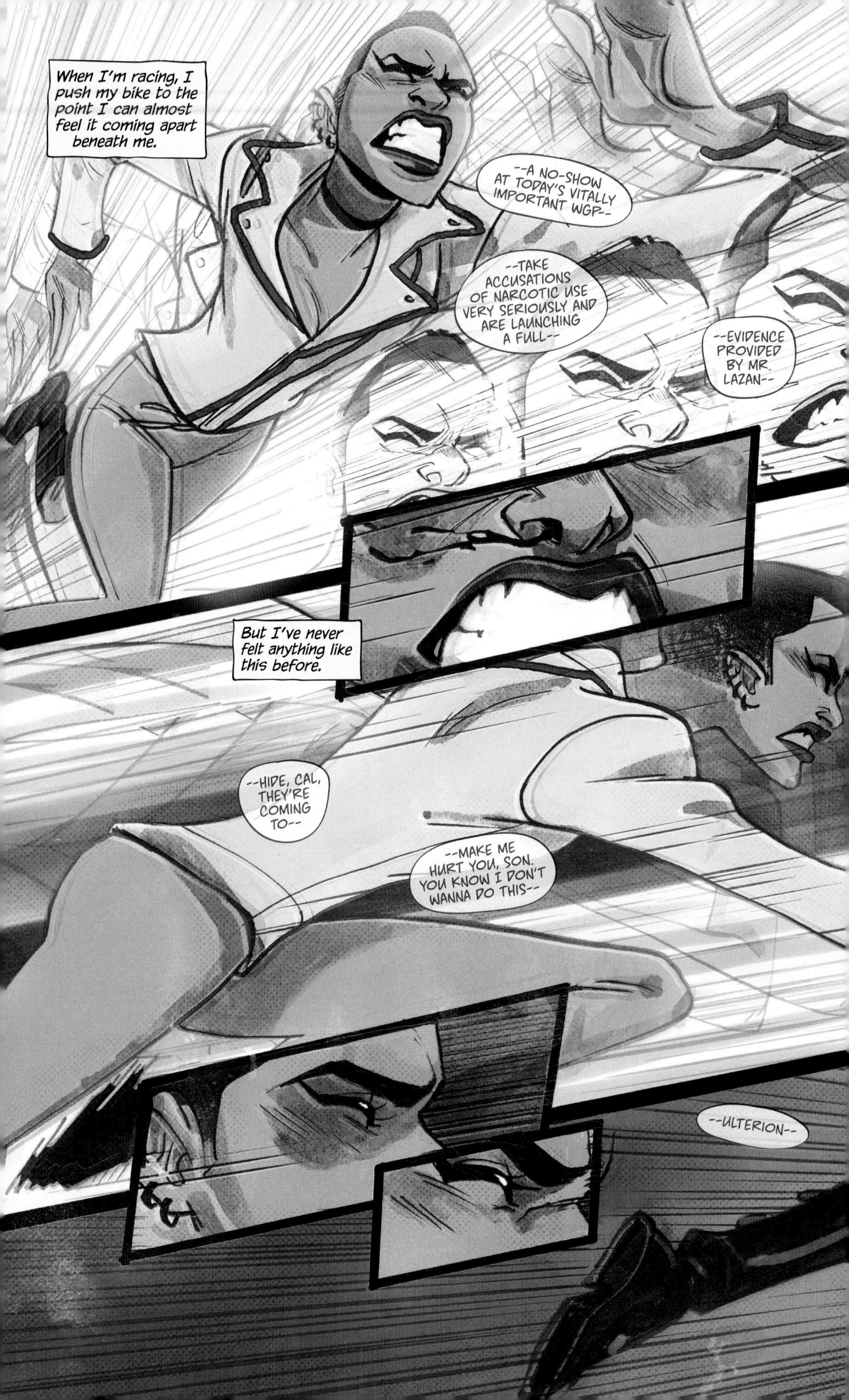
When I'm racing, I push my bike to the point I can almost feel it coming apart beneath me.
--A NO-SHOW AT TODAY'S VITALLY IMPORTANT WGP--
--TAKE ACCUSATIONS OF NARCOTIC USE VERY SERIOUSLY AND ARE LAUNCHING A FULL--
--EVIDENCE PROVIDED BY MR. LAZAN--
But I've never felt anything like this before.
--HIDE, CAL, THEY'RE COMING TO--
--MAKE ME HURT YOU, SON. YOU KNOW I DON'T WANNA DO THIS--
--ULTERION--

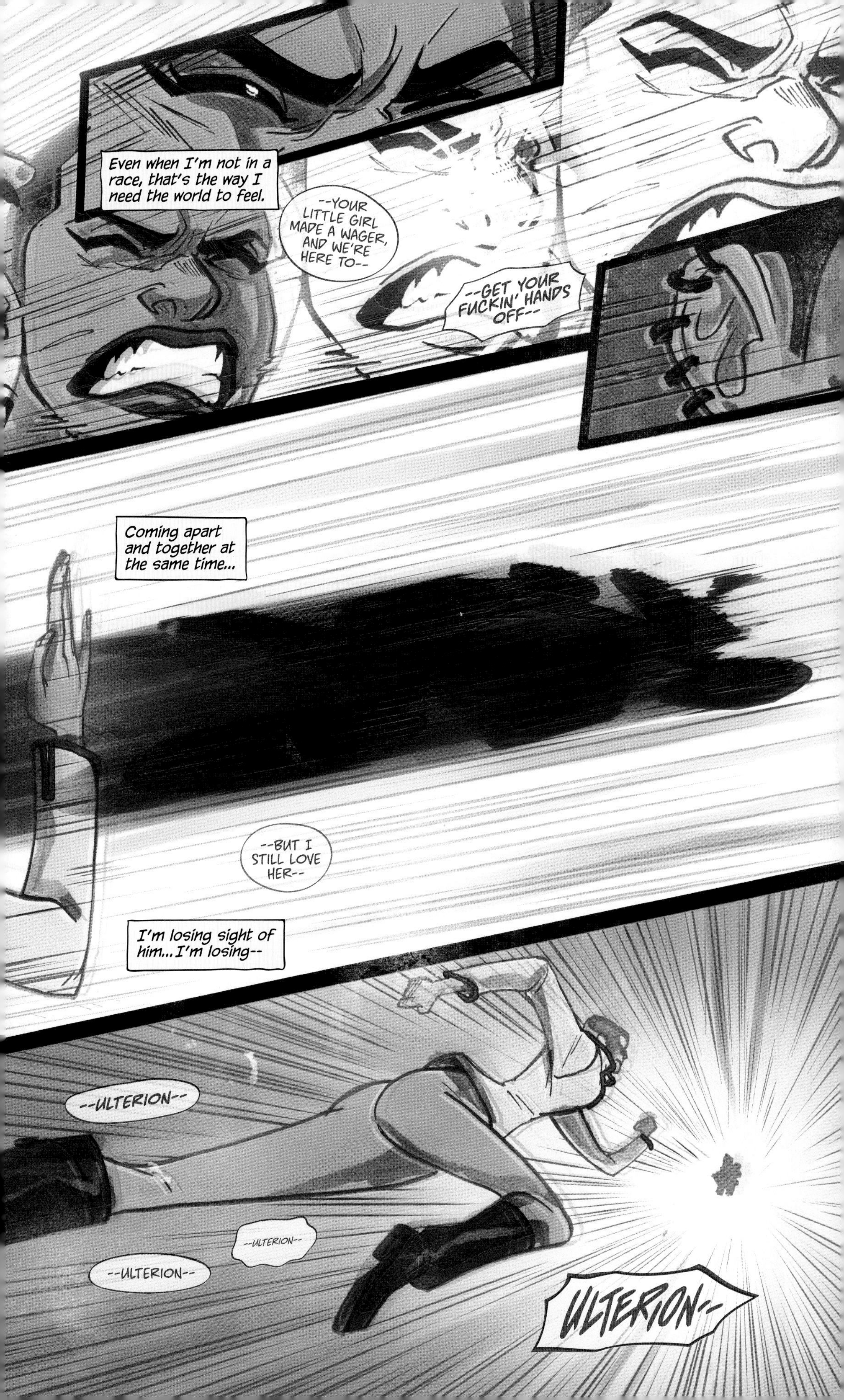
Even when I'm not in a race, that's the way I need the world to feel.
--YOUR LITTLE GIRL MADE A WAGER, AND WE'RE HERE TO--
--GET YOUR FUCKIN' HANDS OFF--
Coming apart and together at the same time...
--BUT I STILL LOVE HER--
I'm losing sight of him...I'm losing--
--ULTERION--
--ULTERION--
--ULTERION--
ULTERION--

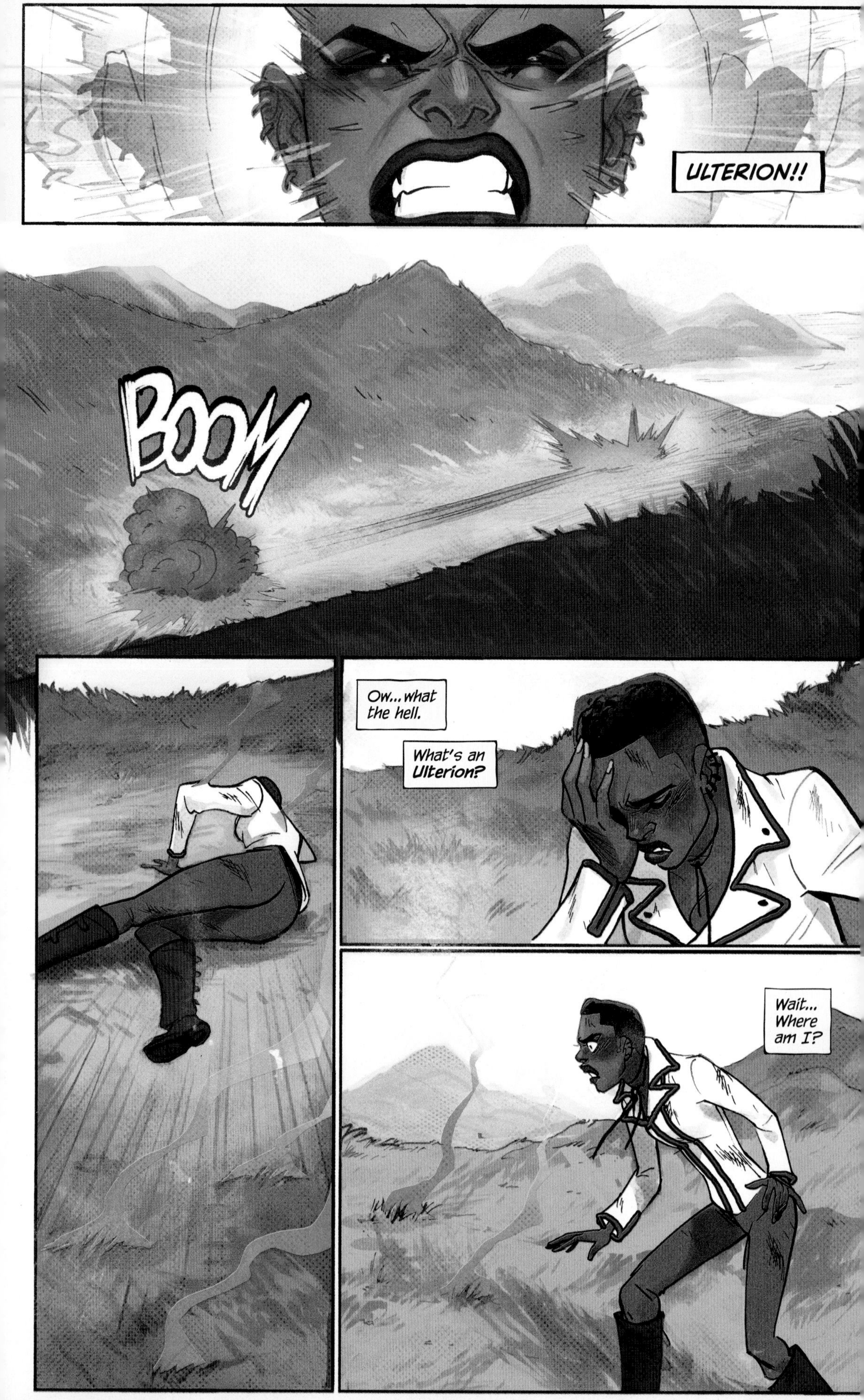
ULTERION!!
BOOM
Ow...what the hell.
What's an Ulterion?
Wait... Where am I?

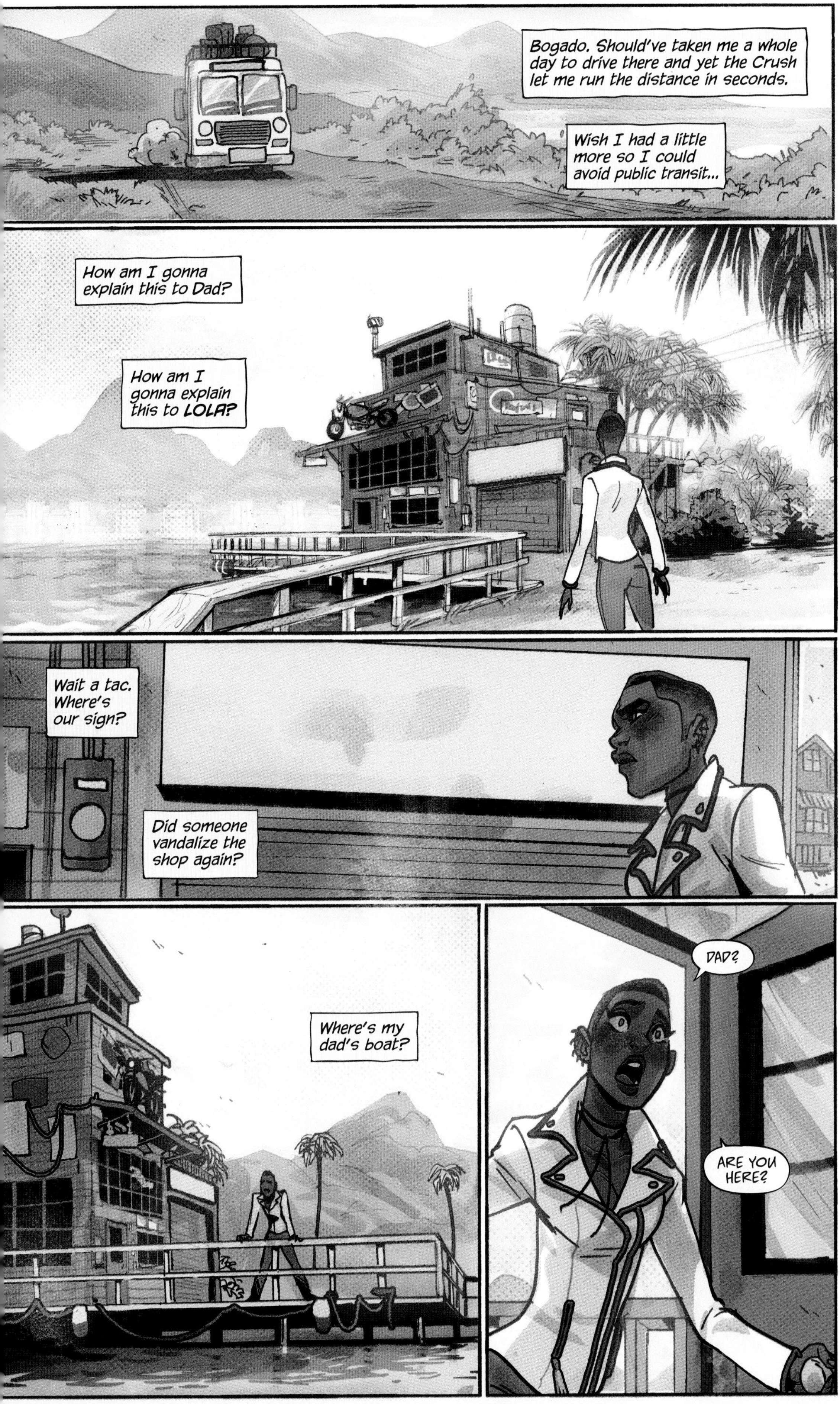
Bogado. Should've taken me a whole day to drive there and yet the Crush let me run the distance in seconds.
Wish I had a little more so I could avoid public transit...
How am I gonna explain this to Dad?
How am I gonna explain this to LOLA?
Wait a tac. Where's our sign?
Did someone vandalize the shop again?
Where's my dad's boat?
DAD?
ARE YOU HERE?

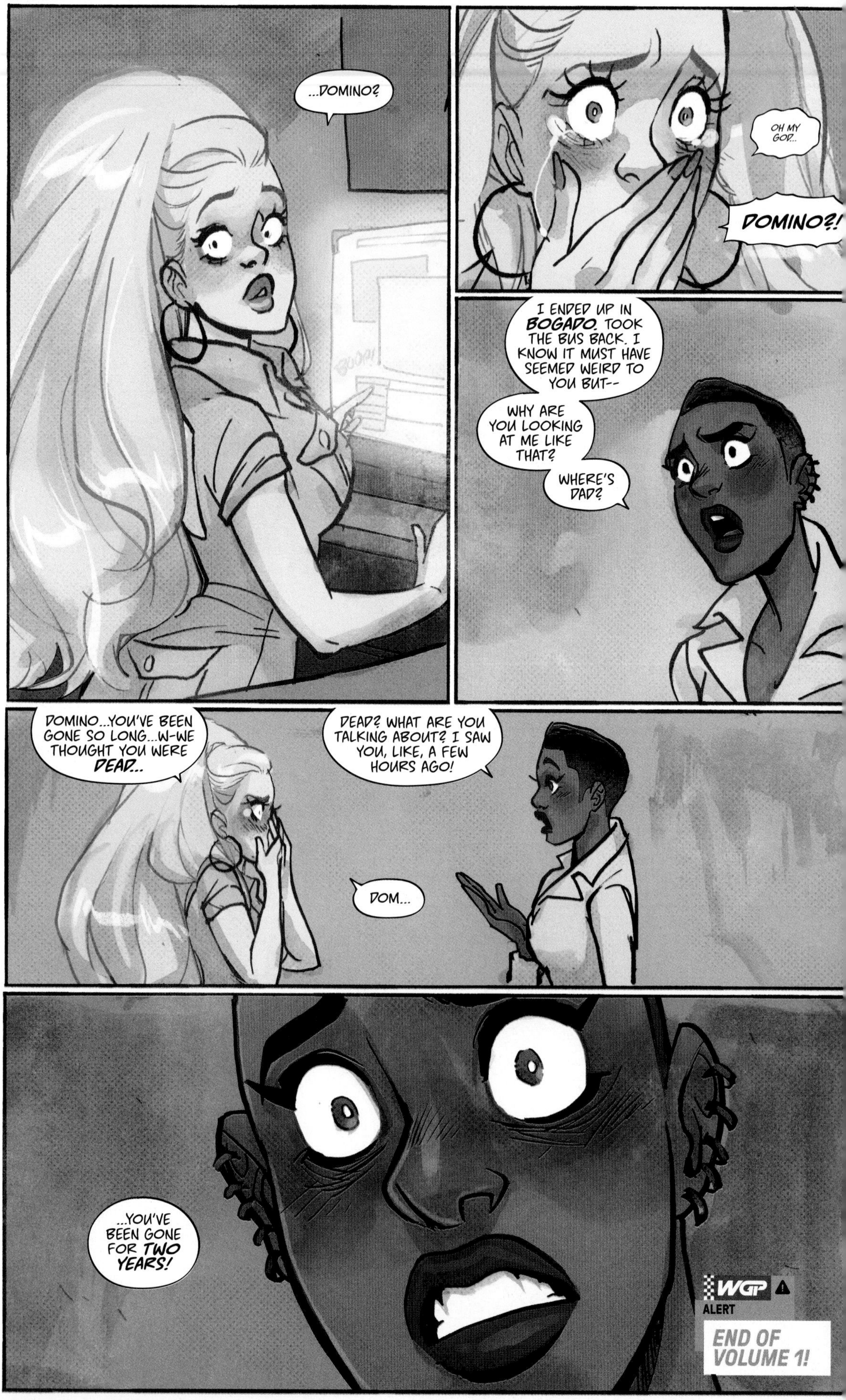
...DOMINO?
OH MY GOD...
DOMINO?!
I ENDED UP IN BOGADO. TOOK THE BUS BACK. I KNOW IT MUST HAVE SEEMED WEIRD TO YOU BUT--
WHY ARE YOU LOOKING AT ME LIKE THAT?
WHERE'S DAD?
DOMINO...YOU'VE BEEN GONE SO LONG...W-WE THOUGHT YOU WERE DEAD...
DEAD? WHAT ARE YOU TALKING ABOUT? I SAW YOU, LIKE, A FEW HOURS AGO!
DOM...
...YOU'VE BEEN GONE FOR TWO YEARS!
WGP ALERT
END OF VOLUME 1!

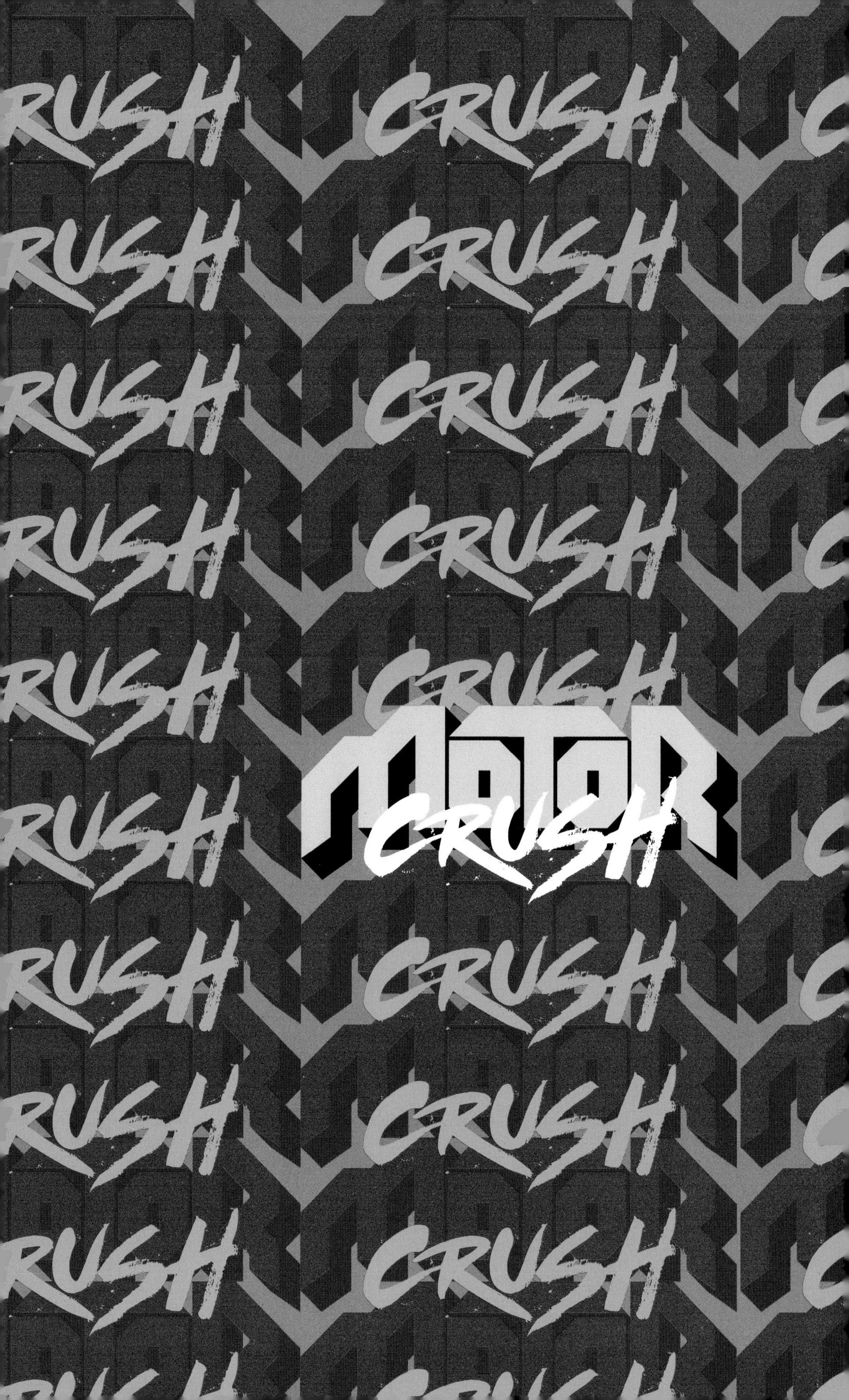
MOTOR CRUSH

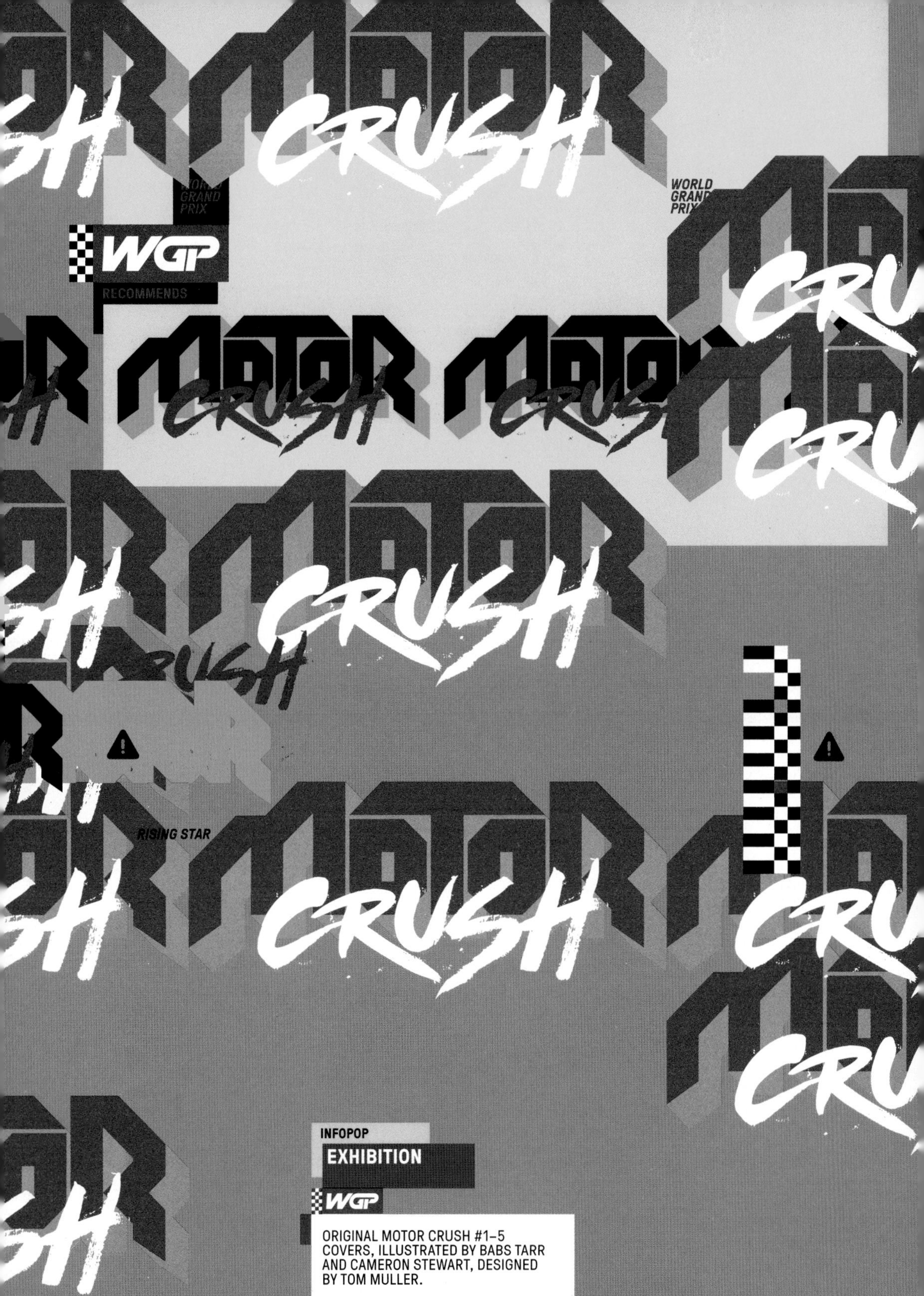
MOTOR CRUSH
WORLD GRAND PRIX
WGP
RECOMMENDS
RISING STAR

INFOPOP

EXHIBITION

WGP

ORIGINAL MOTOR CRUSH #1–5 COVERS, ILLUSTRATED BY BABS TARR AND CAMERON STEWART, DESIGNED BY TOM MULLER.

INFOPOP

MOTOR CRUSH #1 COVER A BY BABS TARR

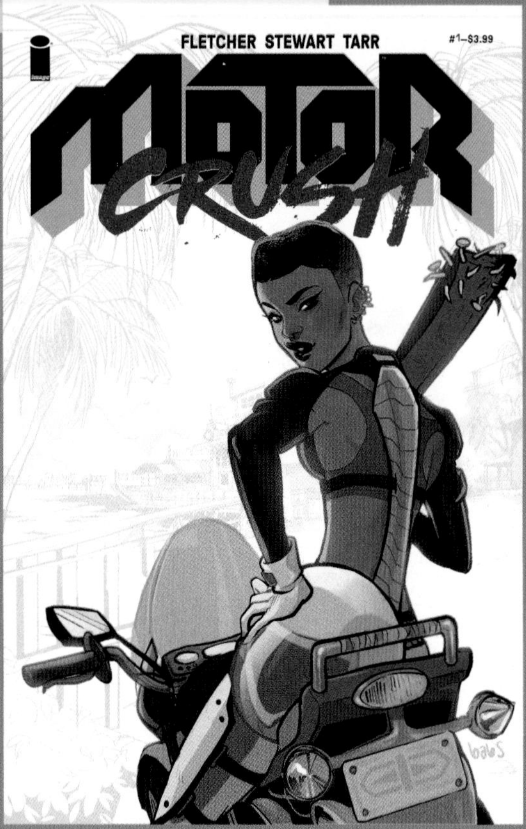
FLETCHER STEWART TARR
#1—$3.99
MOTOR
CRUSH

INFOPOP

MOTOR CRUSH #1 COVER B BY CAMERON STEWART

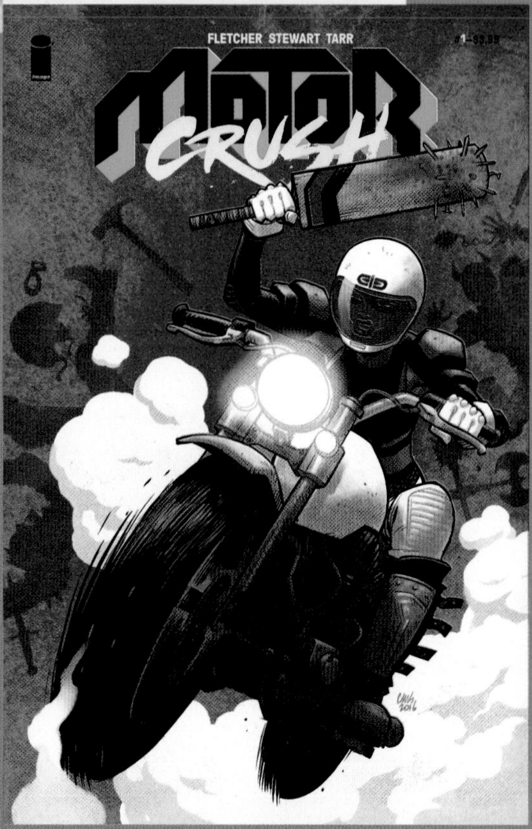
FLETCHER STEWART TARR
#1—$3.99
MOTOR
CRUSH

INFOPOP

MOTOR CRUSH #2 COVER A BY BABS TARR

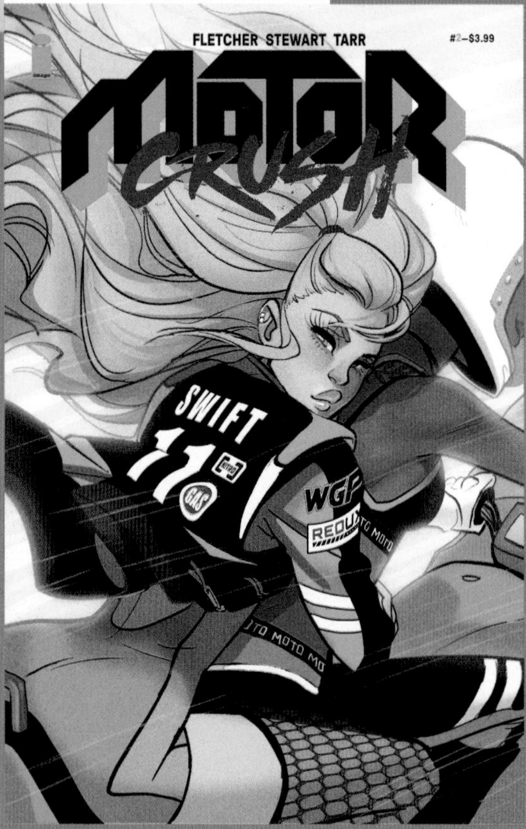
FLETCHER STEWART TARR
#2—$3.99
MOTOR
CRUSH
SWIFT
11
GAS
WGP
REDUX

INFOPOP

MOTOR CRUSH #2 COVER B BY CAMERON STEWART

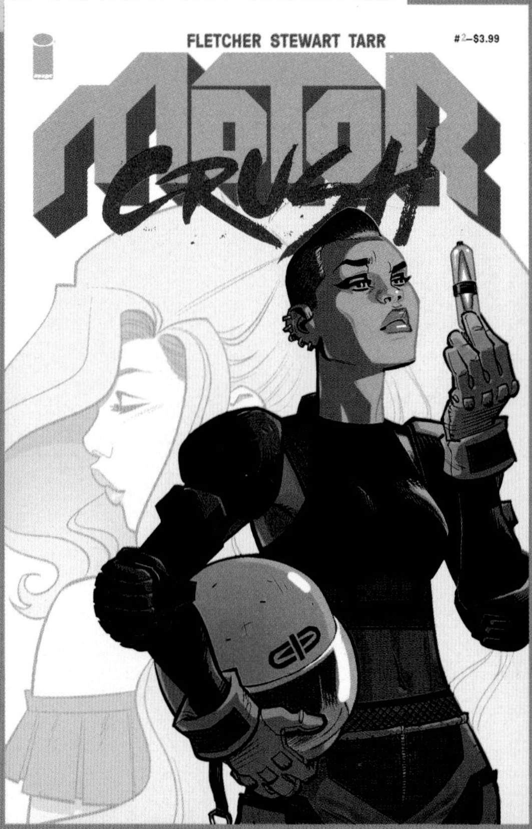
FLETCHER STEWART TARR
#2—$3.99
MOTOR
CRUSH

INFOPOP

MOTOR CRUSH #3 COVER A BY BABS TARR

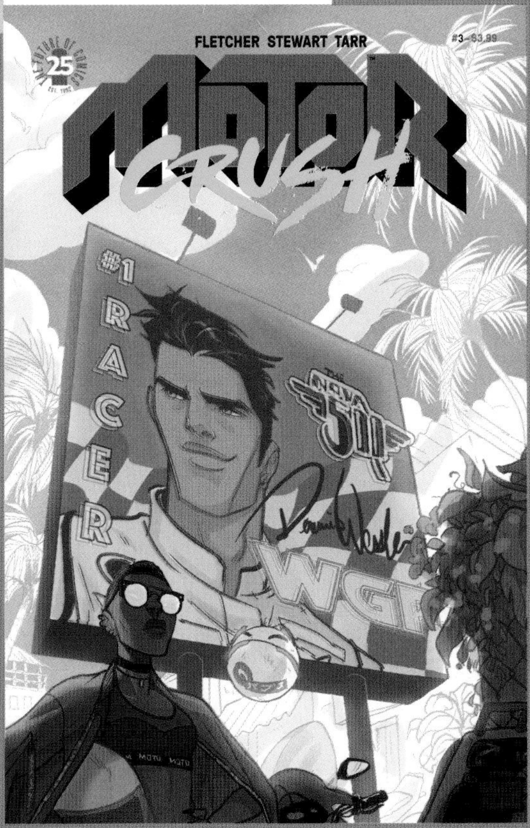
FLETCHER STEWART TARR
#3—$3.99
MOTOR
CRUSH
#1
RACER

INFOPOP

MOTOR CRUSH #3 COVER B BY CAMERON STEWART

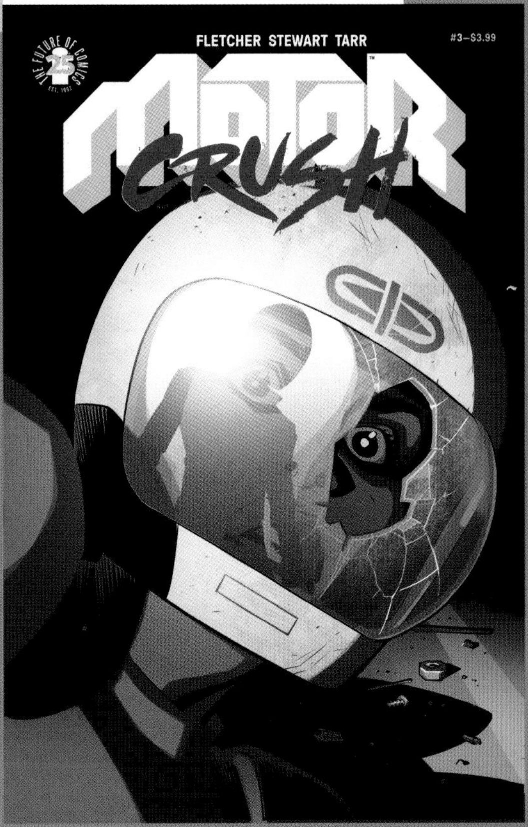
FLETCHER STEWART TARR
#3—$3.99
MOTOR
CRUSH

INFOPOP

MOTOR CRUSH #4 COVER A BY BABS TARR

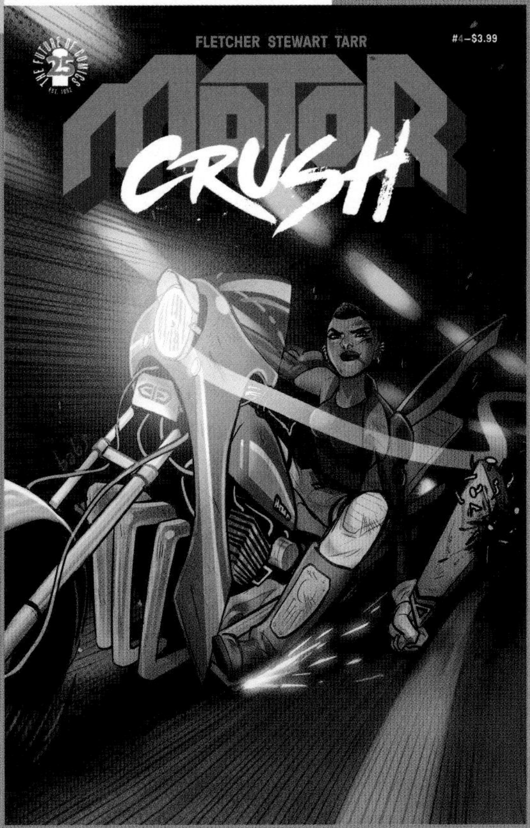
FLETCHER STEWART TARR
#4—$3.99
MOTOR
CRUSH

INFOPOP

MOTOR CRUSH #4 COVER B BY CAMERON STEWART

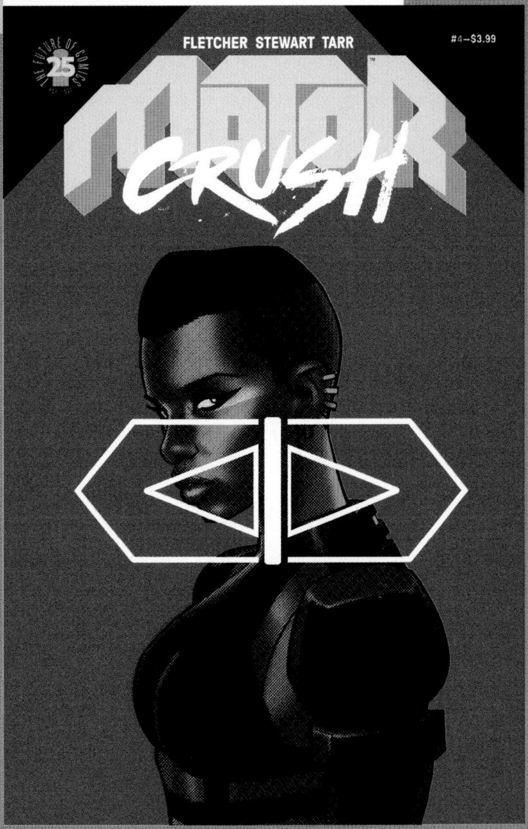
FLETCHER STEWART TARR
#4—$3.99
MOTOR
CRUSH

INFOPOP

MOTOR CRUSH #3 WOMEN'S MONTH VARIANT BY LESLIE HUNG

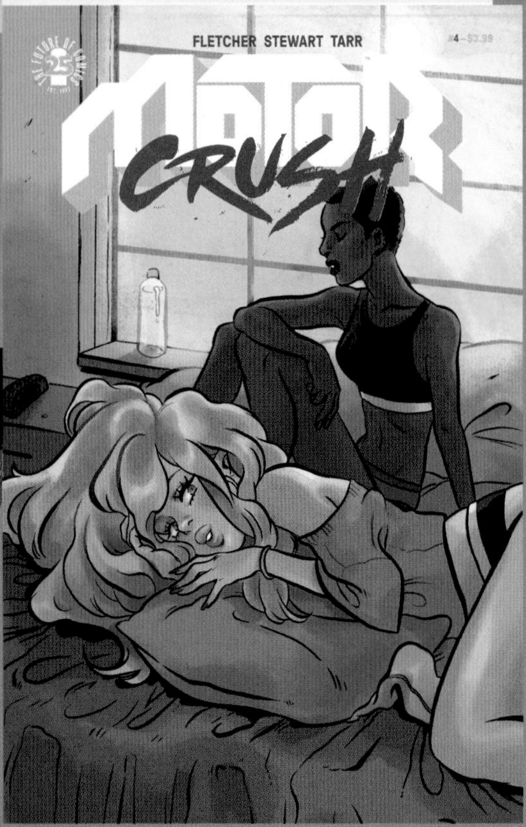
FLETCHER STEWART TARR
#4—$3.99
MOTOR
CRUSH

INFOPOP

MOTOR CRUSH #5 COVER A BY BABS TARR

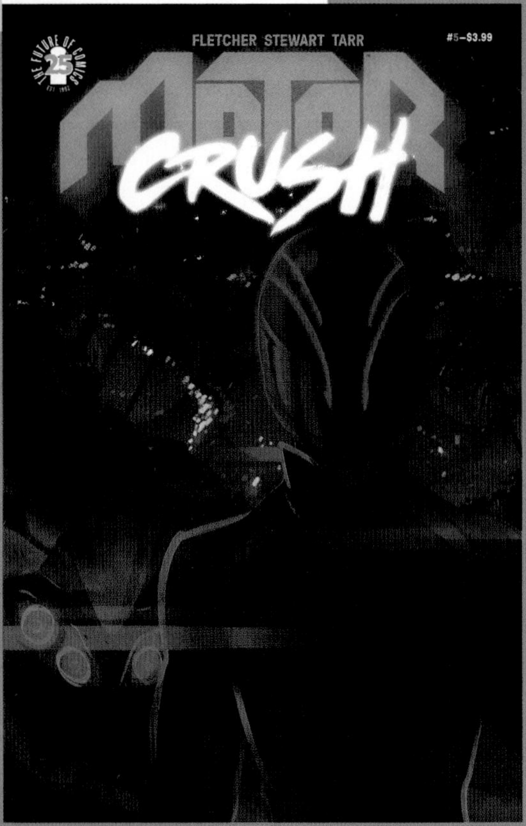
FLETCHER STEWART TARR
#5—$3.99
MOTOR
CRUSH

INFOPOP

MOTOR CRUSH #5 COVER B BY CAMERON STEWART

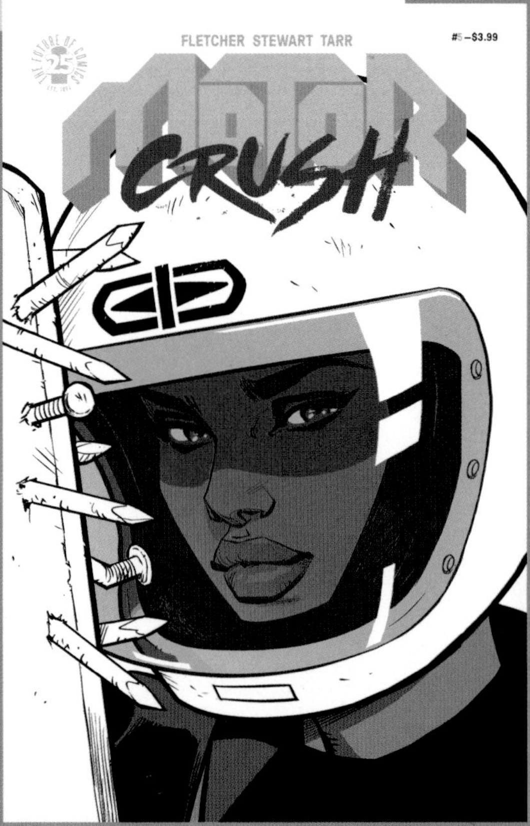
FLETCHER STEWART TARR
#5—$3.99
MOTOR
CRUSH

INFOPOP
SAY HELLO TO BRENDEN!
WGP *RISING STAR*

BRENDEN FLETCHER
@BRENDENFLETCHER

Brenden Fletcher is a writer known for his work on DC Comics series *Gotham Academy*, *Black Canary* and the *New York Times* bestselling *Batgirl of Burnside* with Cameron and Babs.

He contributed the acclaimed *Flash* story to the Eisner and Harvey Award-winning *Wednesday Comics* series and has created comics for brands including *Mighty Morphin' Power Rangers*, *Assassin's Creed*, *Attack On Titan,* and Adult Swim. He lives in Brooklyn, NY with his partner and two cats.

INFOPOP
SAY HELLO TO BABS!
WGP *RISING STAR*

BABS TARR
@BABSDRAWS

Babs Tarr is a graduate of the illustration program at the Maryland Institute College of Art. Before entering comics, she worked in a variety of fields including mobile gaming, toy design, and editorial illustrations.

Spotted online for her personal illustration work, she was invited to join Brenden and Cameron on the *Batgirl of Burnside* revamp for DC Comics and immediately became one of the most distinctive and popular new artists in comics. She currently lives in Charleston, South Carolina.

INFOPOP
SAY HELLO TO CAMERON!
WGP *RISING STAR*

CAMERON STEWART
@CAMERONMSTEWART

Cameron Stewart is a writer and artist best known for his work with Brenden and Babs on DC's *Batgirl of Burnside*, as well as the illustrator of *Fight Club 2*, both *New York Times* bestsellers. His original graphic novel *Sin Titulo* won Eisner and Shuster Awards, and was nominated for Eagle, Harvey, and Stoker Awards.

He has written and/or illustrated a variety of comics, including *Assassin's Creed*, *Batman and Robin*, *BPRD*, *The Other Side,* and many more. Having lived in London, Birmingham, Montreal, Berlin and Glasgow, he has finally settled in his hometown of Toronto...for now.

INFOPOP
SAY HELLO TO ADITYA!
WGP *RISING STAR*

ADITYA BIDIKAR
@ADITYAB

Aditya Bidikar is currently lettering *Drifter*, *Black Cloud*, and *Winnebago Graveyard* for Image Comics, *Night's Dominion* for Oni Press, Grant Morrison's *18 Days* and *Avatarex* for Graphic India, and the *Femme Magnifique* anthology, among others. In a previous life, he's been a comics editor, and has written short stories for the *Faction Paradox* and *Iris Wildthyme* series of prose anthologies.

He lives and works out of Pune, India.

INFOPOP
SAY HELLO TO TOM!
WGP *RISING STAR*

TOM MULLER
@HELLOMULLER

Tom Muller has been designing comics for over 15 years and picked up the odd Eisner and Harvey Awards nomination along the way. He's best known for his design and art-direction on *Zero*, *Wolf*, *Drifter*, *Material*, *Snowfall*, and *The Violent* at Image; his logos for DC Comics' *Suicide Squad*, *Unfollow*, *Survivors' Club*, and *Trillium*; and his design and cover art for Valiant's *Divinity* series, *Ninjak*, *X-O Manowar*, *Bloodshot*, and *Book of Death*. Originally from Belgium, he lives in London with his wife and two cats.

INFOPOP
SAY HELLO TO JEANINE!
WGP *RISING STAR*

JEANINE SCHAEFER
@J9SCHAEFER

Jeanine Schaefer has been editing comics for over ten years. Titles include Marvel Comics' *X-Men*, *She-Hulk*, and the Eisner-nominated *Young Adult Mystic*, *Jonesy* at BOOM!, and the upcoming *Prima* from Image Comics. She also founded *Girl Comics*, an anthology celebrating the history of women at Marvel.

She lives in Los Angeles with her husband and two children, and sporadically runs a Tumblr celebrating the special relationship between nerds and cats.

June 2017. Published by Image Comics, Inc. Office of publication: 2701 NW Vaughn St., Ste. 780, Portland, OR 97210. Copyright © 2017 BRENDEN FLETCHER, CAMERON STEWART and BARBARA TARR. All rights reserved. MOTOR CRUSH™ (including all prominent characters featured herein), its logo and all character likenesses are trademarks of Brenden Fletcher, Cameron Stewart and Barbara Tarr, unless otherwise noted. Image Comics® and its logos are registered trademarks of Image Comics, Inc. No part of this publication may be reproduced or transmitted, in any form or by any means (except short excerpts for review purposes) without express written permission of Image Comics, Inc. All names, characters, events and locales in this publication are entirely fictional. Any resemblance to actual living persons (living or dead), events or places, without satiric intent, is coincidental. Printed in the U.S.A. For information regarding the CPSIA on this printed material call: 203-595-3636 and provide reference # RICH - 736492. For international rights, contact: foreignlicensing@imagecomics.com. ISBN: 978-1-5343-0189-4 Barnes & Noble ISBN: 978-1-5343-0389-8 Kinokuniya ISBN: 978-1-5343-0399-7 Newbury ISBN: 978-1-5343-0411-6 DCBS ISBN: 978-1-5343-0412-3 Forbidden Planet / Big Bang IBSN: 978-1-5343-0413-0 Heroes ISBN: 978-1-5343-0414-7 Big B ISBN: 978-1-5343-0415-4